e4

A SEARCH FOR
SCOTLAND

A SEARCH FOR SCOTLAND

R. F. Mackenzie

with a preface by
T. C. Smout

COLLINS
8 Grafton Street, London W1
1989

William Collins Sons & Co. Ltd
London · Glasgow · Sydney · Auckland
Toronto · Johannesburg

BRITISH LIBRARY CATALOGUING IN PUBLICATION DATA

Mackenzie, R. F. *b 1910*
A search for Scotland.
1. Scotland. Description & travel
I. Title
914 11'04858

ISBN 0 00 215185 5

© The estate of R. F. Mackenzie 1989

Photoset in Itek Janson by
Ace Filmsetting Ltd, Frome, Somerset
Printed and bound in Great Britain by
T.J. Press (Padstow) Ltd, Padstow, Cornwall

Contents

PREFACE

by T. C. Smout

R. F. Mackenzie was a prophet almost without honour in his own country. In a land of educational authoritarianism, he was a teacher of progressive freedoms. In a world that worships the golden calf of economic growth, he was sceptical of the happiness it could bring. In a political climate that nurtured the New Right and rampant individualism, he affirmed an old belief in equality and community. This is his last book, completed during his final illness. Superficially, it takes the form of a guide book or a tour: but like Edwin Muir's *Scottish Journey* fifty years before, it becomes much more than that. It is a commentary on modern Scotland, a moving and sometimes despairing farewell to his native land.

Mackenzie was born in 1910, the son of a rural stationmaster in Aberdeenshire: a respect for trains runs through the book. He went to the local school at Turriff, and then to Robert Gordon's College in Aberdeen, where he became Dux; in 1931 he graduated MA from the University of Aberdeen. The next few years were spent in adventure. He and a friend cycled round Europe and wrote a book about it, *Road Fortune*, published in 1935. He then tried his hand at local journalism, took casual teaching jobs in England (including one at the progressive Forest School in Hampshire) and in Germany, and, when the Second World War broke out, he became a navigator in Bomber Command. His posting to South Africa gave him an understanding of Boer society of which he writes impressively in the final chapter of this book.

He came properly to teaching after the war, going from training college to Galashiels Academy as English master, and moving from thence to Fife, first to Templehall school in Kirkcaldy and then, in 1957 to a new junior secondary school, Braehead in Buckhaven, of which he was appointed head. Buckhaven gave him the opportunity to put into practice the educational theories of his revered mentor, A. S. Neill, and as he taught, he wrote; *A Question of Living*

(1963), *Escape from the Classroom* (1965), *The Sins of the Children* (1967). The following year he was appointed Head of a new comprehensive in Aberdeen, Summerhill Academy. All the success that he had had in Fife for his progressivism turned suddenly and quickly to disaster; in 1972, more than half the staff of Summerhill wrote a formal complaint about his 'unusual and particularly permissive philosophy' and two years later he was removed from his post by Aberdeen Education Committee. His account of the affair, *The Unbowed Head*, was published in 1977, but his teaching career had ended.

There were rights and wrongs on both sides in the Summerhill affair, no doubt, but the conflict was not really between a hidebound local education authority and an obstreperous Head. It was between two educational philosophies, one of rules, discipline and examination, the other of freedom and of teaching as exploration, as the undoing of repression. The marvel is that Mackenzie survived the Scottish Education Department for a quarter of a century, and his main achievement was simply to do so. A. S. Neill had practiced progressive education as leader of a private school with sympathetic governors and parents; R. F. Mackenzie for a decade demonstrated that the same ideals could also be forwarded in the public sector. Perhaps, as his critics said, a relaxed education was not 'practicable' in modern Scotland; but the pupils from Braehead and Summerhill who came to reunions with Mackenzie in 1986 to tell him that they were bringing their own children up in a different way as a result of their education at his hands, had found it the pivot in their lives.

It is far too soon to assess the wider influence of R. F. Mackenzie. It would be wrong to overplay it and wrong to underrate it; his was not the only voice crying in the wilderness, though it was one of the most arresting. Corporal punishment in Scottish schools, against which he had fought all his life, was abolished before his death. The new Standard and Higher grade curricula give a much greater emphasis on learning-by-doing than was thinkable when he entered the profession. But of course the examinations remain and the rules remain. Rightly or wrongly, no-one in authority can imagine a world without them.

A Search for Scotland should indeed be read as the book of a prophet. In points that do not matter greatly, except to academics like myself, he is not always accurate – flocks of Brent Geese do not occur near Stirling, nor grouse near Kilconquhar Loch; Dr Hunter's doctorate was not from Aberdeen University but from Edinburgh; words attributed to Adam Smith are not the phrases he used. Things that an ordinary guide might be expected to mention on a journey round Scotland go unobserved: the physical alteration of Glasgow that has made it, if not 'miles better', at least miles better than it used to be, is not noticed, though the miles of plastic and other detritus that still have to be traversed on approaching the city quite correctly are. The Scottish Development Agency, too, might as well have not existed, presumably because it has developed nothing that Mackenzie would have regarded as important to Scotland's real and spiritual prosperity. In his lamentations over a mode of writing history that emphasises only dynasties and elites and glorifies war, he has not noticed the grass-root vigour of oral history, social history and local history that is about to infiltrate the classrooms in the new curricula with a quite new vision of the people's past, and one much along the lines that he repeatedly calls for in these chapters.

None of this should distract. The reader should rather atune to what Mackenzie is saying about the Scottish condition. We live in a country of extreme natural beauty and our treatment of it is ugly:

> 'In the morning we resumed our journey. There were smashed-up hedgehogs on the road and, off it, a dump of wrecked cars. Smoke rose from a white chimney. Lochs filled in the spaces between the ancient rocks. And then we came down to the trees, ash, and rowan, their berries very red, the ancient trees of Scotland, and larch; and to Lochinver.'

But we need the country, we need its beauty and the reviving force within it for the human spirit far, far more than we need 'economic growth', which in Scotland is so often little more than enrichment for the absent and the few. There are not many passages in the book more arresting and moving than his account of taking the pupils of Braehead Junior Secondary to Perthshire:

'In Rannoch I have seen the vision of Isaiah explode into reality. The mountains and the hills broke forth before them singing and all the trees of the fields clapped their hands . . . After even two or three days at Rannoch, the Fife youngsters became different people. Loud-mouthed, sex-experienced, cigarette-smoking, fifteen-year-old girls lay on the ground, propping their chins in their hands and watching looping caterpillars. They watched the milking of the cows. They saw how Coire Carie had been scraped out by glaciers. Briefly the age of innocence re-entered their lives, and they became almost unrecognisably different. . . . we began to get glimpses of how a Scottish cultural revolution might be set in motion. It would begin in country places.'

Along with this prophetic vision goes a prophetic anger: for an agnostic, it is surprising how often R. F. Mackenzie speaks the language of the Old Testament. 'Is there no balm in Gilead' he exclaims when an Aberdeen father smashes his son's face after he has been in trouble with the police. His rage is at the inhumanity of forms of human authority – the family authority, academic authority, bureaucratic authority. He despises the education system from the SED to the universities, and we wince under the blow even as we think it sometimes unfair. It was no business of Amos or Elijah to be fair. He finds no hope in the politics of left or right, as currently practised; he regards social and political Scotland as duped, and drugged, and the mockery self perpetuated through an education that is still interested in inculcating only good behaviour and blind obedience. In a world where the battle for the hearts and minds of the population is fought out in a circulation war between Maxwell's *Daily Record* and Murdoch's *Sun*, can we gainsay the proposition?

Yet one puts down *A Search for Scotland* not with a sense of having been subjected to sermon and harangue, but with a feeling of having been with a man who was troubled and angry, but who also knew where hope lies. Through all the accurate and arresting observations runs a thread of humane understanding: we are at one with nature, if we but knew it; we are at one in a community, and a community must start on love and gentleness. The world has said of R. F. Mackenzie that he was not a practical man, that he was a dreaming idealist. As we sit in an unlit train approaching the black tunnel of the earth at the end of the twentieth century, do we dare to ignore the little pocket torch the prophet hands to us? Perhaps it might give us enough light to grope towards the communication cord.

T. C. SMOUT

15th November 1988

Orkney

Pentland Firth

John O'Groats
WICK

Butt of Lewis   *Cape Wrath*   *Caithness*

Callanish   Stornoway   Tongue
                 Laxford   *Sutherland*
Lewis   Bridge
                 Lochinver   • Altnaharra
Achiltibuie   *Assynt*   *Loch Shin*
Outer Hebrides Ullapool
                              Lairg   Brora
Harris   *Loch Broom*   *Dornoch Firth*

THE MINCHES   Banff

Uist   • Achnasheen   INVERNESS   *R Spey*   ABERDEEN

Skye   Applecross   *R Dee*
          Wester Ross   *Cairngorms*
Rhum   *Loch Ness*   Braemar
          Mallaig   • Balmoral
          Arisaig
Ardnamurchan   △Ben Nevis
                  • FORT   *Lochaber*   • Forfar
          Tobermory WILLIAM   • Blairgowrie
                  Loch Limnhe *Grampians* DUNDEE
Mull   • OBAN   *R Tay*
                                     PERTH
                  Loch
                  Lomond   STIRLING
                         R Forth
                  Airdrie
                  • GLASGOW   EDINBURGH

Islay   *Kintyre*   Galashiels   *R Tweed*
                  R Clyde   Abbotsford •   Melrose
                              Selkirk •   Jedburgh

                  DUMFRIES •
          Galloway

NORTH SEA

CHAPTER ONE

Introduction

It's like being in a crowded train on a winter night somewhere between Inverness and Perth. Somebody says, 'Where are we?' and we rub the vapour of our condensed breath off the window and peer out into the darkness. But the moon flichters between clouds and most of the landscape is snow and black smudges that could be rock or pines. We search for clues. I look at my watch and listen to the speed of the train, binnerin rhythmically over the rail-joints or unevenly across catchpoints. We thunder through culverts, the noise diminishes as we emerge into opener country. I try to identify a boorachie of lights at the far end of a glen. And then I admit, 'I dinna richtly ken whaur we are, but we could be nearin Dalwhinnie.'

That's what this book is like, searching for clues about where we Scots are as we near the end of a millennium. 'Man is not lost', said the flyleaf to the RAF's handbook on navigation, but I have my doubts about that assurance. There are many areas in which we have lost our bearings. Some say that it is an unprofitable exercise to seek to unearth clues which would give us an inkling on what earth-life is about; they say we'll never penetrate the mystery of where all this to-ing and fro-ing on the planet is taking us. That's unduly modest. I think there's no confining human ability and we shouldn't be headed off from an attempt at solving this, the greatest of all human problems. The way we choose to live our lives depends on the interim answer we set up to this question. Every human being has the right to answer life's basic questions for himself or herself, and a large part of our trouble is that we make do with other people's answers.

The traveller, Freya Stark, sailed down the Aegean in a small boat, calling in at little Turkish ports because, she said, 'I wanted to discover what Alexander found in men's minds when he marched down from the Granicus in 334 BC.' It was a tall order. It's difficult to tell what people are thinking even in our own age. She went on, 'There are too few people in our age who choose to use their own wits in an honest endeavour and, with the facts in a tangle before them, sort them into a pattern of their own.' With that encouragement I set out to present the tangle of facts about Scotland as I have experienced them and sort them into some pattern. As the helicopters, thumping away noisily like steam engines, fly endlessly between the Aberdeen heliport and the North Sea oil-rigs, and the flat-sterned provision boats pass the Torry breakwater on the way out of the harbour, maintaining a lifeline to these vulnerable rigs in the waste of North Sea waters, what related events are taking place in the minds of the Scottish people to whose shores this rich fluid is being piped? It was a search for intelligibility, in which I ransacked my recollection of encounters throughout the century and throughout the length and breadth of the country, trying to extort connections from myths and museums, the face of the countryside, the sayings of gurus and children, moments of insight in random conversations, the solutions that people clutched at in the hope of salvation. This is the story of the search.

CHAPTER TWO

Grampian

We are not polished fighters with our fists, nor wrestlers: but we can run swiftly on our feet and are experts on shipboard; we love eating and harp-playing and dancing and changes of clothes: and hot baths and our beds.

HOMER, *Odyssey*

The search begins at the top of the townhouse of the oil capital, Aberdeen. I've taken several foreign visitors there to get an overall view of the city. A few wing-flaps from the harbour, sea-birds bring up their young on Union Street roofs and the birdlime is like white-wash randomly brushed on slates and granite coping-stones. The River Dee trundles all that water from the Cairngorms down past the prison to the Victoria Bridge and merges with the incoming tide, and the deep water of the harbour provides berth for oil tankers and cargoboats and the Orkney and Shetland ferries and the depleted fishing fleet. Across the water in Torry were the fishermen's houses, built when the steam trawlers poached the white fish from the coastal villagers' hereditary fishing-grounds. Relations of mine, refugees from their parents' villages, lived in Torry in a tenement which had a kitchen and a box bed and an enduring smell of leaking gas, a bedroom, a front room and a shared lavatory on the stair landing. Immediately below the townhouse skyscraper we get a seagull's-eye view of Provost Skene's seventeenth-century house, rudely jostled by brash incomers. Beside it is an area where excavations in 1973 revealed a thirteenth-century midden whose 'layers of decomposed filth were still able in places to offend the noses of twentieth-century diggers'. They discovered also pits that could have belonged to a thirteenth-century tannery. At one end of this area is the insignificant steeple of the old tolbooth, its formidable rough-hewn granite stones almost hidden by newer buildings of polished granite. Inside that grisly building, prisoners in the darkness were shackled to their cell walls, and some of them shambled down the stairs to the gallows whose site is marked by a lozenge-shaped stone in the middle of Union Street opposite Marischal Street. 'He took his last look down Marischal Street' was the way the spectators put it.

There is a monochrome of grey sea and grey granite relieved by the distant red roofs of the College of Education, the brown of two hideous factories built of brick, some streaks of greenery and a long strip of tawny sands extending as far north along the bay as the eye can reach, towards the ancient land of Buchan. Near the mouth of the Don the lofty cathedral of St Machar, built to impress the faithful, is now dwarfed into insignificance by skyscrapers called *courts*, and King's College, five centuries old, is hardly noticeable, like an ancient savant pushed into the background by thrusting oil executives. Two miles inland, obliterated by the oil-office buildings, is a gash in the earth, the dark mouth of the Rubislaw quarry from which they hewed granite boulders to build Aberdeen, shaping them into simple, sedate buildings and ornate buildings bristling 'like a granite hedgehog', as John R. Allan described one of them in *The North-East Lowlands of Scotland*. Lately the industrial grime of a century has been wiped from the face of many of these buildings and their ashlars reassume the soft, comely glow they had on the day they were chiselled from the crust of the Aberdeen earth.

Having had a unified view of the whole of Aberdeen, the foreign visitors are conducted round its ships, towers, domes, theatres and temples, the post office and the Grammar School and the Salvation Army Citadel, all built to the plans of Albert's Balmoral, tenements built to be warrens for workers (lavatories pinned on to them as new hygiene laws required), the main street dominated no longer by local grocers and fruiterers and drapers but by Yorkshire building societies, the new factory sites at Nigg, shopping arcades temptingly warm on the bleakest January days. But I doubt if they would have seen it as a homogeneous whole, the habitation of a community which knows where it is going.

At this point the tour of the city begins to provide too many unrelated stories, like pieces of a jigsaw too multitudinous to fit together into a coherent whole. What is an Asiatic visitor to make of

Aberdeen's statues – Victoria, Albert, Edward VII, the Duke of Gordon, Wallace defying the English, Burns holding a daisy, Byron in front of his school (there was a row about that one) and Simpson, the architect who modelled the present-day face of the city? The ancient Brig o' Balgownie (built in 1320 and rebuilt in 1605) implies a long continuity of civic life here.

The Episcopalian cathedral in King Street tells of another kind of continuity. The American Episcopalians, isolated by the independence war from their English community, had to depend on an Aberdeen bishop for a handing on of the episcopal succession. But these are curios of a history museum. More illuminating for the enquirer is a study of Aberdeen's daily newspaper. It has a community-uniting wealth of local news, oil-rig technical and village simple, together with a lairdly view of foreign news and politics. The local television station reflects the width of east-coast interests from Wick to Dundee, our industries, our legal niggles, our gossip and entertainments, our admiration for English accents, our absorption in social climbing, our changing food preferences. An Aberdeenshire-born journalist, returning after many years to report on the changes he found in his home city, stressed the change in the hotel menus and the absence of change in the local accent. At the next table in an Aberdeen hotel he heard a guest say, 'I dinna like praans wi ma avocadoes.'

The biggest change in Aberdeen during the century has been the opening up of the generation gap. The kirk's counsel hardly counts, mothers go out to work and have less time for their children, the heavy emphasis on the external examinations in the schools has deepened school-class divisions and a sense of rejection amongst many teenagers. They are left much more to their own devices, individuals bobbing about in a turbulent sea. On a Saturday night in February three fourteen-year-olds played snooker in the YMCA. They then went and played snooker in Rose Street. Then they made for the harbour. They played with a trolley. Then they got on to a boat, German they thought, and inspected the engine room and came on deck again and climbed up a ladder to the top of the funnel. They found a knife and used it to cut an orange rope attached to a lifebuoy. A member of the crew saw them and called the police. That was about eleven p.m. The police came and put them in cells separately. One of the parents came for them at one p.m. His parents told one of the boys that he wasn't to keep company with the other two, and was to stay indoors the next evening. He went to his room and barricaded the door and made a row by blowing a saxophone and banging the radiator. In the morning his father hit him in the face and, when he went to wash, turned off the hot water and told him to wash in cold water.

Is there no balm in Gilead? Is there no physician there? Headmastering in an Aberdeen comprehensive in the seventies I found that children's lives were much bleaker than they had been in rural Aberdeenshire when I was a child. There was little balm and few physicians. Parents were buffeted about in an uncharted economic sea and lost their bearings and had rows and, at the end of their patience, took it out on their children. When the father and mother returned tired at the end of their work, there were policemen and school attendance officers chapping at their door asking why they didn't have their children under proper control and did they not know how often their children had been truanting from school? There was nobody to turn to. There was a queue to see the doctor and get sleeping-pills, and the doctor couldn't give you more than ten minutes. They had no dealings with the kirk. And the dominies also were under pressure when Tory newspapers pointed to the truancies in the comprehensives as proof of the failure of Labour education. So, beside themselves, fathers smashed their fists in their sons' faces and told them to wash in cold water.

When pupils truanted, I asked them how they spent their time out of school. Fourteen-year-old Dugald Reid's truancies were mostly spent in the countryside. In Hazlehead park on a fine May day he found the nests and eggs of song-thrush, blackbird and hedge-sparrow; wood-pigeons' nests, but all their eggs were hatched; and there were no rooks' eggs that he could find. He told me the difference between these nests and eggs. In the late afternoon he went to catch sea-trout as the tide came up the Dee. Then he went to Union Street and from there to Northfield where he played with some boys he had met, and when they went home, he slept in a nearby barn. Another day he and another boy went to Newtonhill and watched the jellyfish being stranded on the shore, and he looked at the seaweed. Another day he went to Seaton park, near the Don and the cathedral. Another day he went to the Joint Station and he could give an account of the goods he had seen in transit and their destinations.

Although he had a good appetite, he was so keen to be out in the countryside that he was content to go hungry on some of these occasions. Sometimes he took part in stealing, but one of the boys involved in these thefts said that, although Dugald was equally responsible with the others, he wasn't deeply concerned whether he stole or not. The stealing was not a focal point of his truancies. (I was surprised at a youngster's honesty as a witness and his insight in sizing up Dugald's attitudes.) I believe that a gypsy longing for the open air came over Dugald and he made for the countryside, oblivious of everything else, and, although he liked company, he was equally happy to go alone.

There was nothing wrong with Dugald, nor, I suspect, with his parents. Most people in Aberdeen believed that when he became restive, Dugald should be disciplined. Disowned, and thereby emancipated from the traditional restraints of a Scottish community, the teenagers reached out for other supports and joined groups which would provide the sense of belonging and being protected. The better-off burghers of Aberdeen felt threatened like the Roman senate when the footloose barbarians were pushing down into Italy. The Aberdonians used the same term, calling their assailants Vandals. An Aberdeen fifteen-year-old told a story of a night to remember. There was a mid-week Scottish cup match between Aberdeen and Celtic. In King Street they saw the newly-arrived Celtic supporters, sporting their green, white and yellow sashes, but the police were patrolling King Street very carefully and no trouble arose. Seven o'clock and they were in the football ground of Pittodrie. Bottle-throwing stopped when the match began. At half-time he looked round and saw the Aberdeen gangs. Behind them, in force, were the CREW, to their right the HILTON-FLEET and to their left the TORRY-DERRY who were very quiet that night. Bottles were coming in all directions. The police moved in and made a few arrests. The teams came out for the second half. 'A bobby came in to remove one of the CREW for no apparent reason. What a scrap! Stupid bobby was on his own and he got booted to bits. Then five others appeared to his rescue.' Celtic and Aberdeen both scored within ten minutes. And then, a few minutes from time, Celtic scored. 'We were beat.' They left before the aggro started, not being in the mood for aggro that night. As about twenty of them were moving towards the exit he looked back on the crowd. 'Every bloody gang was watching us. The GRINGO are the most-hated gang in Aberdeen. Just at the back of us were the FLEET. One of them came up and asked if we would help them get the NORTHFIELD TOLL. About fifteen of us went with them for a laugh and a bit of aggro.'

Unaware that they were re-enacting a historical pattern, these groups were fumbling for new forms of association. A sixteen-year-old wrote about a heavily booted gang that was different. 'Their leader was no one, because they did not like being bossed around.' Changes are happening also at the other end of the Aberdeen social spectrum. Robert Gordon's College is housed in an eighteenth-century building at the end of an avenue up from Schoolhill. In an alcove above the front door of the college that he founded for poor children is a statue of Robert Gordon, of Straloch in Aberdeenshire, who was a Danzig merchant. When I was a pupil there, Gordon's still fulfilled its founder's intentions. The fees were minimal and there were very many bursaries and 'foundations'. When Labour came to power and abolished fee-paying in Aberdeen's ancient Grammar School, parents who wanted to pay fees sent their sons to Gordon's. The college's clientèle changed, and, like Eton, Gordon's changed its character. Following the pattern of English public schools, it introduced gowns for the staff, 'houses', prefects. It was accepted into the English 'Headmasters' Conference'. It was part of the anglicization of Scotland.

Aberdeen is less of an integrated community than it used to be. The invasion of oil entrepreneurs has had the effect of detaching the socially ambitious or the suitably energetic natives from the ancient allegiances. Up to the middle of the century Aberdeen was populated largely by past or present incomers from its hinterland. These were the fishing folk, the farming folk and the folk from the highland borders. The fishing communities were very different from the farming communities; they might almost have lived in different countries. They didn't mix much. They had a different outlook on life and on religion, and distinct speech patterns. One season when the fishing was poor a young fisherman went to work on a farm. After a year he gave it up and when somebody asked him why, he said, 'I didna like it. Scartin [scratching] the face o' God's earth a' simmer and throwin neeps [turnips] at a bul a' winter.' Another fisherman, helping to take in the harvest, upset a cartload of sheaves and when the farmer asked him how it happened, he replied, 'I shouted to the horse, "North oot, north oot!" She cam sooth in, sooth in. The ballast gaed a' tae the leeart [leeward] and we landed keel eemost [upmost] in the ditch.'

Their happiness was on the seaways, rowing their brightly painted yoles out of the creek and then raising the sail as they emerged from the lee of the headland into the wind. The fishing hamlet of Whinny Fold from which my mother came was huddled and crammed into a small terrace of level round above the cliffs. Joan Eardley's picture of Catterline, south of Stonehaven, a row of fishermen's houses clinging tenuously to the edge of the land, tells what it felt like to live at Whinny Fold. They looked out across the North Sea, turning their backs on their rural neighbours whom they called 'kwintra folk', a phrase which has the connotation of 'peasants'. (The farming community responded by calling this alien community 'fishers'.) During the First World War my grand-uncle sometimes took me with him in his yole. It was a new element. I looked at the dulse shining brown that swayed in the movement of the water that our passage caused. A solitary figure holding a fishing rod, a 'wand', sat on the Point of Pitscur. My grand-uncle put up the single cinnamon-coloured sail (the colour of the nets which were 'barked' with the juice of oak galls) and made for the open sea. The line of houses on the braeface receded until the land was only part of the framework of a picture. Then he took down the sail and threw out our baited lines and waited. The mast like a pointer traced out a magnified record of our movements in the boat and the water slapped its sides like a playful whale. (Once we did see whales sporting in the water, close to us.) Far out a coaster moved south, leaving a thinning line of smoke, or an Aberdeen trawler bound for the fishing-grounds, and occasionally a dark grey-blue destroyer or minesweeper. The clouds massed and disintegrated and re-formed. The sun broke through and sparkled on the face of the water. A codlin was brought to the surface and spattered in the bottom of the boat. We took in the rest of our lines and rowed to another area, stopping to have a news with the Port Erroll salmon fishermen in their flat-bottomed cobble, emptying their nets. Then we fished again. There would be a haddock, another couple of codlins and three whiting. 'Look, there's the thumb-mark of the Apostle Peter,' my grand-uncle would say, showing me the two dark marks near the whiting's mouth. With the trust and literal understanding of a child I believed him, but also at the back of my mind were unspoken questions which didn't surface until many years later. By what wondrous process was it that Saint Peter's fingermarks on a fish caught in the Sea of Galilee were reproduced two thousand years later on all whitings caught in the North Sea off the Aberdeenshire coast? I didn't know if be believed it himself, or half-believed it, or was handing down the heritage of a memorable saying, a figure of speech, that had enshrined itself in local usage. Adults like to pull children's legs, tell them tall stories and enjoy the open-mouthed credulity of the child. Long ago, I imagine, a bearded fisherman, gutting his catch, told his son that these marks were made by Saint Peter, and the idea endured.

When my grand-uncle felt that the catch in the bottom of the yole justified the morning's launch, he'd put up the sail and we'd sail in a great arc, for the enjoyment of it, towards the cliffs between Whinny Fold and Collieston where, it was said, the Armada galleon, the *Santa Caterina*, sank in 1588. On ledges above precipitous cliffs seagulls nested. A company of gulls and guillemots and kittiwakes squawked in myriad flight and their droppings whitened great patches of rock. The yole bobbed up and down in the swell, perilously (as it seemed to me) close to the fretted knife-edges of granite rock and, to the gulls swooping overhead, an unwelcome intruder. It was a lonely, eerie place, alien to human beings, yet having a fascination, making them cherish the more the warmth and shelter of their own colony a mile or two north, on top of the cliffs.

'Dinnertime,' my grand-uncle would announce, and we would steer for the creek and tie up our boat and carry our catch up the long, steep, twisting path. Our dinner was potatoes and herring. In the afternoon there were other things to do ashore, but I felt that the afternoon was land-bound, grounded like the yole at low tide, and that the real life was afloat, borne up by the water.

But even ashore, life at Whinny Fold was richly different from life in rural Aberdeenshire. Tar and pieces of cork and basket lay here and there on the shore. The flotsam of the high-water line was corks and planks, an occasional fishbox washed off a trawler, a length of rope, and always the chance of some unexpected treasure trove, a green orb of glass which had detached itself from a net, a foreign bottle, a sheep's belly buoy. A shallow cave undercut the rock, and the sound of our boots on the round stones and the clanking of the stones against one another produced low reverberations. A low moaning sound came intermittently from a horn, fixed on a reef not far off-shore which was covered over at high tide. It was strangely in tune with the gulls' cries and the subdued roar of the sea and the sound of the retreating wave rushing through the stones of the shore of the creek. Many ships were wrecked on the reef and my forebears had saved and given hospitality to Lascars and Americans and French. Their houses were full of mementoes of these guests and the stones in the churchyard of St James's, the church on the hill three miles inland, record the story of those who lost their lives.

The danger of their calling thrust eternity into the forefront of their thoughts. They saw themselves as one with those who let down their nets in the Sea of Galilee and, ashore, gathered bait and mended their nets. An echo of Biblical language sometimes gave distinction to their everyday speech. Once my grandfather told the doctor, who lived three miles away in Hatton, that they hadn't seen him in Whinny Fold for a long time. He replied, 'John, they that are whole need not a physician, but they that are sick.' There was a short cut, a narrow track, from the laird's castle at Slains to the kirk in Port Erroll, trodden every Sunday while the old laird lived. But the young laird rarely went to the kirk. The minister rebuked him, but there was grace in the words and in the tone of the voice. 'Sir, your father's path to the kirk is growing green.'

But, back of this religious dignity, there was a sense of fun and occasionally satire, and a lively independence. My mother mimicked one of their neighbours saying grace before meat. There was a loud, attention-compelling snort, a long, confused rising and falling of unidentifiable words and then a definitive snort which meant that they could all start eating. The north-east coast of Aberdeenshire had long been a stronghold of Episcopalianism but after earnest discussion my grandfather and some others decided to leave that faith and they joined the Congregational Church in Port Erroll, and that created no problems in the village. But when others joined the Plymouth Brethren, a gulf grew in some families. A woman said about her neighbour, 'That's him awa to the Brethren meeting wi a Bible under his arm the size of a fishbox.' A husband heard his wife quietly singing a hymn, 'Thou shalt meet the Lord with a contrite heart,' but what she sang was 'Thou shalt meet the Lord with a concrete heart.' He shouted at her, 'Ye feel [fool]! Div ye nae ken fit concrete means? Concrete is steen an lime.'

When you try and get a picture of an earlier generation in your mind's eye, it rarely encompasses the variety that their lives contained. The stories that an uncle of mine, brought up in the village, told me were a surprise. They were about smuggling and gaugers and had a 'Whisky Galore' atmosphere about them. A string of fishwives were tramping along the road, their heavy creels on their backs. When a gauger appeared, one of them, fleeter of foot than the lave, made off guiltily. The gauger raced after her, ignoring the others who plodded on without altering their pace. How was the gauger to know that the girl who ran away was the only one with an empty creel and that the other creels were packed to the brim with kegs of whisky? Another day a gauger stopped two women and asked what they had in their creels. They flung down their creels and attacked him, leaving him at the roadside.

It was difficult to reconcile these artful and pugnacious women with the demure procession to the kirk on a Sunday morning. I become more and more persuaded of the extent to which historians, mostly middle-class and male, got our pre-Victorian great-grandmothers wrong. Another fishwife was followed by a gauger. She managed to get into her house a minute or two before the gauger chappit at the door. But when he examined the creel that she had just laid on the floor, there was nothing but unsold fish in it, and even a gauger wouldn't stop a woman rocking a cradle to see if the white, muffled covering at the end of the cradle covered a baby's head or the top of a small keg.

The storyteller didn't put dates on his stories and I don't know

how many generations back he was talking about. It was like meeting somebody in the village who once knew an old man who
remembered the time when a tree grew on that spot and it was said
that it was always from that tree that a lamp was hung to tell the
smugglers in their boat that the coast was clear.

The longest story was the one I liked best. It was a moonless
night on the north-east coast. A farmer yoked his sheltie into the
gig, lifted the keg of whisky into the back, and blanketed it with
an old horse-cover. It was an unchancy errand he was on and he
was surprised at the amount of noise the horse's feet made on the
cobblestones of the farm close, but once out on the softer turnpike
road they made less. He thought he could make out, in the star-
light, a shadow moving behind the hedge along the end rig of the
ley park. He stopped, and it stopped too. Then he saw that it was
the stilts of the plough at the end of the furrow where he had
unharnessed from it at lowsin time. The white signpost at the neuk,
although he kent it fine, bore an uncanny likeness to a ghost and
the lang stracht had a deserted, eerie feeling about it. Lights seawards might have been stars or gaugers' signals.

He found the merchant he had been seeking but nothing like the
price he had expected. Haggling only put the merchant's back up.
The outcome was that the farmer shouldered the keg and said, 'I'd
raither tak it hame again.' The merchant made no further bid and
followed him outside, and, just as the farmer was climbing into his
gig, he said, 'It's a pity ye tak the keggie back hame. I ken a man that
micht gie ye a price nearer what ye're seekin.'

The farmer looked at him non-committally while the merchant
gave him the address. The farmer turned the gig and, as he started
on the way he had come, the merchant said, 'That's nae the road.
Ye're gyan the wrang road.' But the farmer said only, 'This's my
road,' and trotted away into the night.

Farther up the road, however, when he judged himself out of
earshot of the merchant, he turned off on the right and, through a
maze of by-roads, came out on the house that the merchant had
directed him to. He tied the sheltie's reins to a post and chappit at
the door. A middle-aged man came to the door, peered into the
darkness and invited him in. 'You're a dealer?' the farmer asked
him.

'Ye could say that.'

'I've a keggie oot there. What'll ye gie me for't?"

'What maks he think I buy spirits?'

'Archibald the merchant telt me. Ye needna hae suspicions. Div ye think I'm a gauger?'

'No,' said the middle-aged man, 'but I am.'

The farmer waited for the blow to fall. The gauger spoke.

'Ye say that Archibald telt ye to come here wi the spirits?'

'Aye.'

'Why did ye nae sell the keg te him?'

'He offered me only half the price I socht.'

'Well, I'll tell ye what te dee. Tak that keg back to Archibald an tak the price he offers. But dinna say ye saw me.'

In bewilderment the farmer returned by the way he had come. When Archibald opened the door he said limply, 'I've changed ma mind. I'll tak yer price.'

The merchant helped him carry the keg indoors, drew off a dram from the keg, poured two drinks and took out a money-box. He handed over the money and, as he locked the box, he muttered, 'That's what I call a good nicht's work.'

'Ye took the words richt oot o ma moo,' said the gauger, who was blocking the doorway.

I was the more disposed to believe my uncle's stories after he told me about a much later incident in which he was himself involved. During the 1914–18 war, taking a few steps along the top of the cliff before turning in on a dark winter's night, he saw lights down in the creek and maybe heard voices. They could have come from the crew of a German submarine. 'What did you do?' somebody asked him.

'Do?' he said. 'I was scared oot o ma wits. I rushed tae the hoose and lockit the door and blew oot the lamp and jumpit into ma bed.'

I was relieved by his honesty. All the heroes in the boys' stories that I read showed so much more fearlessness than I felt.

By the time of the 1914–18 war, the village had lost most of its active fishermen. Before the Aberdeen trawlers took away all the fish, the men of an earlier generation on Sunday mornings got up and went for a walk along the braes above the sea, wearing only the long drawers and dark shirt in which they had slept. Then they would say, 'We'd better go back now, and rise.' I can guess what they discussed as they strolled along leisurely and looked out over the North Sea on these beautiful mornings a century ago. The movements of the herring shoals. The numbers of local folk who were leaving the Episcopalians and joining the Congregational Kirk. Man's chief end and how you should live your life. The news in the weekly paper that came to the village and was passed round from house to house: that included the David Livingstone story and also the story of Emin Pasha, Gordon of Khartoum's governor of Equatoria who was cooped up after the Mahdist rising in the Sudan and appealed to Mackay of Uganda (another Aberdeenshire man) for help and who was rescued by Stanley. They discussed the battle of Majuba Hill and Gladstone's proposal to give home rule to Ireland and Salisbury's ceding of Heligoland to Germany. But I doubt if Darwin (who died in 1882) or Marx (who died the year after) figured in their discussions. When the Liberal MP came to the village they asked him about the five shillings they had to pay every year to the Earl of Erroll for permission to fish in his sea. It was called sea rent. 'Don't pay it,' the MP told them, 'and if anything happens, let me know.' They didn't pay it, nothing happened and they were never asked for it again.

The fishermen's houses had a but and a ben and a 'middle place'. The but was the kitchen and living-room. Over its low fire, pots and pans were suspended by black-painted chains from a lever swinging in a horizontal plane called a swey. There were impressive pictures of sailing ships, each with an incredible spread of sail designed to court every breath of wind. There were pictures of their crews and treasured messages from sailors of various nationalities whom the Whinny Fold fishermen had saved from drowning, an outpouring of gratitude. There were much-prized telescopes with which bearded, retired fishermen looked out daily on the traffic up and down the seaways on which they had spent their working lives. Upstairs in the loft, which was lit by skylights and reached by a wooden ladder, were nets, lines, buoys, green glass spheres, corks, cord. Outside in the red-tiled shed were paint, buckets, bait, wands, tar, fish scales. It was a hard life digging for sandeels, shelling mussels, sitting long hours baiting lines, putting out to sea in a small, open boat to earn enough to feed a large family and pay for clothes and boats and tackle and rent. I saw Whinny Fold at the end of a long period of history during which there had been little change. An old story was drawing to its close. The younger men had gone to join bigger herring boats at Peterhead and Fraserburgh or white-fishing line-boats and trawlers at Aberdeen because the money was better.

When my mother left school she got a job sewing at a tailor's in Port Erroll and when she had crossed two miles of sands and got home at night she had her supper and sat for hours in poor lamp-light sewing for the family and for neighbours. Often she told me, 'I sat and sewed and sometimes looked out on summer evenings over the grey sea and thought, "Is this all that I'll do in my life, just sew and look out over this grey sea?" ' Her father said, 'Katie, there'll always be plenty for you here.' I visualize the conflict in her mind, often duplicated in Scottish history. On the one hand her parents worried about the wicked outside world, and her concern for her parents and love for them; on the other hand, the urge of a caged bird to escape and try out its wings in the wide world. She left the village and got a job in Aberdeen. A comment in a reference from one employer, 'Refuses to sew on Sundays', was a recommendation in the eyes of her next employer and she went as a lady's maid to Edinburgh and London and then travelled to the Riviera. Our Aberdeenshire village horizons were widened when we listened, years later, to tales of Bordighera and the boatmen on Como and Bellaggio and the canals of Venice. We heard too of the ongoings of life in what was called 'high society'.

We hadn't realized at the time that Whinny Fold might have closer enduring ties with the continent of Europe than historians thought. Much later my sister, beginning a course in medicine in the University of Aberdeen, was cross-questioned by the professor of anatomy, who was interested in ethnology and made physical measurements of his students, seeking to establish their heredity. According to his measurements she was of Spanish ancestry. Had she a Spanish grandparent? No. All she could point to was that Spanish galleon, the *Santa Caterina*, sunk on the Aberdeenshire coast near her village. The local fishermen would have helped to save the sailors and put them up in their homes. The way home was through English land or over seas patrolled by Howard's and Drake's ships. Did they decide to remain with their hosts and did some of them marry local girls and, nostalgically, give the name of their galleon to a baby daughter? And did the name continue until my mother was baptized with the name of Catherine? Later when I visited Sagres in the south of Portugal and looked over Cape St Vincent, I realized that the Spanish sailors wouldn't have found their new surroundings on the Buchan coast all that different. I wonder if, seated in the ingleneuks of Whinny Fold while the driftwood fire roared up the lum on a winter night, the Spanish sailors would have spun spell-binding yarns about their galleons and the Barbary Coast and Prince Henry the Navigator whose research centre at Sagres had revolutionized sailing by its experiments and initiatives in astro-navigation, compasses, map-making and boat-building and sail-designing more than a century before the Armada. It would have been like telling a tribe in today's Mato Grosso about space exploration and moon landings. And would I be romancing if I claim to detect overtones of Spanish lingering in the speech of Whinny Fold folk? For reasons which I've never seen explained, the Spaniards are not content to use a simple 'o' vowel in a word like 'porto', a port; they twist it round their tongues until they contort it into the diphthong in 'puerto'. That's what my Whinny Fold relations did when they referred to their farming neighbours as 'kwintra folk'.

There was a sense of anti-climax in returning from our summer holidays at Whinny Fold to the turnip-fields of central Aberdeenshire and to a community which had a different speech and a different way of life. Until the mid-century it was still possible, without too much over-simplifying, to accommodate the farming folk of Aberdeenshire inside a few homely generalizations. This is how in 1950 the farming folk were described by a highlander from the totally different society of Lochinver in Sutherland. He had graduated from Glasgow University and spent most of the rest of his life as a schoolteacher in rural Aberdeenshire. The people he was writing about were the parents of the children he taught.

'They are generous in most things, but "careful" also; far keener than the English on understatement in speech, and yet readily enthusiastic; coarse in some things, especially in matters of sex, but with a strong thread of sentimentality – a disposition to talk of loons, quines and bairns almost as tediously as the Italians in their eternal patter about the bambini and Mamma mia. Not really religious (blasphemy is very common) but yet all are members of the

A Search for Scotland

Kirk and regular communicants. Very independent but still inclined to truckle to the laird. Very industrious and full of agricultural initiative (witness, Aberdeenshire has a third of Scotland's poultry and is increasing its pigs daily), great worshippers of Mammon yet not very well acquainted with the possibilities of money, not very keen on the arts but daft on dancing (the sex motif, maybe) and the cinema, on amateur acting and concerts, lip-worshippers of education but not great readers. Low rate of intelligence I should say, and high illegitimacy rate. Appalling to find a girl of the status of a nursing sister who thinks it quite normal to have *one* child before marriage, but bad to have more than one. "I had him before I was married," is a phrase that every dominie knows. So I'd say, hard-headed, notable for sentimentality (witness the unique *Press & Journal*), great respecters of money, and the esteem it brings, great card-players.'

That description of how a highlander saw the lowlanders in the mid-century says something also about the different community from which he came. It is the view of a knowledgeable and fair-minded outsider. The view from the inside a few decades earlier is given by Donside poet, Charles Murray. He recorded the even tenor of rural lives on the west side of Bennachie and gave the feel of the place, its teuchats, the mushroom-shaped rick-foundations, the making of whistles from rowan shoots, the mucking out of the byres. He described a community which felt safe and protected and bedded down in a secure rural civilization which had continued largely unchanged for centuries. That is why he found it congenial to translate Horace into north-east Scots. Murray in the Vale of Alford twenty-five miles from Aberdeen entered sympathetically into the life that Horace lived on his Sabine farm twenty-five miles from Rome. Mount Soracte in translation became Bennachie and Horace's lines,

> Vides ut alta
> stet nive candidum
> Soracte,

became

> Drift oxter-deep haps Bennachie.

24

Cypresses were translated into larches. Horace had a fine, leisurely time of it grafting poplar shoots on to vines; in the same relaxed, unhurried way Murray snedded larch-trees for pea-sticks. Horace went out to the hill and netted a crane; Murray went out to the hill and brought back a ptarmigan. Horace hunted boars; Murray contented himself with taking his dog and ferret to catch rabbits. They both caught hares and ate sorrel; 'sooricks' is the Aberdeenshire word. They both warned their wives to beware of fortune-tellers when they were away, Horace referring to the Chaldean astrologers and their Babylonian numbers, Murray to the spaewife. Horace wrote, 'Drive away the cold by piling high the wood on the hearth.' That's an adequate way of conveying Horace's words in English but Murray's Scots idiomatic translation is livelier. 'Haud on the peats an' fleg the cauld.' Aberdeenshire folk on a cauldrif night huddling up to the glowing peat in the farm kitchen, appreciative of the farmer's prodigality with his fuel, would be feelingly persuaded of what it was like to sit in Horace's ingleneuk.

In his *Apologie for Poetrie*, Sir Philip Sidney said that poetry claps wings to solid nature. Murray's poems did that. There was hardly a native of the north-east who didn't get a lift out of his poetry. I travelled in a guard's van at the tail end of a mixed train between Inveramsay and Insch at the other side of Bennachie from Murray's Alford and the guard recited *The Whistle*, his eyes shining, glee in his voice as we stotted round corners and he steadied his stance by holding on to the brake lever, but never for a moment losing the lilt of the poem. The north-east language, 'the speak of the people', was as perfectly attuned to the feel of the poem as a fiddle to a bothy ballad. In a strange way the speak of the folk influences the folk. When I meet local people who speak the tongue I was brought up with and fall back easily into that speech, I have a sense of relaxation and belonging, of being safe and warm. I can understand better why local groups in France want to re-establish Breton and Basque and Occitan. It's a sense of clinging on to the fruitful earth that bore us, being suckled by its breasts. When we lose our native speech, a birthright, we lose something of our wholeness, our integrity. We have too easily accepted the prevailing argument that north-east speech is a picturesque anachronism, a hindrance to progress. We have to balance up the profit and loss again. Maybe the accompanying alienation affects our mental health more than we had supposed.

A generation later than Murray, Lewis Grassic Gibbon also was sensitive to what he called 'the speak of the people'. And also to the dark background of history that shaped us; and to the folds of the terrain, its geology and plant cover and the climate that moulded and milled and transformed these things. Like Thomas Hardy in Wessex, he grew out of the soil. Hardy had a poem about green leaves in May, 'delicate-filmed as new-spun silk', a hawk in the dusk alighting on a wind-warped upland thorn, the hedgehog's furtive run over the grass, the full-starred winter heavens, and he said he wanted to be remembered as 'one who had an eye for such mysteries'. So also Gibbon. His territory of the Mearns and ours of central Aberdeenshire met at the long, low Hill of Fare. His Aberdeen novel, *Grey Granite*, ends like this:

> Over the Hill of Fare, new-timbered, a little belt of rain was falling, a thin screen that blinded the going of the light; behind, as she turned, she saw Skene Loch glimmer and glow a burnished minute; then the rain caught it and swept it from sight and a little wind soughed up the Barmekin.

Contemporary with Murray, the artist Joseph Farquharson also conveyed the spirit of the place, like Gibbon sensitive to the changing face of the countryside. His pictures traced the brightness and coldness of a winter's sunset on Deeside, trees and oat-ricks and houses blanketed by a thick snow-covering, flames of the setting sun hitting the fir-tree trunks and the fleeces of the sheep, the feeling of what it was like to live here. When the dark set in, the farmer lit candles and put them in the lamps of his sleigh and, thickly mittened and muffled, had leisure to survey the snow-laden firs and beeches and the softened outlines of bridge and cottage as the sleighbells tinkled and the horse trotted easily, enjoying the exercise. We responded to winter in the same way as did the folk of Shakespeare's Cotswolds. Dick the shepherd blew his nail and Marion's nose looked red and raw, great armfuls of logs were borne into the house, the pails of milk were frozen, birds sat brooding in the snow, and there was continuous coughing in church. In the evening the family gathered beside a big fire in the kitchen, turning the frayed wristbands of a shirt-sleeve, going through the events of the day and the parish.

In spring and summer the Garioch of central Aberdeenshire is a smiling landscape for more of the time than the legend would allow us to believe. The morning hillside was dew-pearled, the sound of larks and peewits filled the air, the shepherd moved quietly among the lambing ewes. The rough winter earth has been torn up, ploughed and grubbered and weeded, to make a bed for oats and barley and turnip seed, the seeds have been bedded down and tucked in comfortably and the roller has evened out everything into a brown tidiness, ochre when it is dry and a rich soft brown when it is wet. In April and May there is a clear, sharp light that makes the newly budded trees vivid and sparkles on granite buildings and on granite chippings on the road. We enjoyed the gleams and glooms of a morning in early May after a night of rain. I was just in time to see the last of the hand-sowing of oats. When the sower went forth to sow, he put an old thick shirt over his jacket and trousers and paced along the field rhythmically scattering handfuls ('gowpenfus') of seed, now the right hand, now the left. Like the Bible community we entered into the idiom of good shepherds, tares, barns, seedtime and harvest. For children the identification with Biblical customs was total. We believed that Jacob's farm was like local farms and we visualized it down to the last detail of the cart-horses' harness, the build of the carts, the red and blue and green paint, and the shining brass plate inscribed with the name and address of the farmer. In the Sunday school my father asked a class how it came about that Jacob's sons, visiting Egypt for corn, didn't know their long-lost brother Joseph, but Joseph knew *them*. A hand shot up immediately with the pride of sudden insight. 'Joseph would have seen the name on the carts.'

There is a Biblical simplicity in that reply. I visualize country children seeking to make sense out of the insufficient material accorded to them, like jigsaws with pieces missing. We all long for the security of full comprehension and we improvise the bits missing. The children saw Jacob as a rich Aberdeenshire farmer. It was bound to be a big farm since there were all these sons working it. Probably they bred shorthorns and the byres would have been decorated with red first-prize tickets won at agricultural shows all over the north-east and even furth of our region. Pharaoh was a laird in alien country several miles south of Aberdeen who had fee'd Jacob's son, Joseph, as farm-grieve or overseer. Jacob's sons had washed out their carts and spread straw in the well of the carts and put on their Sunday clothes and harnessed the horses and began the long journey ben the turnpike. They arrived at Pharaoh's farm unbeknown to Joseph and stabled their beasts and went in for their supper. In the gloaming Joseph was taking a dander through the close and came on these strange carts and he went up to one of them and in the fading light read the lettering on the burnished brass plate,

JACOB & SONS,
MAINS OF SHECHEM,
DOTHAN.

I used to laugh at the innocence and incongruity of their imagining. Isis and Osiris, the mummified bodies in the pyramids, the hiero-glyphics, Nefertiti and Nefertari, were civilizations away from the Aberdeenshire farm-touns. But lately I've been wondering. Maybe childish intuition was better founded than I thought. Maybe Nefertiti wasn't really different from a country queyne, powdered and painted for a village dance; and there were Pharaohs among our farmers.

We were aware of our Biblical roots. We knew less about how much we had in common with peasant Europe. One day returning from delivering a telegram I saw a notice pinned on a tree announc-ing that there would be a 'Love darg' (a darg is a task, and a love darg is a task done for the love of it and without payment) to hoe the tur-nips of a crofter neighbour whose leg had been broken by a kick from a horse. Much later in his book *Mutual Aid* I read Kropotkin's description of that custom and of similar customs in mediaeval and modern Europe. We did not know that we were members of such a wide confederacy of rural communities.

An awareness of such connections grew in a random way. We read *A Midsummer Night's Dream* in school and it very slowly dawned on me that these country folk were like us. On fine winter nights when I cycled through woods and across open, rough country with a late telegram, I was one with Shakespeare's night-wanderers, enjoying the moonlight, the deep shadow of the woods, the rutted tracks, the trinkling burn, the star patterns and gauzy clouds half-hiding them, the comforting lights in small windows. What were Shakespeare's travellers thinking when they ventured abroad at night? Did they believe in Jack o' Lantern? Probably not, but there was so much tavern evidence of night travellers who had been misled, and of milkmaids who had had stools unaccountably pulled from under their bums, that they couldn't be sure. It was later still that I learned that Shakespeare's country folk spoke of their bums. The word had been censored from our school copy of *A Midsummer Night's Dream* and, although we were sharp enough to smell a rat because of the break in the rhythm, we didn't dream that a Great Poet would use what we were taught to regard as a vulgar word.

About the same time I learned from Milton's *Il Penseroso* (and later from *Paradise Lost*) and from Gray's *Elegy* and Hardy's novels and poems just how much country folk in different places down the centuries, in Warwickshire and Horton and Stoke Poges and Wessex, had in common with us in twentieth-century rural Aberdeenshire. We were all Jock Tamson's bairns. But that was not what Literature was about. Literature was about Great Poetry, not about our common humanity. The teachers of literature interposed a filter excluding the homeliness, making everything grey and abstract. But some things got through the filter. *Il Penseroso* speaks of the mower whetting his scythe, an age-old sound which I frequently heard. It has the sharpness and the rasp of the peewit's call. Later we got to know about Horace's Odes and Virgil's *Georgics*, and later still I read Sholokhov's *And Quiet Flows the Don*, and learned also about the rich earth of China. We might have felt at home in the Han civilization, digging the alluvial soil of the Yellow River basin five millennia ago. We were one with the cultivators of Galilee and Latium and the Ukraine.

Like those others, we were a closely knit, warm community. From the age of four to sixteen I delivered telegrams (or 'wires' as they were called) to an area within three and a half miles of Wartle Station and knew every person and house and road and farm-track and dog. Sometimes I got a gruff 'Nae reply' but usually I was invited in and got a jam piece or a sweetie or a drink of 'reamy' (creamy) milk. It was a friendly community, not censorious. The sociable postman was sometimes offered so many drams that he lay down, at the roadside. The news got to my father who was subpostmaster and he cycled to the place where Jimmie had, as they said, 'foundered', and took his letters to the post office and then helped him home. Nobody complained. On one of these occasions I remember Jimmie in the post office taking his pipe out of his mouth and, his eyes shining, declaiming lines from *Tam o' Shanter*.

> 'Ah, Tam! Ah, Tam! thou'll get thy fairin'!
> In hell they'll roast thee . . .'

and Jimmie paused to give emphasis to the next words, 'like a herrin'!' And then he laughed loud. Like Tam he was glorious,

> 'O'er a' the ills o' life victorious!'

Burns's words like 'glorious' and 'roarin' fu'' (which meant the same as Shakespeare's 'reeling ripe') and his poetry were part of the currency of everyday speech. The imagery in local songs was vivid because it was drawn from daily experience. A song about a rural wedding describes the dancers as revolving like chaff and broken straws and light grains in a sieve.

> They gaed roon an' roon aboot like sheelocks roon a riddle.

On a Saturday afternoon a stationmaster on our branch line who was a bee expert was called away to deal with a farmer's swarm and he told the guard on the down train that if on his return journey there were any passengers waiting, the railway office would be open and would he issue tickets from the ticket-case and leave the money in the till. Between trains at another station the signalman made furniture and the floor of the signalbox was ankle-deep in wood shavings. These men did not do their work less well because their leisure interpenetrated their work. The Great North of Scotland Railway, whose main line ran from Aberdeen to Elgin and whose branches went to Peterhead and Macduff and Ballater, was small enough to give its members a unity, loyalty to one another, an intimate sense of belonging. A railway guard on the Aberdeen to

Elgin train was confronted at Huntly by the Catholic priest. The conversation went something like this.

Priest: Could you tell me the name of the ticket inspector at Aberdeen who checked the tickets of passengers joining this train?

Guard: Has your brother offended you?

Priest: Yes. I consider he was most discourteous.

Guard: Is it the first time your brother has offended you?

Priest: To the best of my knowledge, yes.

Guard: The scriptural injunction is, thou shalt forgive until seventy times seven.

And with that the guard turned and walked back to his van.

The members of that society had the close-knit relationship and the independence of a mediaeval guild. Most of them weren't all that concerned about promotion, and that immunity gave them a freedom of opinion and expression that has been reduced by our growing emphasis on material gain. One stationmaster, on receiving a high-handed and what he considered an undeserved rebuke from the headquarters office in Aberdeen, replied fiercely, quoting Shakespeare,

> 'Man, proud man,
> Dressed in a little brief authority . . .'

The general tenor of their lives was relaxed and friendly. Our chickens and turkeys roamed and scratched over the railway loading-plank, picking up corn, and laid eggs in the straw-pile in the goods shed. Once a light Sussex hen settled in comfortably among sacks of oats going to Aberdeen and the porter didn't notice her when he tied a tarpaulin over the railway waggon. We didn't know that the little white hen had been missing until, next morning, the porter drew back the tarpaulin from a waggon shunted into our goods shed and there, among our village imports from Aberdeen, perhaps sacks of sugar and rolls of stiff leather, oilcake for cattle, Mustad horseshoe nails from Sweden and gardening tools, snug amongst a heap of straw, sat the little hen, none the worse for her venture. A railway porter at the Waterloo goods depot in Aberdeen had found her and noted the place of origin of the waggon and probably put her into a closed place and later transferred her, just as they were tying the tarpaulin over a waggon consigned to Wartle. We liked to think that the wee hen had laid an egg on her way to Aberdeen and that her protector took it home to his children and told them the story of the hen's odyssey.

But changes, large and small, were infiltrating into our rural economy. When an order came out saying that railwaymen had to retire at seventy, the engine-driver on our branch line had to go. This break in age-old continuity came to him as a rude shock. 'If I had thocht it wasna to be a permanent job,' he said, 'I would never have ta'en it on.' On farm-touns the introduction of the eight-hours' day was regarded as an infringement of the laws of nature, a violation of the rhythms of feeding times and milking times. We didn't realize how piecemeal our society was changing. There was always somebody getting into the lead with some innovation or other. Somebody would bring home from Aberdeen a magic lantern and stick a towel on the kitchen wall and blow out the lamp and turn a handle and there on the white towel were pictures of men jumping about in a jerky fashion all over the place. Somebody else would dig up a family stereoscope and visitors sitting round 'the room' fire on a Sunday night (the only night when a fire was lit in 'the room') gazed with wonder at the three-dimensional reality of the Lucerne memorial and houses and landscape. People liked reaping the reward of a neighbour's astonishment. The greatest wonder I saw was a small box which had an immense horn growing out of it. The box was on a chair in the barn and the straw had been pushed well back, and a voice, which didn't come from anybody hidden in the straw but from the box itself, was singing the hymn, 'Yield not to temptation.'

There were kaleidoscopes, belt-driven motor bicycles, centri-fuges to spin off the cream. A small engine that drove a threshing machine caused the mill-dam and the mill-lade and the water-wheel to fall into neglect. There were visits from relatives who had gone to work on the prairies or on a milk-round in Detroit. Slated houses were going up and thatched houses were falling down. Water-closets close to the house replaced the earth privies (incon-gruously called 'wateries') in the garden. Turnpike roads were beginning to be tarred and that made cycling easier. The small railway was swallowed up by the London and North Eastern Railway and from Doncaster, the waggon control centre, a new word was communicated to Aberdeenshire farmers and crofters, *demurrage*. That was the extra money they paid if they didn't at once cart away their goods from a waggon in the loading bank; previously they had taken their time to it. A Labour candidate, a farm-workers' representative, came third but with a respectable vote, in a by-election. There were pictures of James Smillie, a railway union leader. There was a railway strike. A revered highlander, formerly my father's dominie at Aberlour and then rector of a large academy at Banff, leaned out of a delayed train one Saturday morning (I remember his severe face and beard of formal cut) and asked, 'Who are the blackguards?' I hadn't heard of black guards. Our railway guards wore a blue uniform. My father explained to me that a blackguard was a scoundrel; the dominie was saying that strikers were scoundrels.

David Toulmin, novelist of the north-east, who spent most of his working life as a farm labourer, described farm life in a phase of change. It wasn't all an idyll, the peaceful march of the seasons, rural mirth and healthy ribaldry and sweet content. There was another side to it, poverty and monotony, one furrow after another, swathe after swathe while the sun crept so slowly across its circular orbit and you straightened your back and gave yourself the luxury of listening to the lark, a brief intermission before you bent your back again. The prospect of this treadmill for yourself and your children for ever and ever. The professor of political economy in the University of Aberdeen explained to his students that there could be something of value in monotonous work. 'I enjoy weeding my garden.' A farmer's son commented, 'He wouldna have said that if he had to do it a' the time.' Even if you could lay your hands on some money and get a place of your own, you still had to work hard. Neighbours of ours sold their milk and brought their children up on tea and bread and treacle. Siren voices were beckoning the farm-workers to lusher pastures and making them dissatisfied with the simplicities of seedtime and harvest. In *Harvest Home*, Toulmin tells of his infatuation with Garbo and Dietrich and Dorothy Lamour. One night, when he returned from seeing *Rose Marie* in a

Fraserburgh cinema, the blue and white cow, Gorgonzola, calved and, with the Ave Marias of Jeanette MacDonald and Nelson Eddy ringing in his ears, he helped deliver Gorgonzola of a swarthy bullock.

Toulmin had found the land of pure delight that we Scots have sought all down our history to escape to from our pent-up dissatisfactions, the non-realization of our dreams. Long ago we thought Saint Ninian could lead us to it. We thought we could find it through the rituals and incense of Roman Catholicism, the austerity of Calvinism, the unction of the Revivalist preachers, in materialism and respectability, in whisky (*uisge beatha*, the water of life, an elixir that gave us the same euphoria as the Europeans gained from *aqua vitae* and *eau de vie*), and in heroin and cocaine. For a time in twentieth-century Scotland, Jerusalem and Rome and Geneva had been replaced by Hollywood. Religious pessimists say we'll never find this land of pure delight. I think they're wrong. Rural life does hold the prospect of happiness if we have enough food in our bellies and are free from back-breaking toil, so that we feel free to enjoy the sight of the dew-pearled hillside and the snail on the thorn.

But in the twenties all these social and mechanical changes, even the wireless aerial that the blacksmith set up on his kitchen lum, caused only a few ripples on the surface of the ever-moving stream that had flowed apparently unchanged down the centuries. Scythe and sickle were replaced by reaper and mower, but we took them and even the complicated binder in our stride. Rural history was full of precedents showing the ability of farm folk to react to the pressures of nature, and adjust and initiate and evolve. The expansion of China, wrote Professor Keith Buchanan, was largely 'the history of the expansion of a specialized agricultural economy whose technological roots go back to the first elaboration of a "hydraulic civilization" in the valleys of the yellow-earth country more than four millennia ago'. Ingenious farm-workers within my telegram area had enough of the skills of saddler, sailmaker, mechanic and blacksmith to cope with the preparation of the binder for the harvest. The binder, a triumph of man the toolmaker, was still a manageable tool that the farm-workers could fully understand and service. David Toulmin's description of a binder at work shows a total comprehension of its working parts. He detailed the links in the chain of operation – the blade in lightning motion slashing the feet from the ripened corn, the packer arms bundling the stalks into the amount of a sheaf, the wooden butter tidying up the ends of the sheaf, the knotter tying it and the knife cutting the twine, the delivery arms tossing the sheaf on to the ground at intervals. We enjoyed cultivating new skills and displaying mastery of a new craft. In each railway station a centrally pivoted needle tinkled out more messages. On a still summer afternoon the youthful railway clerk would open the office door and the back door of the station and go out and sit on his bicycle only just within hearing range of the needle and, holding the telegraph pad on his left hand, transcribe the incoming message.

As Gray's elegy said, village life was circumscribed; but there was always this movement at the periphery, gingerly pushing out, always wanting to try a step farther. It must often have been a humorous story, the story of the innocence of human beings equipped with nothing but ancient experience with which to essay an advance into the unknown. When the telephone was put into Wartle Station a farmer begged to be allowed to use it to send an urgent message to Inveramsay (known as 'the Ram') three miles away. He shouted into the mouthpiece with all the power of his lungs, and the railway porter said, 'John, man, they could hear ye at the Ram withoot a phone. Ye dinna need to buly [bellow] like that.'

The 1946 official report on primary education in Scotland said that because of remoteness from outside influences, speech in the north-east had remained more unchanged since mediaeval times than elsewhere in Scotland. And attitudes also were unchanged. A local farmer's son who became a medical consultant in Aberdeen, rose to high rank in the 1939–45 war. When he was on leave in his native area a local farm-worker said, 'Hullo, Wullie, I hear they've made ye a corporal.'

'Corporal be damned,' he replied. 'I'm a bloody brigadier.'

Maybe the local man had read that Hitler, like Napoleon, had been a corporal and had assumed that that was the highest army rank available to anybody. The incident shows how our isolation saved us from the reverence for army rank, mandatory elsewhere.

It's difficult to fathom what was in the minds of local people. There were reports that some people, coming unawares on the roadman breaking stones all day at the roadside, heard him swearing at his enemies, such as the chairman of the local council (who wanted to keep down roadmen's wages), as he brought his hammer down sharply on an intransigent stone. On life and death we weren't supposed to ask questions. That would have been arrogant, like querying the doctor's diagnosis, a lack of respect for the people, the experts, who looked after such things for us. You kept your questions to yourself. Once in a blue moon you might venture a hesitating question on first and last things if you had a deep trust in the man you were putting your question to and knew that he wouldn't make fun of your naïveté or bamboozle you with abstract words. 'Agent,' said a neighbouring farmer to my father one day, 'Agent, what does the versey mean where it says,

> The moon by night thee shalt not smite,
> Nor yet the sun by day?

We sing it often in the kirk, but . . .' If Alec had dared a further elaboration of his question he would have added that he didn't want to hit the moon or the sun anyway, such an idea had never entered his thoughts; so why . . . ? My father explained that it was a promise that neither the sun nor the moon would hit us, and Alec said, 'Oh, aye,' and left it at that. There was a vague assumption that the ministers of the kirk, like the doctors, the dominies and the distant politicians, had everything well in hand, and we accepted and didn't interfere. Most of the community theoretically supported the kirk, and even those who used their sabbaths for a long lie in bed, and the repair of farm machines and flat bicycle-tyres, felt it prudent to maintain their lines of communication by attending the twice-yearly sacrament of the Lord's supper, not enquiring too much into the meaning of the mystery of the bread and wine. They tolerated mutants like 'the chapel folk' (Episcopalians) and the Plymouth Brethren, but were suspicious of the very few Catholics in the same way as present-day Americans are suspicious of Communists, uneasy about them, wondering what they might be up to. In the kirk they sang, with becoming gravity, verses that were doggerel.

But yet the Lord that is on high
Is more of might by far
Than noise of many waters is
Or great sea-billows are.

Aberdeenshire children were brought up in the insecurity of half-information. There was, for example, an absence of reliable information about the Devil. He went about like a raging lion, we were assured. The picture of him was filled out by random details, like a present-day police identikit picture of a dangerous criminal who is at large. He had a tail and cloven hooves, a neat, pointed beard like the French cardinal Richelieu and a mischievous look like Bernard Shaw. He was obviously highly intelligent, a fallen angel, the leader of a degenerate Cavalier gang providing all the fun that our Roundhead kirk denied us. 'If it's Heaven for comfort, it's Hell for company,' said a Barrie character. There was no doubt about it, the Devil had charisma, as we say nowadays. The luxuriant imagery of the Revivalists made our interest in him compulsive. We were hooked on the brimstone, blazing in the fiery furnace, the appealingly rich vocabulary of velour iniquity, the lures of the flesh, Sodom and Gomorrah, Babylon, foul fiends, witches in cutty sarks (not all wizened witches like those that Macbeth encountered on a desert heath near Forres, but – Burns assured us – some comely wenches, too), drink and fornication, dancing, theatres, card-playing.

We had no cards in our house but on winter evenings when I delivered a telegram to a remote dwelling and saw people playing cards under the lamplight, I was attracted by the rich tapestry of wickedness in the clothes of the courtly figures, king, queen and jack. The kings and jacks had jerkins of red and gold and blue and black and had elegant moustaches shaped like the sound holes of a violin. Dancing was robed in the unco aura of a witches' coven. Later when I went to the theatre in Aberdeen I had a delicious sense of overstepping the bounds of virtue and entering the abode of sin. Our fantasies, like Tam o' Shanter's, showed us the tantalizing benefits of a compact with the Devil, a document we might be lured into signing. For us, exactly as for the ancient Greeks participating in the bacchanalian feasts at Delphi and in the ceremonies of the

Eleusinian mysteries, there was a shivering, ravishing sense that longs for consummation in untold wickedness at whatever cost and for a glimpse behind the veil of forbidden knowledge. John Buchan's *Witchwood* gives an inside story of douce Presbyterians escaping from their religion and exploring forbidden realms.

But in spite of the vividness with which we perceived a sector of activity called 'sin', the identity of the Devil, and even his existence, remained in doubt. For all the traditional imagery he was a shadowy figure. We went through our childhood not knowing if he were a real being or a character in a fairy story. Children have a greater capacity for understanding, and a more urgent need for sure ground under their feet, than adults imagine. They would gain in self-confidence if the ministers and dominies said more clearly what they believed, and explained that other people believed other things, and left it to the children to reach their own conclusions. But they waffle and haver, and children are left groping in the dark, trying to fill in the missing bits of the jigsaw for themselves, to produce a feasible scenario of life and death. We were brought up to believe in a heaven 'above the bright blue sky' where the soul went when the body died. When the daughter of our crofter neighbour died, my sister, believing that the afternoon of the funeral would be the time when the soul ascended, sat on our garden swing and watched and waited, and saw nothing, but believed that the mystery had taken place during a moment of inattention. The flight of the soul, probably in the shape of a dove, was even more elusive than a glimpse of a corncrake in the long grass, but nevertheless available to those who had the patience to watch and wait.

An Italian novel, Carlo Levi's *Christ Stopped at Eboli*, said that Christianity never penetrated far from the Mediterranean and that the Apennine interior of Basilicata was never really Christianized. Was central Aberdeenshire Christianized? The minister was often a kind, upright man, guiding and helping his flock, but was their neighbourliness and loving-kindness due to his teaching or would they have been good neighbours anyway? What were the roots of the good neighbourliness? I'm not sure. We need more enquiry. We didn't produce Chicago gangsters like the hilltowns of Basilicata. We had no Al Capone or Johnny Torio. The people who went to the kirk regularly and those who rarely went were equally kind. There was a duality in the community, the kirk folk and those who, although nominally Christian, didn't give religion much thought, the 'non-pratiquants', as they are called in France. We lived in a climate of reservation about some of the kirk's teachings. (Part of the doubt was due to the kirk's reluctance to say clearly what some of its teachings were.) Some of the commandments were in doubt. The first commandment said, 'Thou shalt have no other gods before me', but nobody wanted to set up an altar to Baal at the Maiden Stone at the foot of Bennachie. There was no disposition to worship graven images. Of the commandments that were clearly understood, we mostly kept those that it was in our nature to keep: we honoured our parents, we didn't kill or steal or bear false witness, and covetousness was not a besetting sin. Sex was different. At dances, farm-workers pressed close to the breasts of their partners but they had a vague idea that they weren't suppposed to do that. The non-kirk folk had a free and easy attitude to sex and spoke about it naturally. I remember seeing a young farmer filling up his cart with sacks of artificial manure from the Milling Company's or the Lime Company's store beside the railway loading-bank. He was a bachelor and had a young housekeeper. He was accompanied by an eight-year-old boy, red-cheeked, smiling, well cared for. 'That's a bonnie laddie ye have with you,' said the storekeeper. 'Did ye mak him yersel?'

About the age of seven I spent much time at the neighbouring croft. The hens strolled through the kitchen and sat comfortably on cushions on the dees. On butter-making days I watched the plump-churn and the process of an age-old wonder (as old as domesticated animals), cream precipitated in yellow, flocculent scraps and then firmed into substantial butter. The crofter's wife had a simple ceremony to mark the consummation of the process. Country folk like to mark occasions, in both senses of the word to *celebrate* regularly recurring events. They had cliack sheaves marking the end of the cutting of the corn, and harvest homes, and yule bannocks. The production of the butter was marked by the presentation of 'a thoomed piece', a 'quarter' of newly-baked oatcakes on which the new butter had been spread by her thumb. When her morning's work was finished and the dinner dishes cleared away and washed and stacked, she washed herself from a basin on the kitchen table.

The presence of a child didn't embarrass her. 'Would you like to see my paaps [breasts]?' she asked me, as she took off her blouse. It was my first view of the mature female form, an ample one. At the age of seven I knew intuitively not to recount the incident to my parents. They were practising Christians and had taken aboard the sexual inhibitions enjoined by the kirk. Even at that early age the kirk was prising open the generation gap, separating me from my parents. The crofter's wife belonged to an earlier dispensation. Although there was much neighbourliness between her home and ours, my parents faintly disapproved of her. Maybe it was the Christian dis-approval of a still-enduring paganism. I recall two incidents which may be significant. When their old grandfather died, as a sign of special esteem they presented my mother with a small piece of cloth cut off his grave-clothes; and this she politely refused. And when the crofter's wife came to inspect the bookcase my father had got the joiner to make, she said that the books in the case looked fine but it would have been bonnier if my mother had used the case to display her best china.

Twice a year they dressed in black clothes and harnessed the Clydesdale work-horse called 'Mallie' and drove to the kirk to par-take of the bread and wine. What was in their minds as they bowed their heads over the white napery of the pew-shelf in mute accept-ance of a solemn act of worship? I doubt if there was much sense of awe, but they did have a sense of community participation in cele-brating a required sacred rite. The general attitude was passivity and I never heard any questioning of the rite. Nor among the main body of the folk was there much political questioning, just a dour acceptance. Many farm-servants were numbed and desensitized by poverty and wet clothes and the prospect of trudging along an end-less furrow. They retaliated by 'rochness'. 'Roch' is the same word as the English 'rough' but it means much more than that. The roch farm-servant pretended to be indifferent to cold and wore no scarf or mittens or overcoat; he was indifferent to good manners and responded with the coarsest vocabulary he could think of; he was indifferent to hygiene. His hero was an Aberdeenshire farm-servant whose feats of rochness projected him into a legendary figure. He was called 'Roch Tam'. His fellow-workers vied with one another to impress him with their roch initiatives. They lived in a farm bothy or 'chaumer' and for breakfast they made brose and supped it with milk which had been poured into milk bowls for each of them the previous night. A thick layer of cream topped the milk when the farm-worker sat down to his breakfast. One morning a farm-worker, to impress Tam, having poured boiling water into a kaap of oatmeal, took it outside and pissed on the ground as he stirred it. Tam gave a snort of contempt and decided to teach the youngster a lesson in the real meaning of rochness. The legend has it that he took up his bowl of milk and, instead of a spoon, used his cock to ease the cream off the side of the bowl.

Much rural accommodation was dispiriting. We had a kitchen, a bedroom and 'the room' which was used for special occasions. When our parents felt that one bedroom was insufficient for five people (them and my two sisters and me), the railway company refused to add a bedroom unless my father paid an extra rent of ten per cent. The house was damp and wallpaper peeled off the bedroom. In some airts of the wind the kitchen chimney wouldn't draw and the reek was blown back into the kitchen, suffocating billows which dimmed the light of the paraffin lamp and covered the shining-white, newly ironed clothes with a myriad of black smuts, and my mother wept tears of frustration. The railway architect came to inspect the lum and put a taller chimney-can on it. It made no difference and when he returned he said there was nothing further he could think about to alleviate the down-draughts (smoke, it seemed, was an act of God) and what would she suggest? She replied, 'You're the architect.' Finally the blacksmith shaped a piece of iron which hooked on the bars of the grate and reduced the space for the air-intake. Always the first questions addressed to friends who had moved to another house were 'Is the house damp? Have you smoke?' My mother was a perfectionist and liked to do well whatever she undertook – playing the piano or mandoline, singing, embroidery, fine needlework, cooking, drawing. Her laundering bore the same mark of excellence. Later when I looked at seventeenth-century Dutch paintings and the pearly white of their newly-laundered clothes, I realized that my mother was akin to those Dutch craftswomen housewives. There isn't much in the school histories that reveals the ability of our forebears and the frustrations that dampened and often quenched the flame of

artistry seeking to illuminate their lives. Complementary to that
artistic love of excellence was the spirit of enquiry, which also runs
like a thread of gold through working-class history. Luther pre-
eminently asked questions. They were about religion but inadver-
tently he stimulated questions on politics, since the spirit of
enquiry is indivisible. However much the English squires like
Cromwell and Pym and Hampden tried to douse political enquiry,
that smoking flax was not quenched. My father was in that tradition, seeing the reformed religion and a reformed politics as
indivisible, and alike accessible to the question of those who were
making an independent search for a way of life and an attitude to
the universe. In his younger day, in the evenings in rural railway
stations between trains, he had read D'Aubigné's *History of the
Reformation in Europe.* (One of the laird's guests, arriving early to
meet a train, told him the correct pronunciation of D'Aubigné.) He
searched the scriptures diligently. He attended a local weekly
prayer-meeting where they studied Biblical texts. The carpenter
quoted. 'These are they which came out of great tribulations,' and
my father corrected quietly, 'Tribulation.' Even though it interrupted the flow of his argument, the carpenter maintained the
correctness of his quotation. My father said, 'All right, then. We'll
look it up.' They turned to the seventh chapter of *The Revelation*
and there it was, at verse 14: 'tribulation'. I think of that scene, its
Rembrandt quality; the little ante-room of the corrugated-iron
village hall, a table in the middle, cupboards holding Bibles and
hymn books, an oil-lamp hung from the ceiling, maybe half a dozen
local men peering reverently into the recesses of the holy books
seeking a lamp to guide their steps. In this tradition that derived
from Luther and Knox, Abraham Lincoln was reared. Lincoln's
biographer, Carl Sandburg, said that Lincoln 'would sometimes
correct a misquotation of Scripture and give chapter and verse
where it could be found'. But no less important than this scholarly
insistence on getting a quotation meticulously right was their
determination to get back to basics as they saw it, not to accept the
word of any human authority. One spring evening, my father, digging the garden as I returned from the university, stopped to ask me
what I thought of something or other. I had started to say, 'Professor So-and-so thinks . . .' when he interrupted me. I still remember

his hand moving in a slight gesture of impatience. 'Never mind what the professor thinks. What do *you* think?' An incident like that put me into the way of asking questions – a casual exchange of views on my way between the garden gate and the supper table in the kitchen, and its enduring memory.

The Scottish schools and universities didn't much contribute to this independence of thought. A Scottish poet, reflecting on his schooldays in a Donside academy, threw some light on the process by which Scotland restricted freedom in its schools while gaining an international reputation for literacy. 'The three highest classes used to be taken together for English. So when I was in the fourth year I had to write "essays" on the same subjects as the fifth and sixth were given, and we read the same books. *King Lear* was one of them and we had to write an essay on the character of Edmund. What had I, son of a village tailor, to say about the son of the Earl of Gloster? By racking my brains and stretching my imagination, just enough to fill half-a-page. The boys and girls in the Sixth, though – young men and women, they seemed to me – got off to a flying start (a very good class they were from the examination point of view) and filled several pages. Most of them got high marks; my attempt was dismissed not with a sneer but with a casualness that was as good as a sneer to me. I asked one of the Sixth afterwards to show me the essay for which he got alpha+; I wanted to see just how any-one could fill five pages as he did on a subject which had left my mind clawing desperately at the empty air. Then I saw the recipe for success. You quoted Shakespeare first of all. That was a good one! I felt I'd been the victim of a trick. You took your Shakespeare and copied out what he had made Edmund say. I'd never have thought of that. If the stuff was printed, why write it? Then you quoted Bradley's *Shakespearean Tragedy* and you linked all these quotations with little sentences of your own. So that was how it was done. I made up my mind to try it – and I did – with an essay on Keats. We had a fair number of books at home – that gave me con-siderable advantage over a great many of my fellow-pupils in that village school – and among these books was a very decayed copy of Mason's *History of English Literature*. There was also a book called *The Achievements of Youth* which my brother had got for good attendance at Sunday School. There was a section on Keats with the odd quotation about the *Quarterly*'s savage attack and fortunately Mason gave a long quotation from Jeffrey's *Edinburgh Review*. With them, a few quotations from such of Keats as appeared in Palgrave (I liked the bit in *The Realm of Fancy*,

> And the cakéd snow is shuffled
> From the ploughboy's heavy shoon

because I'd seen that at the village smiddy and my mother used to call shoes "shoon"), with them and a few sentences of my own there was an essay in literary criticism fitted. I handed it in; I got it out – and the headmaster who took us for English really began to take me seriously. This brought me mixed pleasure; what I wrote myself was of no value at all; what I copied from books was – the goods! I liked the high mark, but did not much like the way one had to go about things to earn it.'

Later when he became a teacher of English in a prestigious fee-paying school in Aberdeen, he had an encounter with the head of his department who was instructing his assistants in the marking of examination papers. As he described it, the encounter went like this.

Question:	Write a sentence in which you use the word 'genius'.
Boy's answer:	The man was a genius.
Principal Teacher's comment:	He can't get full marks for that because he hasn't shown that he understands the meaning of the word 'genius'.
Question:	Write a sentence in which you use the word 'hydrogen'.
Boy's answer:	Air is composed of hydrogen and oxygen.
Principal Teacher:	Full marks. He understands the meaning of the word 'hydrogen' and he has conveyed information.
Assistant Teacher:	But the information is wrong.
Principal Teacher:	Is it?
Assistant Teacher:	Yes, of course it is.
Principal Teacher:	Nevertheless, he has tried to convey information. Full marks.

That's in the Scottish tradition. The principle (of conveying information) is more important than the practice (the information conveyed). The form is more important than the content. This rarefied, cold, austere thought, superior to the satisfactions of sensuous living, has a bleak appeal for us. The asceticism about this devotion to first principles is maybe a hark-back to the monastery and its insulation from the tempting vulgarities of the market-place. In our village the blacksmith's son left school at the first opportunity and in his father's smiddy tinkered with motor bicycles. I stayed on at school and learned the first principles about magnetism and electricity. I couldn't make a broken-down motor bicycle work and envied him his empiricism and its satisfactions – making his motor bicycle work, and flying up hill and down dale on it, his bonnet turned back to front and his breeks flapping in the wind.

The dissociation between the theory and practice of knowledge has bedevilled learning, and the Asiatic visitor might enquire into the role played in Scotland by its world-renowned education. (Aberdeen had two universities when England had still only two.) The purpose of King's College in Aberdeen (as defined by the Borgia pope, Alexander VI, when the foundation of the university was sanctioned in 1494) was to help 'rude and barbarous' men to profit from 'the pearl of knowledge, which shows the way to live well and happily'. Whoever wrote these words for Alexander was aware that a university could help the people of the city and its hinterland to find their way through life, a kindly light in the encircling gloom. But to extort from knowledge the essence which will help us to live well and happily required a skill which eluded most of the scholars. They could compel the truth from ancient texts, amending and remaking our image of the earth's history and of the convolutions of its thought, but for many students the study of the Latin texts became an end in itself. There were scholars who spoke out against this tradition. Seven centuries ago Roger Bacon said, 'If I had my way, I should burn all the books of Aristotle, for the study of them can lead only to a loss of time, produce error and increase ignorance . . . Cease to be ruled by dogmas and authorities; LOOK AT THE WORLD!' John Stevenson, professor of philosophy in Edinburgh (1730–5), replaced the study of

Aristotle with modern philosophy, natural philosophy and logic. A century and a half ago in Aberdeen Professor MacGillivray, physician and botanist, gave geology lectures on the site. He said,

> A single-minded man may by the right use of his eyes, anywhere that the sun shines, and the wind blows, and the rains fall, find abundant matter for observation and instruction.

From his journeys through Deeside to Braemar there emerges an enjoying spirit exulting like Linnaeus in the wonder of creation. Nobody who had walked the Deeside hills in that spirit was likely to be over-respectful towards ancient texts. Today more of the university teachers are following in his footsteps. The extramural lecturers have had a concern for the whole community.

Outwith the scope and care of the university and on the other side of Bennachie from the poet, a railway clerk was conducting his own enquiries into the nature of life and society. He was brought up on a small farm at the Kirtown of Rayne. He left school at fourteen and got a job as a railway clerk. He told me later, 'At seventeen I suddenly woke up and realized I had been asleep for the preceding part of my life.' He started reading everything he could lay his hands on. He had read that David Livingstone studied a Latin grammar while working at his loom at Blantyre near Glasgow, and he too studied Latin. But he quickly gave it up. He bought secondhand books in the gallery of the New Market in Aberdeen. Not a new planet but a new universe had swum into his ken. He read about history, physics, economics, politics, religion, philosophy, astronomy, literature. He read widely, voraciously, submitting everything to a vigorously independent judgement. At Inveramsay, the junction where a branch line to Macduff left the main Aberdeen–Inverness line, he and a shunter shared a two-roomed shack which they called 'Utopia'. One half of it was partitioned off for sleeping. In the other half there were two chairs, a table, scores of books later gathered into shelves, a paraffin lamp and a paraffin stove that went glug-glug as occasionally we sat into the night discussing everything in heaven and earth. He became a socialist and got the *Daily Herald* daily.

In the nineteen-twenties, Scotland was in transition from the dominance of religious disputation and the quoting of scripture. There were other questions to dig into, other quotations to cite in evidence. I was a university student, a docile professional; he was the enquiring, irreverent amateur. My university lecturers talked, largely, about 'transitions' and in their classrooms we were invited, in a vague, abstract way, to envisage the process of a transition in history. In a shack at Inveramsay I was privileged to observe the small, homely details by which a transition takes place. It's the process by which large numbers of people doff an old allegiance and don a new one, giving up paganism for Columba's Christianity, giving up Catholicism for Knox's Calvinism, giving up religion for socialism. It's like the details of the metamorphosis by which a caterpillar changes into a butterfly. I was watching one of these changes in slow operation.

It started amusingly with rural disrespect. In those days we were brought up to salute the pillars of society when we met them on a country road. He told me, 'I've decided to stop saluting the laird. I'll salute the doctor and the minister and the dominie because they contribute to the community. But not the laird.' Then, in a sudden glint of a smile, he would descend from this high seriousness to country humour. 'The laird's nae what you could call very intelligent. There's naething in him except what he puts in with a spoon.'

This was not the dour stereotype of the enquiring Scotsman. There were many railwaymen like him who in the previous generation were asking questions about religion and now were transferring their interest to politics. But the religious component didn't disappear suddenly. At that stage these enquirers were asking courteous questions about the kirk. The clerk and I spent many spring and summer Sundays visiting kirks within bicycle range to discover what was on offer. Usually we came out by that same door wherein we went. Like the university, the kirk had become unaware that throughout the north-east there was a market for the words of eternal life. In an undramatic way we were seeking for salvation, for a way of life that would command our total allegiance. What we mostly got was Paul's epistles, which we didn't understand, and dull homilies which we quickly forgot. We enjoyed some of the hymns which retained something of the poetry and the buoyant vision which swept people off their feet in Galilee. I remember vividly the Rev. A. J. Gossip in Beechgrove Kirk in Aberdeen on a summer Sunday afternoon reading the last part of the Sermon on the Mount. He read it with such unselfconscious naturalness that the words leapt out of the text.

> Not every one that saith unto me, Lord, Lord, shall enter into the kingdom of heaven . . . Many will say to me in that day, Lord, Lord, have we not prophesied in thy name? . . . and in thy name done many wonderful works?

> And then will I profess unto them, I never knew you: depart from me, ye that work iniquity.

He glowered over his specs as he looked down on the people he was addressing, and spoke the words, 'I never knew *you*.' If he had added, 'Get to hell out of here,' it would have been totally appropriate. Briefly we had a glimpse of reality, a village carpenter's outburst of anger at the characters whom today's *Private Eye* describes as the Pseuds.

Inveramsay junction could be a cold place and the occasional passenger would be invited into the warm, well-lit porters' room. If he had known about the books in the shack, he might have accepted the invitation with less alacrity. Politicians, provosts and ministers of the Church of Scotland may have misinterpreted the welcome implied in the invitation but they had hardly time to thaw out in the blaze of the fire, fuelled with engine coal, before they found out. How was the unsuspecting minister to know that the railwayman who was entertaining him had just read, very carefully, the preface to Bernard Shaw's *Androcles and the Lion* and had been waiting for just this opportunity to make use of the arguments with which Shaw had provided him? 'How do you explain,' the minister would be asked, 'the difference between the first three gospels on the one hand and St John's gospel on the other?' Or he would be confronted with questions about what Luke meant by 'The Kingdom' and what proof he had that Matthew the publican and Matthew the evangelist were one and the same person.

On their shelves I noticed a book called *The Art of Conversation* which I imagine they had studied as they might have studied a book on chess, because the most harmless-looking opening gambit welcoming the traveller to scrape the snow from his boots and draw the chair up to the fire usually led in half-a-dozen moves to something like 'Check!' Once in the midst of a discussion a minister was asked, 'Have you ever committed adultery?' While he was fuming at the effrontery of the question and fumbling for a reply, the railwayman referred him to Matthew 5, 28 and quoted the verse. 'Whosoever looketh on a woman to lust after her hath committed adultery with her already in his heart.' Checkmate.

They were even harder on politicians. 'Do you know how many tons of coal Britain exported last year?' they would ask, in a softening-up process. I admired that one because there was almost no answer to it except a reluctant 'No', which drew the triumphant reply, 'Well, I'll tell you. Britain exported . . .' No quarry was too big for these railway highwaymen to swoop down upon, firing explosive ideas that they had drawn from the arsenal of Wells and Bernard Shaw and Bertrand Russell and John Stuart Mill and following up with some incendiaries of their own manufacture. From their reading of Shelley, Masefield, Emerson and Bagehot (whose name they mispronounced), they developed confidence and a humorous disrespect for the arts departments of the universities and their high priests of learning. 'Aye, aye,' said the railway clerk to me one evening as I stepped on to the platform after listening to a day's lectures at King's College in Aberdeen, 'and what was the [pause] PROFESSOR [pause] saying today?' Since then I've never been able to hear the word 'professor' without hearing the faint hiss of air escaping from a punctured academic balloon.

The railway clerk was invited to tea with a Church of Scotland missionary newly back from India and the host afterwards expressed amazement at the facts and up-to-date figures which the clerk had produced with ease out of what seemed an extensive background of knowledge. The missionary couldn't know that only the previous day he had read and committed to memory a double column about India in *John o' London's Weekly*, and went to the missionary's house, as he went to every discussion, with the facts at his fingers' end. Once he was caught napping, though. An undergraduate came in, the son of the local joiner, who later became a professor at Princeton in the USA. They had a conversation on the lands of heart's desire, Avalon and Atlantis and El Dorado and Shangri-la and Utopia. The undergraduate asked, 'Have you read More's

Utopia?' Since the clerk had to say no, he told him about it and at great length. Afterwards the clerk told me, with a humour that was for once unconscious, 'Ach, I bet he knew all that only because he had been reading it up for an exam that week.'

One summer he and I went to London for a holiday. We travelled free because he was a railwayman and I was the son of a railwayman. One night we saw Drinkwater's comedy, *Bird in Hand*, and we discussed it as we walked back from the theatre to our lodgings near Gray's Inn Road. We'd enjoyed the play but I pointed out that it wasn't really a good comedy. I had been reading Meredith's essay on comedy for an examination at the university. Meredith laid down the law that a comedy must castigate some of the faults or foibles of the age, as Molière's comedies do. But Drinkwater's play, I said, didn't attack anything. It was a humorous, good-tempered story about life in an English village, but not really a good comedy. He asked me by what right Meredith claimed to lay down the law on comedy and I replied that everybody accepted Meredith's essay as the last word on comedy.

'That's not true,' he said. 'I don't.'

'Do you think you have the right to contradict Meredith?' I asked. I was aggrieved that this amateur should play the game of dramatic criticism with rules of his own making, ignoring the regulations which the professionals had imposed on themselves. It was like an anarchist playing cards and making up his own rules as he went on. I repeated the question. 'Do you think you have as much right to an opinion as Meredith?'

He stopped and considered it further and then he delivered his answer. 'Yes.'

Many years later I conceded that he was right. The professionals methodize and draw up the rules and expound; the students make notes, and the opinions handed down take on a venerable air. Scotland needs disrespectful amateurs to keep the balance right. He introduced me to Wells's *Outline of History*, not a book recommended by the University of Aberdeen. He astounded me by telling me that, halfway through, the book had got only as far as the decline of the Roman Empire. Scottish school education hadn't focused on the perspective of time. History before 55 BC was a gloom, like a November night, and we weren't encouraged to peer into it. There were disconnected constellations in that night sky, the Pharaohs, the Hebrew Prophets, the Greeks, the Romans, but they were out there free-floating, inaccessible. I'd have liked to know more about Ur of the Chaldees but it was only an incantation. Wells, another disrespectful amateur, came and integrated all that and put it into focus. It was as if he gave us a map to tell us where we are and where we might want to go from here. I was amazed, and then delighted, at the chapters on Caesar and Napoleon. Wells was saying, 'I am a man. They were not more. Let's have a look at them.' These were words of emancipation. They were keys that fitted the locks with which any school and university education had enclosed me in a prison of ideas, and particularly ideas about GREAT MEN. They dominated the Aberdeenshire landscape. The literature we were taught was scattered with memorable quotations about them. 'Others abide our question, thou art free.' They bestrode the world like a Colossus and we small men crept under their huge legs to find ourselves dishonourable graves. Wells said about his own early days that he felt that Oliver Goldsmith held his hand. I felt the same indebtedness to Wells. Deep down were those doubts about the worshipful texture of Aberdeenshire ceremonies and doctrines that I hardly dared to articulate and I needed all the comfort and encouragement I could lay my hands on.

The clerk was a member of a large family. None of them followed his example, least of all when he packed in his job and superannuation and insurance and trade-union membership and high-tailed it for London. But they had a smiling, affectionate admiration for him. He was a character, they said. He was 'an affa laad'. I heard from him at intervals. He had hitch-hiked on a railway engine across Perthshire. He was working in a pub in Putney, and enjoyed the encounters, no doubt employing all the arts of conversation on the bar customers that he had used on the railway passengers in the porters' room. I met him once or twice. Once, in the New Forest, he told me of another discovery he had made.

'You know all these newspaper articles on "the problem of sex"?'

'Yes,' I said.

'Well, there is no problem.'

That was in 1935. An intelligent youngster from the parish of Rayne in Presbyterian Aberdeenshire had broken through a traditional inhibition and reached (and practised) his own way of life. When the University of Aberdeen told me about transitions in history, they didn't illustrate it by such easily comprehensible examples.

I'm writing this book from the point of view of a Scottish school-teacher appalled at the stagnation of Scottish life at the end of the twentieth century. And therefore I need to ask, 'From where did this railwayman draw his inspired questioning of everything?' And the corollary, 'How come the rest of the people of the parish weren't asking the same basic questions?' Historians have attempted to explain why Greek questions flourished between the sixth and second centuries BC, and then died down. And there was that period when the Arabs illuminated the darkness with their searchlights. Engels spoke of 'the joyous free thinking of the Arabs'. They kept the flame of enquiry burning brightly when Christianity was trying to douse it. There was Averroes (Ibn Roshd) of Cordoba, physician, philosopher, lawyer, and Avicenna (Ibn Sina) of Bukhara who studied skin diseases and asked, 'What is disease?' and tried to understand what the universe is about and described plants and wrote poetry in Arabic and Persian. And Ulug Beg, grandson of Tamburlane, astronomer, who built a sextant deep into the rock at Samarkand (its huge arc is still there) and on whose observations the first star catalogue since Hipparchus was based.

What is it that makes some people questioners and others accepters? I think the answer is that we all start as questioners, bur-rowing into everything to investigate, but that our education and upbringing bear down upon us from a very early age, channelling our thoughts, as agriculturists channel the course of a river. Occasionally the River Dee near Aberdeen has changed its course. The melting of extra-deep snow in the Cairngorms, a weakness in a containing bank, a random obstruction like uprooted trees, and the river gushes through, flooding the surrounding fields and some-times issuing into the sea by a new course. The agriculturist seeks to restore the status quo, stopping a breach here, damming the water there, building strong new levées until the force of the surging river has been contained. An outburst of questioning is equally random. The wind bloweth where it listeth. A casual comment, a question that won't go away, the whole drift of a book, and an individual and then a community is set on a new course. The culturists, the minority entrusted with directing the flow of the community's thoughts, move in to shore up the old defences and restore the current to its old channel.

A friendly critic maintains that it is simplistic to believe that we are all naturally questioners. There are (he says) many natural conformers and some questioners; acceptance is the norm and questioning the anomaly. I would concede that the railway clerk was the only member of a large family to break the mould. But in the old junior secondary (secondary modern) schools I found the questing spirit widespread as in young animals, seeking freedom to explore. The apostle Peter said, 'God hath showed me that I should not call any thing common . . .' As a schoolteacher I tried to put his advice into practice. I found that most pupils woke up when we took trouble to present the story to them in clear, concrete terms.

One theme of this book is that, with encouragement, many young Scots would become lively enquirers like the railway clerk. The schools should be presenting to us a more flesh-and-blood story of our forebears in a way that leads each child to think, 'These were *my* great-great-grandparents.' There were the incomers in dug-out canoes who coasted up to Aberdeenshire. What made them come ashore in Aberdeenshire and decide to settle? They left flints and shells and bones at Nigg and Belhelvie and Banchory, and used deer antlers on a pole for a hoe and the thin bones of birds' legs for needles. Excavations beside the town house in Aberdeen showed that the area had been the scene of human activity for 6000 years. Detectives examining pollen grains and flints estimate the dates when early man cleared the landscape here. The Beaker people, incomers from the Rhine who settled in the Garioch, amused themselves drawing squiggles on their clay pots before they fired them. We'd like to have a news with the folk who built forts like Dunnydeer and Bennachie and a barmekin like Echt. They would have tales to tell us about the wild country outwith their protected clearings, the forests where wolverines and wild boar, beavers and cranes and capercailzies roamed freely. I think these forebears of ours would have felt more restricted than I did. I wandered at all hours over the countryside without fear. There was nobody and nothing to be afraid of. On the other hand they weren't under the same pressures to work harder and increase production and pass examinations that their later children had to endure. Into their territory came the Romans, marching. They crossed the Dee beside Culter. It was a good place for a camp and there is still some evidence of it. A writer in the Deeside Field Club's magazine discussed the possibility that the big battle against the Picts, the battle of Mons Grapius, was fought at Durno. I used to deliver telegrams at Durno but I had no inkling that history might have been made there. The dominies presented us with the Roman point of view of that campaign. They didn't help us to see it from the Picts' point of view, any more than USA schools encouraged their children to view the US cavalry from the point of view of a Navajo child, watching the invaders create a desert which they then called peace. That was partly because the Romans left some account of what they did and thought but we have no written Pictish records. I wish I could commune with the Pictish artists who sculpted the Maiden Stone at the foot of Bennachie, chiselling out patterns that look like the interweaving of strips of willow. Like the railway clerk sitting on his bicycle and transcribing the faint tinkling of a morse needle, they liked to show their mastery over their craft. They chiselled out also an arrow and an elephant and what could be a mirror or a fried egg in a pan. Why, in the name of all the gods they were brought up to reverence, why an elephant? The Aberdeenshire dominies should tell their teenagers the true story of the Picts (as far as it can be pieced together out of obscurity) and invite them to recreate in their imaginations what these Pictish sculptors had in mind when their fantasies trickled through their chisels into these runes on the Maiden Stone. If we are to understand our past, we do need our children to help us. Children are more imaginative, more artistic than adults, who have generally had the artistry hammered out of them.

I wish I could enter into the thoughts of our ancestors who built shelters in a huddle round the Castlegate of Aberdeen for protection against the Vikings, scared of a night attack. And into the thoughts of the Vikings. What was biting them that they endured the cold and loneliness and misery and the hail-showers of the North Sea in open boats, so feelingly detailed in *The Wanderer* and *The Seafarer*? Our history teachers made them out to be downright bastards but I'd like to hear their side of the story. More than a thousand years later a Swede, Vilhelm Moberg, gave a clear account of what moved thousands of his countrymen last century to endure the privations of a voyage to America and set up a new home in Minnesota. The novelist's homely and crude details are more riveting and comprehensible than the scholar's generalizations. The emigrants had love affairs that went wrong (says Moberg), they saw little prospect for the future in biding where they were, they had come up against the little Caesars, one of them was escaping from a community which gossiped that he had had sexual relations with a cow. Human beings who find life in their village or parish unendurable for a score of reasons, clutched at a new way out of their miseries.

Into our Aberdeen speech have been stirred immigrant words as currants and raisins into a Christmas dumpling. Words from Sweden (dreich, douk, gowk, hoast), Iceland (caller), Germany (dambrod, flesher, wappinschaw), Denmark (swack), Holland (hotch-potch), Flanders (youkie), France (ashet, grossart). There are Gaelic words remaining – bannock, brogue, gollach. These words were naturalized into our speech in the way that mowers and reapers and binders were absorbed into rural life.

Detective work in ancient middens holds the attention of the young. Any amount of clues there about how our forebears lived after the Vikings had long gone home – flax seeds, mignonette for dyeing cloth, bog myrtle also for dyeing cloth as well as spicing beer and repelling fleas and making besoms, left-overs of rasps and figs and cereals and rabbits. In the moss with which these mediaeval Aberdonians wiped their bottoms there have been found eggs of stomach worms. In the seventeenth century, swine rooted about and grunted amongst the slops thrown from buckets into the streets of Aberdeen but a contemporary account says that the houses were 'cleanlie both within and without'. In the Wartle area, farm names like Bogend and Mosside describe the post-Ice Age desert from which the colonists, racking their bodies, extorted thin crops. These are douce, homely names, but what of Auchentarph, Baldyquash (pronounced Baddyfash), Jimpack and Folla Rule, also on our doorstep? Strange to think of all these forebears of ours yabbering away in Gaelic all over the north-east lowlands and that, after they had gone west, only their farm-names survived into the English-speaking occupation.

But what I'd particularly like to engage the interest of our teenagers in is the psychological warfare which the bigwigs of the north-east have conducted against us all these centuries, and so successfully. On a late evening in summer I used to see a middle-aged man leading by a rope a majestic Clydesdale stallion on its way to its next service on the morrow. The man's razor and towel and change of socks and underclothes were strapped in a little-bookit parcel on the saddle of the stallion's broad back and the man walked on the grassy edge of the road, the two of them a peaceful symbiosis in the cool of the evening. But what would have happened if somebody had told the stallion that it was all a bluff and that with one powerful movement of his glittering sandal he could have kicked his guide into the middle of next week? It's a parable of our history. High up in Crathes Castle we can still see the room where the prisoner, facing the laird, stood immediately under the royal coat of arms on the ceiling as he awaited sentence, but we feel as much out of place there as he did. The Burnett lairds were related to the Gordons and all the other lairds, and they made a cosy company, an officers' mess, defending their land tenure against the brutish populace. They controlled regiments and kirks and colleges, and we, the ordinary folk, are still living in the shadow of that dispensation.

It extended everywhere. My father bought for us every week the *Children's Newspaper*. It was full of improving articles on history and geography and art, but I rarely read them. I looked forward to the humorous cartoons of a monkey called Jacko and to the serial stories. It never occurred to me to ask why these were about upper-class English public school boys and never about children like us. I identified myself with them. In one of the serials the heroes, when they visited the neighbouring village, met a village boy, the son of a boatman. He was an excellent chap and they became friendly with him. It turned out that he wasn't really the son of a boatman but had been saved from a wreck by the boatman and brought up as his own son. He was from an upper-class family. I felt that I couldn't be the son of a village stationmaster and wondered by what turn of fate I had landed up in these modest surroundings. From the

Children's Newspaper serials I progressed to John Buchan, whose
Presbyterian antecedents made him persona grata in an Aberdeenshire home. In the Richard Hannay stories, Buchan had a hero
called Sandy Arbuthnot, the scion of a Scottish land-owning family
seeking his fortune in London society. I was enthralled by the
opening words of a Buchan story. It was high summer, nothing was
happening and there was nobody in London. Various distin-
guished characters were scattered about the empire on proconsular
duties or in Scotland for the grouse. 'Sandy was keeping an eye on
the Middle East.' As a child I could conceive of no greater glory
than identifying with the splendours of this powerful empire. If
they had gone into detail, my Walter Mitty dreams might have
taken some such shape as this:

His Majesty's Secretary of State for Foreign Affairs: Mackenzie, what
are you doing over the long vacation?
Me: I have no plans, sir.
HMSSFA: That's good; as you know, London is empty during the
summer months. Always the chance that something
might blow up abroad. We should be on the *qui vive*. I
have a mission that I would like you to undertake.
Me: Yessir.
HMSSFA: I want you to cycle inconspicuously through France
and take a tramp steamer from Agde to Beirut. I'm told
you speak Amharic like a native. I'd like you to wander
disguised through the bazaars of Aleppo picking up
information about an Abyssinian plot to seize Damas-
cus and start a new jehad. Something strange going on
there. I want you to keep an eye on the Middle East.

We all seek for a model which will encompass and tie together
our higgledy-piggledy perceptions of life, something which will
make sense of our experience and give direction to our lives.
Buchan, like a ready-made tailor, was saying, 'Try this for style and
size.' It fitted, and I wore it for years. What should we Scots do
when we see our children spellbound by these wizards, the singers
of Lorelei songs, the pied pipers who lure our children away from
their homes into a romantic land? The 'arid intellectualism' of

Scottish education only increases our youngsters' appetite for candy floss. Scotland can do better than that.

What Scotland lacks (and what probably all countries lack) is a sense that we owe it to our children to give them an *integrated* account of how the world of their great-great-grandparents grew into the world of their grandparents and into our world. The episodic, staccato history that we offer the young is incomprehensible to them. Like priesthoods down the ages, Scotland's educational priests use that incomprehension, which is due to bad teaching, as evidence that our youngsters are too dim to understand history; that is, as proof of their caste system, of their theory that the majority of Scots are unintelligent and should entrust the running of their lives to the clever minority, the bright boys of the Scottish Education Department in Edinburgh and their colleague-priests in other departments. My religious forebears believed that we have to pass through a sense of sin before we reach a state of grace, and I'm beginning to wonder if there may not be a deep psychological truth in that statement. These arrogant characters in Edinburgh, full of themselves, have little sense of sin. I am maintaining that if we were good teachers, every time our pupils didn't totally understand what we were saying we should stop and ask ourselves, 'Why don't they understand? Whose fault is it? We would then have to fall to, and explain in clear, concrete terms, how the circumstances and hopes of one generation evolve into the life-style of the next generation, how the rough tracks linking a scattered Aberdeenshire parish into a community grew into the turnpikes and how the railways came and gave to a region the sense of community previously felt only by the parish.

Having re-read that statement I realize that it is too posh and priestly and computer-like to make sense to the questioning fifteen-year-olds. What really happened was much less structured and more humorous and clumsy. We have to tell the young about the tricks that their smart-Alec great-grandparents got up to, to avoid paying the turnpike toll at the tollhouses and about the similar tricks, on a larger scale, that the greedy entrepreneurial capitalists played, to do down their competitors. The American movie-makers, imaginative characters, were much better at seeing and portraying the drama and humour of their railways, striking

out westwards, than our educators are in telling the story of how
the Aberdeen–Port Elphinstone canal was superseded by the railways. When the negotiations about the purchase of the canal were
protracted, like present-day arms talks, an exasperated contractor
broke the canal bank and let the water run out into the Don, so that
barges were left stranded, and the canal (about to go out of business
because of Watt's engines) had to be repaired and refilled so that
the barges could float out.

The canal had been a triumph. At 8 m.p.h. (slower than our
pupils cycle) it carried lime for Aberdeenshire's agricultural revolution, and iron and corn and passengers. And then, suddenly, as the
railway began snaking its way towards Inverurie and Huntly, all
that pick-and-shovel work went for a burton. The railway engineers
were in the driving seat. To persuade travellers from the south to
use this route to Inverness, they speeded up some trains, the 41
miles from Aberdeen to Huntly being completed in 45 minutes. A
century later it took 52 minutes.

Although (or maybe because) it was a small railway (a main line
from Aberdeen to Elgin, and branches) it was called The Great
North of Scotland Railway. I thought it would last for ever. Today
the branch lines are grassed over, eroded by rain and gravity like
Roman roads and earthworks. Our teenagers, realistic and down to
earth, always glad to see their elders taken down a peg, would smile
indulgently and realize that history is made by people like them.
It's a serial story, one instalment merging by a multitude of changes
into the next. There were some abrupt, dramatic changes but until
the mid-twentieth century it was a story of slow, earthy change.

At the end of the First World War, Russian prisoners, due for
repatriation, were asked where they lived and would answer,
'Beside Ivan's mill.' Their community was no wider than ours
before the turnpikes and the railways came. In a blizzard in the
twenties when the roads were blocked, local folk, their day's work
over, put on luggit bonnets and gravats and greatcoats and puttees
and foregathered in the railway station office where the tinkling
morse needle was their sole contact with the outside world. My
father interpreted. 'The Alford line's blocked . . . The Buchan
lines are blocked . . . The Deeside's blocked . . . The Macduff's
blocked . . .' Everybody looked grave, and with a child's love of

drama, I hoped against hope that the shutdown would be total. After a long interval the news came through. 'The main line's blocked.' Now our community was on its own, as in pre-history. As the gathering prepared to scale, my father announced the final message that the railway snow-plough would come through at ten o'clock. A crofter said, as he wrapped his gravat round his face, 'That's an affa wind. Maybe the telegraph wires will be down. What should I dae if they're broken?'

My father replied, 'Whip the two ends round a paling wire in the field.'

I was impressed. The Great North of Scotland Railway's communications were ultimately dependent on the paling wire round a crofter's field.

We were allowed to stay up to see the snow-plough. It was the most magnificent sight I had ever seen in my life. The engine came at great speed scattering the deep snow piled high in the air as if it were of little account. A blizzard was an act of God and here was man beating the blizzard, forcing a line of communication against the worst that Nature could throw at us.

There was no baker's shop in the village. For over a week we were fed by hampers of food from the baker's shop at Rothie Norman, four miles away, transported by the railway. People came on foot and in horse-sledges to collect bread and baps and pies and even cakes, and the station collected the money and kept the accounts and indented for further supplies. The railway extended the boundaries of the community. So did the telegraph. It literally extended our communication and speeded it up. The doctor lived half a mile from the railway station and post office, and his remote patients felt reassured that their call for help could reach him so speedily. 'Come to Mike in bed with his back', said the text, and the doctor would be on his way. That enlarging of our small, close-knit community meant some diminution of intensity with distance but it was still as if the farmer widened the circle of chairs round the kitchen fire when strangers came chapping at the door on a winter's night, we still felt the oneness of the people of the community, our thoughts and dreams and jokes fitting conformably into the idiom and accent of our common speech. I imagine that Horace's neighbours felt the same about their corner of Latium and the Russian

POWs about the land served by Ivan's mill. For millennia the size of a community had been set by the horse, its radius and pace and rhythm. Ours had grown somewhat bigger; we belonged to a region.

These are the terms in which we should try and convey to the young how we interpret our story, answering their queries in clearly comprehensible, 'hameower' language so that they can choose for themselves where their allegiances lie and not be lured away from reality when minstrels come singing Lorelei songs.

The Second Book of Kings has a story about a husband and his wife in Shunam who gave hospitality to the prophet Elisha when he passed that way, bread, and a little room furnished with a bed and a table and a stool and a candlestick. The prophet was grateful and offered to recompense them. 'Wouldest thou be spoken for to the king, or to the captain of the host?' I hadn't expected an outspoken guru like Elisha, cherishing his independence, to have had at his disposal the favours of royalty and the army high command. But what stands out pre-eminently from the story is the warm, couthy values of the Shunammite woman. She replied simply, 'I dwell among mine own people.' These values survive down the millennia in spite of the glitter of the metropolis, Jerusalem or Babylon or Nineveh, and in spite even of some of the prophets. We Scots have got to have it out about this. I'm not saying that we have to dissuade the go-getters from emigrating to the metropolis, only that the young should be given time to reflect calmly on their values. Which do they prefer, the gawds of career and high office or the homely fare of dwelling among their own people? We owe it to them to make clear that there *is* a choice. There *are* different views of the nature of reality and of the things that give satisfaction to the human spirit.

At the end of the millennium some people are adopting different views from those which presented the high road to the metropolis as the noblest prospect. Young Scots should get an inkling on how the Bretons and Basques and Catalans see themselves, and visit these regions to learn if they have any relevance to ours. I'd like them deftly to discriminate between the realities and the myths. We were brought up on tales of Robert the Bruce and Bonnie Prince Charlie and Robbie Burns and we were passionately partisan about Bannockburn and Flodden and Culloden and would have boasted of being Scots. But we didn't *feel* a sense of community with the rest of Scotland except in a vague way. We belonged to a region. Outside that region was different. I had a sense of entering foreign parts when I climbed into a south-going train at Aberdeen. We were venturing outwith the familiar jurisdiction. The GNSR engines were painted green relieved by black and yellow and red. In the fief of the North British Railway everything was different. Instead of the homely, tall smoke-stack of the GNSR engines we saw the short, thrusting, austere smoke-stack of the NB; the rolling stock was painted different colours. The farther we travelled, the more different was the speak of the people. We were in alien country. It was the same if we went west of Elgin and entered the territory of the Highland Railway.

CHAPTER THREE

The Land of the Three Rivers

The history of human mental development has been
a history of removing the human mind farther and
farther away from the reality of the world we live in.
JEREMY RIFKIN, *A New World View*

A city's hinterland becomes indistinct at the edges. Aberdeen's
boundary of influence varies according to whether it is measured
by the people who put their advertisements in the local paper, or
travel to Aberdeen to shop, or watch football, or attend the university. More than most places of its size, Aberdeen was composed of
country folk who have happened to migrate into it, and these
migrations moulded its character as glaciers and rivers moulded its
river valleys. The moulding process never stops. The character is
always changing with the flux of immigrants, of industry, and con-
sequently of ideas. There is an inconclusive battle between those
who try to make permanent the existing pattern of ideas because it
is comfortable for them and those who want to change it because it
isn't. There is an inconclusive battle inside the heart and head of
Aberdeen children between the influence of their lowland-born
adults, prosaic, material-minded, and their highland-born adults,
more emotional and visionary.

Children are sensitive to these changes in atmosphere. When we
were children we went for holidays to my father's mother who lived
on Speyside. Somewhere about the no man's land of Keith we passed from the prose of the north-east lowlands into the poetry of the
highlands. The hills were higher, the burns fast and brown and
frothy, the delicate tracery of the birches and their silver bark more
fairy-like. The smell of the larches was richer, the air softer, the
speech of the people softer. The train snaked past a long loch and
through the ravine of the Fiddich and emerged on Strathspey, a

new world. At Craigellachie, a Swiss-like village, we crossed the platform into the Aberlour and Boat of Garten train. We had a glimpse of Telford's magic-like bridge over the Spey and entered a tunnel and then, emerging, saw the deep, dark water of the Spey churning round in the fearsome Tunnel Pool. And then we were at Aberlour and my granny had always a wonderful supper ready for us. After supper the leavings were thrown into the Lour Burn at the end of the garden where eels seethed to gobble it up. Where the trees had been cut down at the Linn of Ruthrie for shoring up trenches in Flanders, we collected firewood every evening when the air was full of the smell of the resin of the felled fir-trees and my granny rewarded us with cocoa before we went to bed and we fell asleep listening to the chatter and bubble and murmur of the Lour Burn.

It was the land of salmon. Beside the river was a notice about smolts' parr, strange new words. My uncle, until he joined the Gordon Highlanders, was a water ghillie on the Spey. He was killed near Arras and there was a military funeral at Aberlour. A young officer, wearing a Gordon-tartan kilt, walked up and down the column of soldiers, giving orders, and, the showman again, I wished I were a kilted officer in the Gordon Highlanders, giving orders. Shots were fired over the grave and the pipers played 'Lochaber no more'. It was the most beautiful music of sorrow I have heard. This is a strange thing, that human beings, forcing breath through the wee holes of a chanter as my uncle's body was returned to the Highland earth, could soften the limp, empty sense of irreparable loss by channelling it into haunting, abiding music.

On the day that my uncle announced that he had decided to enlist, his eldest brother, a tailor in the Scottish industrial belt, was visiting his parents. 'What have *you* to fight for?' he demanded; 'six by two?' It was the first searching question I heard, the first jarring note in the symphony of patriotism.

A generation and a war later my wife and I, newly married, returned while on leave to Aberlour and camped on the thick turf close beside the Spey. We made camp fires of alder and birch and fir and pine-cones and watched a solitary water-wagtail balancing itself on a big stone in the middle of the amber-coloured river. It was daylight at midnight because of double summer time. On two mornings a very small seven o'clock shower made us think that the day was washing its face before starting work. There were hay coles beside the white suspension bridge and Scotland was going energetically and optimistically to the polls to make a better post-war world. But it didn't work out. Another generation later we are back to the drawingboard. What I'm really trying to discover is what ails us that we are so ham-fisted at politics. I am reluctant to believe that politics, revitalized by a more sensitive system of education, is incapable of resolving the frustrations of the human condition.

Country folk, they say, are 'not political'. A century ago when hunger drove many Aberlour young men to Canada, the laird turned up at the railway station to wish them bon voyage. They attributed the hunger to an 'Act of God' and not an act of the laird, and, even so, tradition and the kirk headed them off from criticizing God. Besides, there were many compensations for poverty that are good-naturedly remembered, exploits of poachers and smugglers and pipers and heavyweight athletes, humorous stories, stories of the supernatural, stories of unusual characters in whom any community could glory. My father told me of the reputation of Macarthur, the bonesetter, who was an older porter at Aberlour Station when my father was a junior porter. 'Laddie,' he would say when a patient turned up on the loading-bank in the middle of a summer afternoon, 'Laddie, if you hold him doon, I'll put his joint back in.' There was a quick, skilful movement, a moment of pain, and the patient (on whom the doctors had given up) was restored to full movement of the joint.

Above the village in a line with the main street there is a steep road which leads to a distillery. One sleepy summer afternoon a horse was coming down the hill with a cartload of whisky casks. The horse fell and the casks dropped on to the road, ran askew into a wall and against one another, and burst open. The whisky raced downhill in the convenient angle between the camber of the road and the high banks, and in a few minutes was flowing like the rainwater of a sudden summer thunderstorm between the village street and the kerb. The somnolent village sprang into sudden life. Grocers rushed into the street and back into their shops for pails, cans, basins; housewives came with porridge pots and soup tureens. There were jelly jars, china basins from washstands, berry pans, butter churns, vases, cocoa tins, honey containers, shaving mugs, wooden platters and hastily swilled chamberpots. Desperate men, bachelors or folk from outbye, lay down on their bellies on the road or the pavement and drank with their mouths in the current. Then the flood eased off. But its effects weren't fully seen until the sun had disappeared and the full moon shone serenely on the village. The scene was like a battlefield. It had been a great victory.

Annals like that, a beautiful countryside and a majestic river give to a community a pride of belonging that saves them from the emotional need of being over-respectful towards any metropolis whatever. Scotland's felicity depends on de-centralization. That's a short but arid way of saying that our cultural resources should be used to help our children to feel that they 'belong' to the land that begat them. On a fine evening the folk of Aberlour go for a walk 'along Spey', reassured as a baby is by the closeness of its mother and by her lullaby. After a summer thunderstorm they say 'Spey is in spate' as if they were newsing about a neighbour. The Dee and the Don, although affectionately regarded, are still rivers; Spey is a local deity, the familiar spirit of the place, a life-giving source.

The Spey is the river I like best. Moray District Council show to visitors a film biography of the river from its birth in Loch Spey and its infancy in the trackless country near Spean Bridge and Loch Lochy and the Corrie-yairack Pass, its childhood in Laggan and Kingussie, gathering strength from the melted Cairngorm snows and particularly from the Avon, reaching stately middle age above Aberlour, sweeping under the Telford Bridge at Craigellachie, increasing its pace and emptying its peaty water a long way into the Moray Firth offshore from fishing villages painted blue and white, yellow, green, red, lilac, grey. The water-music accompanying the film gives an appropriate lyrical quality to the river's life-story, deepening the impression that it has an individual existence. People who live alongside the river absorb something of its peace and serenity and music.

Speyside owes it to the young to reinforce that sense of belonging by giving them a clear picture of the valley in geological and historical time, an understanding that *they* are acting the present instalment in a long serial story. Some places are rich in concrete annals, on which we can draw. Forty miles upstream from Aberlour is Rothiemurchus in the vicinity of the Cairngorms that rise suddenly, inky-blue, from the plain. Elizabeth Grant, in her *Memoirs of a Highland Lady*, described life here at the end of the eighteenth century. They made their own fleeces and clothes, blankets and carpets. They sowed lint-seed to make sheets, shirts and sacks and they wove dambrod-patterned table-linen. They made their own bread and beer and ate red deer, roe deer, hares, grouse, ptarmigan, partridges, chickens, salmon, pike, char, trout, cranberries, raspberries. Wine, groceries and flour were all that they bought in from afar. They tanned their own leather, made spoons out of horn, made their own candles. They played 'ba' – shinty. The big occasion was the Floaters' Ball, the annual dance for the men who floated the timber down the Nethy and Spey to the coast. There were two sets of fiddlers to maintain the dancing, punch was made in the washingtubs, the lighting came from tallow dips. When the lad led his lassie to her place in the reel, he 'preed her moo' before the dance began.

A guide from Glenmore Lodge, taking our pupils through this part of Rothiemurchus, asked them why fir-trees, which like a drier habitat, were growing out of waterlogged soil. We searched round and found the ruins of dams built last century to raise the level of the water and ease the floating away of the newly sawn tree trunks. This practical problem-solving, and its investigation, appeals to the young; they like getting their teeth into real problems.

Elizabeth Grant described their journey north from London, averaging thirty miles a day. At the old inn at Blair they had 'a particularly good pudding, a regular soufflé', which had much whisky poured over it. Farther north they had hotch-potch, salmon, fine mutton, grouse, scanty vegetables, bad bread but good wine. The inns had no carpets or cushions or curtains. Equally significant is it that the battle of Waterloo rates only one mention in the book.

This is the story of Scotland that I'd like our young Scots to be familiar with, experiencing the leg-ache of following its contours, the inn-aromas of its mouth-watering history, the sense that our valley and not some alien metropolis is the centre of our world, that our values and not imposed alien values are those against which we measure our lives. Elizabeth Grant took an unimpressed,

Rothiemurchus view of the shenanigans of the 1822 George IV reception in Edinburgh, the Hollywood spectacular designed to win friends for the House of Hanover seventy-six years after the eclipse of the Stewarts at Culloden. Elizabeth said coolly, 'A great mistake was made by the stage managers' in presenting George IV in highland dress at the levée. She was under no illusion about the nature of her society and didn't hesitate to give chapter and verse in the charges she made against it.

> One incident connected with this time made me very cross. Lord Conyngham the Chamberlain was looking every-where for pure Glenlivet whisky; the King drank nothing else. It was not to be had out of the Highlands. My father sent word to me – I was the cellarer – to empty my pet bin, where was whisky in wood, long in uncorked bottles, mild as milk, and the true contraband. Much as I grudged this treasure, it made our fortunes afterwards, showing on what trifles great events depend. The whisky, and fifty brace of ptarmigan all shot by one man, went up to Holyrood House, and were graciously received and made much of, and a reminder of this attention at a proper moment by the gentlemanly Chamberlain ensured to my father the Indian judgeship.

She didn't think much of Parliament. 'No one thought of their country's good in these days, the general interest was of little account compared with the individual's fame for *speaking* – very little being *done* in Pitt and Fox days.' Nor of Oxford, of which she had inside knowledge. (It was her uncle who had to write to Sir Timothy Shelley about his wayward son.)

> Two facts struck me ... the ultra-Tory politics and the stu-pidity and frivolity of the society ... There was little talent and less polish and no sort of knowledge of the world ... The Christian pastor, humble and gentle, and considerate and self-sacrificing, occupied with his duties, and filled with the 'charity' of his Master, had no representative, as far as I could see, among these dealers in old wines, rich din-ners, fine china and massive plate. The religion of Oxford

appeared in those days to consist in honouring the King and his *ministers*, and in perpetually popping in and out of chapel.

The territory between the Inverness–Perth road-and-railway, and Aberdeen is dominated by the three rivers, Spey, Don and Dee. These glaciers, literally making their way from the basalt and granite of the high interior, scarified the face of the landscape, and gave different characters to the valleys and the people who lived in them. If one of these recalcitrant pupils said, 'What does that mean?' I'd reply that *scarify* comes from a Latin word meaning to scribble or write, and that a character is an engraving, and that when we get into this territory of discussing the effect that the place they live in makes on people, we come right up against the difficulty of transferring ('carrying across') ideas from one human being to another. The scribbles, the inscriptions, made by ice and water on the skin of the earth, were different in different river-valleys. I'm maintaining that the difference in the terrain of the river-valleys made a difference in the people who inhabited them. But always I have in mind the pupils who ask the searching questions. 'How can you prove it?' This chapter is an attempt at an answer.

We walked to the source of the Don, its simple beginnings near the roof of Scotland. From here we got a god's eye view. A neighbouring river the Avon (pronounced A'an) was making for a link-up with the Don but its road was blocked and it flowed north instead and was joined by the Spey; but it was a near thing. A light brown track, closely paralleling the twists of the Avon, like a graph demonstrated the nature of the terrain, difficult for humans. Our forebears used their intelligence to establish themselves, make them feel at home even in the high places of the earth's crust, by cooperating with nature, accepting their conditions of life, accepting that the easiest way to go from one place to another is to profit from the river's experience of reconnoitring it. From up here we investigate the spaces between the ridges as an anatomy student traces the blood supply to the muscles between human ribs. It is rich terrain and repays study. It is surprising, the premutations and combinations of colour and material, the variety of life, that is concocted out of such basic things as soil, air, sunlight, water, frost and gravity.

In her book, *A Land* (1953), Jacquetta Hawkes tried to establish our oneness with all animate and inanimate creation. 'I think we are returning to an awareness of our unity with our surroundings.' The Greeks, she said, sharpened a knife ('literate self-consciousness') that cut man away from his matrix, but, for a thousand years before the Renaissance, 'the mind of an agricultural society was rocked by the comforting seasonal rhythm'. The sharp spirit of enquiry of the Renaissance isolated us again and left us naked and lonely and feeling insignificant. But we are reverting to a union.

Amongst the young I sense a nostalgia to return to this belonging, this one-ness. They grope through paperbacks about Anglo-Saxon sorcerers, learned in plant lore, and Neanderthal and Cromagnon people discovering the terms on which they may live in easy communion with their mother earth. It's only by metaphors that we can give shape to our dreams. The words we let slip out bear witness to our sub-conscious dreams. We talk of 'the rock from which we were hewn'. Tennyson describes our leaving of the earthly scene as the turn of the tide, 'when that which drew from out the boundless deep, turns again home'. There is more in that choice of words than he was perhaps conscious of, because it was in the boundless deep that life developed before it colonized the dry land. Our Scottish children reach out for fulfilment of this part of their nature, aware of a presence that is not to be put by. They and we do get random clues about how we should be living, occasional bright intervals of serenity or elation which tell us when we are getting warmer.

A rich life has colonized this high land near the rounded Grampian tops and I know what Jacquetta Hawkes meant when she wrote that we are part of it, flesh of its flesh and bone of its bone. There was a soft south wind, clouds and blue patches of sky, white gems of snow in the Cairngorms. There was lark-like birdsong and a piping note that came maybe from a dotterel. There was a moth in the heather. There was rufous-coloured sphagnum moss. As a child in the First World War I had spent hours cleaning sphagnum moss, removing grasses and roots. It was then dried and sterilized and sent to Flanders as dressings to soak up blood from the wounds of Scottish soldiers. Elsewhere on the open hillside there were wild geraniums, cotton grass, butterwort, orchids with spotted leaves, bleached moss, whitened heather stems, shells of grouse or ptarmigan eggs. When we stopped to listen, there was a soft silence and we could distinguish the quiet noises that inter-rupted it such as the wind in our ears when it rose slightly. Jacquetta Hawkes thought back to the aeons when Scotland's ancient rocks were 'without memory of life'.

> No-one inured to the din created by our species can con-ceive the silence of a calm day on pre-Cambrian earth. I cannot use the word *hush* which perhaps best conveys the sense of a closed-in silence for it also implies a world of life that has fallen silent. This was a negative and utter quiet. For us, in addition to our own noise – the racket of cities that must in fact penetrate the surrounding country – and that of animals, birds, and insects, there is a fine tissue of imperceptible sounds; vegetation growing, leaves and flowers moving, all the stirrings of growth and decay. Then there was nothing. Perhaps in the heart of deserts that ancient stillness may persist, yet we cannot experience it, for wherever we go we take a humming community of life with us – ourselves.

Like a naturalist trying the more fully to savour an experience and make it his own by choosing the right words to record it, Stevenson wrote of 'essential silence' in the hill-recesses,

> For there, among the flowers and grasses,
> Only the mightier movement sounds and passes.

Water-trickles on the hillsides gave themselves away by green wrinkles sometimes thickening and widening where more water collected. We went up the slope following the main wrinkle fur-rowing the hillside, to the place where the Don starts. Above that it has not yet assumed the individuality of running water; it is just seeping water. Lower than that there is a black scar of peat; but where the peat was drier, it was brown. All round about were patches of heather and grass and sunshine. There were bird drop-pings, frogs, a rabbit skull with hair on it, some rabbit fur weathered into downy hair. Our shoes crackled on dead or dry grass and heather, and squelched through rich greenness. Mosses and lichens had struck up a partnership for mutual aid. Right in the midst of a welter of Gaelic names on the Ordnance Survey map were three English words, Well of Don, like Davie Crockett alone in a pow-wow of Indian braves.

We came down from the heights. At a ford over the mile-old Don where the track descended and rose steeply, the car stuck. With a breadsaw and screwdriver we cut away earth and grass and stones and then raised the wheels with a jack and put stones under them. It took us an hour to get away. Meanwhile a fawn raced up the hillside and leapt on to the horizon, red grouse and their chicks ate heather shoots. The broom grew richly yellow and the hill-slopes on the north side of the valley, ribbed for tree-planting, had the texture of a thickly knitted jersey, very dark brown.

Outstanding on the plain beside the young river is the startlingly white Corgarff Castle, a Hanoverian outpost, surrounded by a white curtain wall. I imagined frightened redcoats (no cunning camouflage in those days) manning the two-feet slits in the curtain wall or venturing out on patrols up the Lecht towards Tomintoul and, at the end of the exercise, mighty relieved to be back within those thick walls. It was hostile territory even in summer. They wouldn't have had a chance to notice the marsh marigolds that grow in the burn down from the castle, nor the lady's smock, nor the mimulus yellow with maroon spots, like the material for a girl's summer dress. A medical student, looking through binoculars, detailed his observations of a bird that was sitting on a deer-fence post, uttering alarm calls. It was as if he were recording symptoms to make a diagnosis. 'Red legs. Tail grey. Red beak. Black wing-tips. Light brown top of head. Breast pale grey with darker grey stripes. Black under the wings, pale brown on top. A speckled bit below the eye, that is on the cheek.' We were checking up the details in the bird book. No doubt about it. It was a redshank. It flew off over the marshy field. It had a repeated single note of alarm and jerky wing movements. Near by were oystercatchers.

This bird-identification business. I'm not sure about it. Do we think we're an élite because we identify a highland wader as a century ago the MPs thought they were an élite because they could identify a Virgil or Horace or even Thucydides quotation in parliament? Do we validate the study on the ground that it gives us an insight into natural history in the same way as the classicists claimed that their study made them cultured? We should let the young ask questions about the value, or lack of value, of every study.

Upper Donside is a simpler, less wooded countryside than Deeside; it has the appeal of quiet, unassuming country and I'd like fine to bide there. Farther down there is an area of birches, each with plenty of space separating it from the next. A friend of mine had a book about the trees in his area, each tree being accorded a paragraph of biographical detail, the planting, growth and development, appearance. I hadn't thought of trees as having individuality, an individual 'Christian' name to prefix their botanical family name. The comely Donside birches, enjoying space and sunshine and freedom to develop and display the network of their tracery, gave a feeling of spaciousness to the landscape, making it memorable. It was still a highland strath.

Five miles from the river, on the borders of the north-east lowlands, is the village of Rhynie. Geologists, hammering open the stones of a local farmer's field-wall, liberated fossilized plants which 350 million years ago grew here in a peat bog. Lava, containing silicate, poured down on these plants and petrified them. They now call the plant *Rhynia*. To look at these plants, which have survived throughout aeons, smashed back the boundary walls defining our history and gave a new concept to the dimensions of Scotland's past.

The River Don swells as it comes into the broader plains, the rich farmlands of central Aberdeenshire, but it still retains traces of its origin. Nearer Aberdeen the manufacturers poured pollutant into it for many years.

The Dee gets higher marks for tourist attraction. The best way to see it was from a train on the Deeside railway but Beeching closed the railway on the grounds that it didn't pay, not imagining that more and more folk, city-pent, would gladly pay to make the forty-mile trip to Ballater just to relax and enjoy the sight of this lovely river. Near Aboyne there is a stone that claims to mark the Highland boundary but the transition is too gradual to permit of such definition.

At all seasons of the year, motor cars compensate for the demise of the railway. A Sunday outing is to go out along the North Deeside road and back by the South Deeside road. Tenements in streets and even semis cheek by jowl in 'avenues' are prisons, and on Saturdays and Sundays folk escape briefly into Deeside. Although most of them no longer go to the kirk on Sunday fore-noon, they share the longing of our kirk-attending forbears, who sang

> I to the hills will lift mine eyes,
> From whence doth come mine aid.

Sometimes the outing is elucidated by tantalizing notes from the AA's excellent *Illustrated Road Book of Scotland*, which gives glimpses of megalithic and Celtic remains, mediaeval castles, local characters and hill tracks.

Even in January the colours are much more vivid than people imagine. There is the bright maroon of the birch-trees, their silver stems sometimes covered with the same grey-green fungus as the drystane dykes; the glowing green of the firs, their mast-like trunks near black; the lemon of the larches; the tawny leaves of the beech hedges; the green and russet of the young willow stems; the light brown of the bracken; the brown winter overcoat of the heather, happing the earth; the brown roadside quarries which look like a door opening on geological history; the inky-blue mountains. The rain, which can fall with a sodden persistence in June and January alike, provides compensations.

The Glenshee ski-ing had been rained off and on a January after-noon the hotel bar in Braemar was full of skiers, knocking back their pints. The social anthropologist from the Third World would have found richly rewarding clues in the furnishings, throwing sidelights on our upbringing and beliefs. There was a Gordon tar-tan carpet. This was Gordon country. The local regiment is Gordon Highlanders, and a popular music hall song declares that

> The black Watch is braw, the Seaforths an a',
> But the cocky wee Gordon's the pride o' them a'.

The anthropologist would need help with that richly allusive line. The chief of the Gordon clan was called 'The Cock of the North', the best, or maybe just the busiest, penis of them all. Above the hotel bar were two stuffed wildcats, sinuous like stoats, their tails barred like a tiger's. Beside them a fox, and the head of a deer. There was a picture of the old Braemar–Ballater horse-bus about to leave its terminus, showing clearly at the back of the bus the handle to work the wheel-brake. There was a picture of soldiers in red uniforms. There was a picture of languid Victorian aristos in deer-stalker hats, a fine-looking ghillie, the lower orders unobtrusively in the background. Outside the hotel is a brightly coloured coat of arms. Working-class skiers, upwardly mobile, were being inducted into the *mores* of the class to which they ultimately (some of them) aspired. It's heady stuff, like the beer, which helps.

How little the spirit of the Highlands has changed since the day, a hundred years since, when the photograph was taken. My fellow-countrymen have a sturdy independence, an upstanding self-confidence, but within the system. They are respectful; they 'know their place', and acknowledge their 'superiors'. The Gordon Highlanders and the British Legion can be friendly, hospitable, aggressive, no nonsense, bawdy on occasion, but coming smartly to attention and saluting when they come into the presence of an officer. We are deeply steeped in the tradition. We drink it in with our mother's milk. It clings to us like ivy, it is as pervasive as fog, as persistent as the earliest of bad habits. Our vocabulary is tinctured by the feudal system. The royalty propaganda is at its most potent in Deeside. Cairns commemorating Victoria's family surmount the hills. A stone marks the place where she happened to meet soldiers about to embark for the Boer War. At a country house where she went for picnics near Lock Muick she first heard about the death of the Duke of Wellington. Ballater's former railway station contains the most posh lavatories in Scotland, their basins decorated with floral designs. This was where kings and queens, and maybe the Czar, relieved themselves before they got into motorcars to take them the rest of the way to Balmoral. The town's streets are bright with coats of arms above shops which sell goods to Balmoral. It should be the function of Scottish schools to encourage the young to ask questions about these customs. 'Last Sunday your parents took the car to see the Queen going to the kirk at Crathie. What was the nature of the satisfaction that they found in watching a woman going to the kirk?' Do we have a thirst for magic that can be quenched only by the deification, the apotheosis, of certain human beings? No accident that these words that we apply to queen-worship come from the Romans and the Greeks. Some of the pupils will have seen the farther reaches of deification in its disastrous effect on the mind of Caligula in Graves's *I, Claudius*. It is at this level of understanding, or at least questioning, how we satisfy our imaginative urges that the remaking of Scotland begins.

From Ballater a road goes south to Glen Muick and Lochnagar. Above the road there are rickles of stones of a long-deserted Clachan, the shapes still enough defined to give the imagination of our pupils something to be let loose on, to recreate the function of these structures, and the way of life of the people who lived in them. Their environment was the same as it is today. They would have had their spirits lifted as ours are by the smell of bog myrtle, the deep, deep blue of the butterwort, the orange anthers of the bog asphodel, the glitter of mica schist, a curlew, a wheatear standing on a boulder and bobbing up and down, the rich variety of cross-leaved heath, bedstraw, heartsease. We came on Scottish asphodel and the pupils would have been tolerantly amused to find that the botanists disagreed on its description. The Rev. C. A. Johns said that its flowers are greenish yellow; the Rev. W. Keble Martin said they are greenish white. But there's a lesson to be learned from their disagreement. It is not that one of them is necessarily wrong. Reality is sometimes difficult to imprison in the existing words. The young should realize that our vocabulary doesn't measure up to the multitudinous variety of natural things and that therefore they shouldn't subdue their experience to make it square with the words with which others have tried to describe it. Maybe there was a simpler explanation. Our plant was nearer the description offered by Keble Martin. Maybe the Rev. C. A. Johns never came to Glen Muick to see what the Scottish asphodel looks like here.

If education had a tradition of enquiry, like medicine, we'd try to find out which educational experiences made an impression on the young. I think they would like to be much more involved in making their own discoveries. I wish they could have taken part in a study that cunning geographers of Aberdeen University made of the Dee valley. Burns from the surrounding hills and lowlands emptied into Loch Kinord, bringing their cargo of eroded earth and pollen grains which was distributed on the floor of the loch and built up, layer on layer. The geographers took a plug one and a half metres deep from the bed of the loch and from it deduced five thousand years of history, the thick primordial forest, the clearing of the trees, the extension of agriculture in a warmer climate, the nature of the vegetation and eventually the fertilizers seeping into the loch. The geographers were good scouts. Pupils, genned up on such studies, are more likely to keep a weather-eye open for any sort of clues their sharp eyes may alight on, in the valley, the ruins of limekilns and grain-driers, the grass greener where the land was formerly cultivated, stumps of trees above the present tree-line. Just as the excavation of thirteen-century tanners' pits in Aberdeen was supplemented by archive information that there was a man called John the Tanner living there in 1317, so the study of the Deeside landscape is supplemented by the records that Glen Lui was first cleared for sheep in 1763 and then for deer in 1820. It is in this way, I believe, that pupils, wanting to know more about their inheritance, begin to take an interest in how different forms of community overlap, the feudal earls of Mar co-existing with the chiefs of the Farquharson clan, and apply that knowledge to present-day systems of community.

On a June crossing of the high plateau of Scotland from Braemar to Rothiemurchus, from the Dee to the Spey, in which thirty teenagers took part, we discovered a little of the enquiry and discovery that appeals to them, the experience that gives them enjoyment. We left the Linn o' Dee at nine in the morning and stopped four miles later, near Derry Lodge, for breakfast. Some had sandwiches. One gourmet fried bacon and eggs; we thought he would go far. We followed the less frequented track of the Lairig-an-Laoidh up the Derry Burn, past ancient Caledonian pines, quiet, flat-topped like the mediaeval bonnets that Aberdeen professors wear for graduation ceremonies. The gouging out of two neighbouring corries has left between them the tight-rope of an arête but we had twenty miles of tough walking ahead of us and there wasn't much time to look at it. A. S. Neill, kindest of critics, said that we were compulsive teachers, too keen to offload geology on our pupils. I imagine he was right because when we stopped for mid-morning break to eat a sandwich and gulp lemonade, the pupils were much keener on dropping rocks in the burn to throw up a cascade of water and soak their unsuspecting companions than on listening to a cascade of geological information. Nevertheless I thought it was worthwhile as we resumed our packs to tell anybody who felt like listening that that red flower with a pouting mouth was a bartsia, that this other innocent-looking blue flower had its leaves coated with glue that caught the flies that alighted on them and sucked the juice out of the flies and then released the dry remnants of wing- and body-fabric and let them float away in the wind; that this plant which had red flowers growing on one stalk and blue flowers on another was a vetch and that it was probably the poorness of the soil, the lack of phosphates, that just prevented the blue flower from graduating into redness; and that series of tiny dots on the Ordnance Survey map indicated rough pasture (that is, grass for feeding animals) and therefore it was not surprising to see, close to the track, heaps of stones that were all that remained of a clachan of houses where people had made a living and made love and brought up their young.

If you suggest to teenagers that it might be worth considering a life like this among the mountains, you get a fairer hearing than from brainwashed adults. Children from an industrial area, usually more independent than country children, will weigh the pros and cons. Children are the real philosophers; 'Thou eye among the blind,' wrote Wordsworth. Moths fluttered up from the heather, violets decorated the side of the track, a curlew uttered its plaintive call. We rose above the tree-line and saw, away to the west, like a square of snow, a hut at the side of Loch Etchachan. 'Couldn't we go there some day,' said a pupil, 'and make journeys from there?'

We came to part of the roof of Scotland, the watershed dividing the waters that flow east into the River Dee and into the North Sea at Aberdeen, from those that flow north and empty themselves finally into the Moray Firth. A little farther on, we stopped at a bridge that carries the track over the River Avon. Beside it was a bothy built of slabs of rock laid on layers of softly binding peaty earth, and beside the bothy a signpost marked with arrows pointing north to Ryvoan and Glenmore, east to Glen Avon and Cock Bridge, south along the way we had come to Derry Lodge and Braemar, and west to the Shelter Stone and Cairn Gorm itself. At this crossroads of high valleys between upheaved masses of mountains, a chaos of rounded shapes, we stopped and had our lunch and the teachers composed themselves for slumber. The warm air and the subdued monotonous roar of the burn induced sleep. An old pattern of life was briefly re-formed, adults resting and children energetically playing in the burn. I watched them drowsily. They went farther and farther afield to fetch bigger and bigger boulders and drop them in the deepest part of the burn, just for the sake of hearing that deep and satisfying 'plomp' as they hit the water and fell to the bottom and the spray settled back over the water.

The compulsive educationalist tries to gather some crumbs of validation for his own over-serious classroom preoccupations. The sixteen-year-old, staggering in his self-imposed task of carrying a half-hundredweight boulder, legs apart, is learning about density, the feel of granite, the musculature of the human skeleton, the endlessly entertaining phenomena of this miracle substance, water. In the classroom, pupils of mine were totally absorbed in Jack London's story of a puppy, accustomed to the water of a flowing river, and of its astonishment at the discovery one winter day that the frozen water supported its weight. Other pupils, heating glass-tubing, started revolving the thin threads like a skipping rope or a lasso, astonished at their discovery of the plasticity of heated glass.

It comes back to the full meaning of the word *know*. What is knowing? We repacked our rucksacks after the midday siesta, laced up our boots and resumed our journey. High above us, near the summit of Bynack Nor, great citadels of rock stood out of the evenness of the mountain slope. 'The Barns of Bynock', they are called. With the exuberance of youth, three pupils struck off the path and started the climb towards them. From time to time we could just make out their tiny shapes on the skyline, seven hundred feet above us. Few people can sit down and read a musical score and hear the music; few people can read a map and imagine the terrain, forecasting the view that opens out from the head of Cairngorm pass. A classroom education is largely a two-dimensional education, a life in Flatland, and the experience is as flat as drinking lemonade without the fizz. The only way to know these hills is to climb them. Sweat and the aching calf muscles is an integral part of the understanding. The North American Indian says 'You haven't worn my moccasins.' Our pupils were being, in Shakespeare's phrase, feelingly persuaded of what life was like for our predecessors who took their cattle to the summer shielings. There is no fatigue in looking at the fifty-foot contour lines tightly packed together and therefore not much understanding of the lives of people who deserted pastures we'd seen on the Lairig an Laoidh pass, of the effect on them of living in daily contact with that huge bulk of mountains, shutting out the sun, their flanks scarred with burns and waterfalls and sudden geological revolutions, sometimes menacingly imposing their presence on a thinly scattered population scraping a living out of the thin soil.

After the next ridge, it was all downhill, the first consistent downhill progress of the day's journey. We had walked up an intercostal space to the backbone and were now descending another similar space. Ahead of us lay the unremarkable plateau of the Monadhliaths and, more inviting, the Spey valley all the way up to the Moray Firth. Looking over the shoulder of the mountains we were descending, we could see its tributary the Nethy and the huge bulk of Cairn Gorm. We rested beside a bothy by the Nethy and again beside the Green Loch. Some of the pupils had thin shoes but even in the last miles of the twenty-mile trek the aches and blisters were endured without fuss. The last part of the journey through fir-trees was warm. At seven in the evening we reached Loch Morlich just as we had planned but, because of a breakdown, the bus to take the pupils home didn't turn up till nine. But there was not one word of complaint out of the thirty of them. A stop for fish and chips on the way back was, they felt, an appropriate finale and celebration.

Our day's journey confirmed what we believed to be the basics, the building bricks, of education. These are: The young are OK. They *need* freedom. They flourish best when we respect the individuality of every one of them. If we study what gives them enjoyment, we won't go far wrong.

We rarely know how much of a day's journey through the mountains rubs off on these young Scots. I think many of them are sensitive to the feel of the region, responsive to the changes of terrain. The indescribably pure green of the new grass and briard oats in the lowlands in May. An old railway-line in the process of being re-absorbed into the natural landscape of grasses and wild flowers, healed over and forgotten or existing only as a wrinkle on the face of the countryside, visible only to the trained eye of a historian telling his students about the brief, hundred-year venture of a railway that followed the river valley. The enduring earthworks on which had been raised a castle, now a ruin, which predated Robert the Bruce. The Alpine freshness and brightness of the high places. The animal instinct of seeking out a sheltering hillock in the lythe of which to eat your breakfast. A corrie gouged out by a glacier into the shape of their grandfather's comfortable armchair. The freedom and loneliness of the high places and the comfort of the return to human habitations. The soft soughing of the pines above Nethy Bridge and the extraordinary clearness of the atmosphere, the quality of the light. (I sometimes wonder if I am imagining things, in the elation, the intoxication, of striding out through that incandescent atmosphere. I wrote that I had never seen such pure light except once before, in the hills of Jugoslavia, and I was later reassured when I read in her book, *Black Lamb and Grey Falcon*, that Rebecca West also bore witness to that clear light in Jugoslavia.) I wonder what the inhabitants of the high places, dotterel and redshanks, grouse and ptarmigan, made of the invasion of their territory by these incongruent, alien contemporaries, humans from built-up housing, city nests. Our pupils were a motley crew, kitted out in red knitted bonnets, yellow jerseys, brown anoraks, thin shoes and nylons, walking boots and thick socks, blue waterproofs, scarves, jerkins, and blue jeans. They sometimes behave in strange ways in city warrens but up here in the heights they were, as you might say, in their element, much simpler characters, one with the animal world. A few of them have found pleasure in recording a sensation in words or paint or clay or music, the sun shining cinnamon on the fir trunks, the feathery effect (accurately reproduced by Corot) of the sun shining on the brown foliage of the birch-trees. But I believe these things imprint themselves on the wax of the memories of all of them. You never know.

CHAPTER FOUR

The Mearns, Angus, Perth, Stirling

The dark backward and abysm of time.
SHAKESPEARE

From Aberdeen, the oil capital, a dual carriageway now encourages motor cars to speed on the coast road south to Stonehaven. This used to be a forbidding landscape, a post-ice-age desolation of peaty soil and bleak houses, but prosperity has refurbished the houses with more glass, bathrooms, extensions and greater comfort. It happened so slowly (over forty years) that change was almost imperceptible until one day the completion of the dual carriageway marked a milestone in local history. Factories, warehouses and a supermarket covered the rushy fields. A film that compressed forty years into an hour would help us to grasp its significance and gauge our future direction.

Beyond Stonehaven, linked to the mainland by a vulnerable neck of land, is the embattled castle of Dunnottar. If the University of Aberdeen had had a concern about bringing the light of understanding to *all* the people of its hinterland, it would have made a film of Dunnottar's tenure of this headland, compressing its fifteen century span into two or three hours. The story would start with Ninian who brought Christianity to the Picts within their drystone walls here, long before Iona or St Andrews or Edinburgh lit lamps in the encircling gloom. Their schoolbooks tell our children, 'St Ninian brought Christianity to the Picts,' It's not a very helpful statement. It brushes in no real picture, just leaves a blank. The phrase suggests a sandalled friar driving up in a delivery van and opening the tail door and shouting 'Are you the Picts?' and they'd say 'Aye,' and he'd say, 'I've a crate for you. Sign here.'

'We werena expecting a crate. What kind of a crate?'

'It's your Christianity. It's the latest religion. Everybody is changing over. I was told you needed it here.'

'Does it work?'

'Oh aye. It comes wi a guarantee. Once you get this fitted up,
you'll live happily ever after. And now I must away. I have to take
their Christianity to several other places before it's too dark. Can
you tell me how to get to Aberlemno?'

What really happened? Fifteen hundred years later (a century
ago) a succession of missionaries from Scotland went to 'darkest
Africa' following the pioneering trail blazed by David Livingstone.
There were Laws of Livingstonia, Mackay of Uganda, Mary Slessor
of Calabar. She was born in Aberdeen, worked in a mill in Dundee
and decided to devote her life, selflessly, to the natives of Nigeria,
bring them the light of the Christian gospel. It was as heroic an
adventure as Ninian's journey from Candida Casa in the south-
west of Scotland into darkest Pictland. I imagine the dangers, the
resistance and the reasons for the ultimate proselytizing were similar. Why did the Picts 'accept Christianity'? Did they say, 'Many of
us have been thinking lately that this is no way to live? Frightened
of our enemies. Brud here, he says he just likes to sit and watch the
waves breaking against the headland and the skuas fanning out
their tails as they glide. We've never time to enjoy life. Always on
the alert. Every summer there are the daisies and red campion and
cinquewort and camomile and bluebells but we hardly notice
them. Always the chance that some bastard will slink up on you and
slit your throat.' Was there argument about it and about, concerning this idea of loving your enemy, and taking no thought for the
morrow, and leaving it to a heavenly father, above the grey
Dunnottar sky, to provide the things that his earthlings need? Did
Saint Ninian promise that, if they embraced Christianity, it would
be different from now on? If he did, he was deceiving them because
it wasn't. Vikings came. And the English. Sir William Wallace
burned the English garrison in 1297. A hundred years later the
Great Marischal of Scotland built a castle on the rock, and
royalty visited it – James IV, Mary Queen of Scots and James VI.
On 'Tuysday, 26th May' 1640 there was 'schooting of ordinans'
'betwixt ane English schip and ane Scottis schip' below Dunnottar.

Four years later Aberdonians sent their wealth for safe keeping

because the Earl of Montrose was on the rampage. He set fire to
Dunnottar. It was defended against Cromwell's army in 1652. Scotland's crown and sceptre and the king's 'rich hangings and bedds,
plate and other furniture' were in the castle. Cromwell took the
castle, but he didn't get the crown and sceptre. Thirty-three years
later the Convenanters were imprisoned suffocatingly in an over-
crowded vault, as Scott tells in his introduction to *Old Mortality*.
The Nazareth carpenter's ideas, which Ninian communicated to
the Picts, hadn't had much of an innings at Dunnottar. I'd have
liked to see the film bring that out with cutbacks to the converted
Picts, wondering what glorious future the new gospel had opened
up. Then in the anti-climax the film would give the Picts a glimpse
of present-day visitors to Dunnottar, as doubtful of their future as
the Picts were and maybe less hopeful, seekers groping in the dark
backward of time to see if they can lay hold of some wisdom
matured here, as in a cask, over the centuries.

Today's tale of visitors is a girl attorney from Philadelphia, a
couple from Denmark on a motor bicycle and members of foreign
orchestras taking the afternoon off from a music festival in Aberdeen. Do the violinists hope to benefit from their visit to Dunnottar
as from Beethoven and Haydn? Or is it a ritual visit as obscure in its
effects as Ninian's rituals were to the Picts, who similarly went
along with them? Is twentieth century culture as obscure to its par-
ticipants as fifth century Christianity? Today's visitors would have
found it difficult to say what benefits or insights they drew from
their visit. All we're left with is the scaffolding that supported the
lives of the Dunnottar garrison. These are the stables and the livery-
master's quarters, the substantial bakery and brewery providing for
a considerable community, the wash-house, the stone structure
that held the cauldron in which they boiled their water. From the
land side it all looks a restricted area in which to live but when you
walk up the alley, paved with an intricate, interweaving pattern of
rounded stones, into the castle you find that, like Edinburgh Castle,
it is a collection of buildings, a clachan, a farm-toun, and the inhabitants would have had little sense of restriction. The bowling green
was 40 yards by 35 yards.

We try to recreate the circumstances of their lives. A sally down
the watergate to the jetty to try and push a boat out and get provi-

sions from Stonehaven during a siege. The jetsam they'd collect from the shore, their pets, clothes, children's games, boats, gossip, beliefs, hygiene. We can see the runnels for channelling the urine over the cliff. Were they well-informed about the political currents that washed over them or did they just accept the Earl Marischal's views in the same way as most of the people of the Grampian region today accept the opinions propagated by Lord Thomson's Aberdeen newspapers? I try to repopulate the ingle neuk of Dunnottar when the brewers and bakers and liverymen on a wild night shut out the howl of the wind and the thunder of the waves and listened to the minstrel's song about bogles. Did they believe in bogles? They would say no but, still and on, some of the shadows louping at the other end of the rush-lit hall werena mouze, and if there came a hammering at the muckle yett, nobody would be in a hurry to rise and give admission to a belated traveller.

The landscape of the Mearns and Angus is a living museum exhibiting the story of change. Patches of reed-growing bogland reveal what most of this now-fertile plain looked like at the end of the last Ice Age. Heart-breaking and back-breaking ditching and digging and clearing compelled food out of the earth. Recent ditches show that it is a continuing process. Within a few miles of Kirriemuir there are a Pictish earth-house and an underground air-raid shelter at a derelict aerodrome. In dire emergency we still seek protection within our Mother Earth, but slowly people venture out with that protection. Fear is built into those redoubtable castle walls and their narrow slits of windows. Then small houses crept out from the protection of the castle. They had little glass lozenges of windows and skylights which expanded into dormer windows. More recently town-dwellers bought the deserted farm cottages high up the cultivated slopes and replaced the living-room wall with one giant window which gives the inmates the illusion that they are living in the muckle furth. Bathrooms were built on to the back of cottages, red tiles replaced the grey-blue slates. Doocots, built to provide food in winter, have been preserved because they are picturesque. Tollhouses survive the turnpikes that they financed. Ducks still swim in farm-ponds although the farm's waterpower no longer comes from the mill-lade. Dominant multi-nationals have taken over the once-proud shop-signs and squeezed the shopkeeper's name into a corner. The traveller is lucky who sees a horse in a day's journey. Standardized bungalows make the landscape less individual than it used to be and prosperous farmers speed along wide straight dual carriageways. But in the lee of the mountains among places which have history-haunted names like Cortachy, Airlie and Menmuir, the old narrow road twists round old kirks and large manses and war memorials and past drystane dykes, not letting change get out of hand, like a village worthy who makes no concessions to new ideas. You can't speed up on these ancient roads. And the framework of speech (old idioms, and a manner of speaking attuned to the slow process of the seasons and the speed of the horse) slows down change in attitudes. Feudal respect is decreasing. The kirk's voice on sex is not heeded and one result of experimentation is fewer Saturnalian volcanoes like the Ball of Kirriemuir. But I imagine the Tory philosophy is in good heart in Angus, and I know one large school where the staffroom are segregated and where, even in the coldest January, girls and women teachers who wear trousers are frowned upon.

The wee village school at Kingsmuir outside Forfar is part of the museum of Angus, soberly reminding us of how our grandparents looked at life and what it meant to be a child in Scotland less than a century ago. On 9 November 1983 a plaque was unveiled at Kingsmuir to the Scottish educational innovator A. S. Neill whose father was dominie here. We were shown a brief history of the school from 1874 and the delayed, reluctant introduction of an inside lavatory. In a shed in the playground there was an old soup-kitchen containing a boiler for the mass-production of soup. Inside the school were hot water bottles of the time, and wallie (porcelain) dogs that were the required ornaments for every house, a butter churn, a school register that had to be meticulously kept, slates and slate-pencil that often squeaked when you wrote with it, and inspectors' reports. At the turn of the century the report on pupil-teacher Alexander S. Neill was, 'This candidate is warned that his work all round is weak.'

Neill's daughter, smiling pleasantly to the pupils, unveiled the plaque. Speechmakers said the appropriate unexceptionable things about caring for children, and a young minister said a prayer. Neill himself would have smiled sardonically.

The transition from the nineteenth to the twentieth century in the Mearns and Angus was defined in the work of two local writers. James Matthew Barrie wrote as if he had got it all taped, not only this smiling plain and its people but the whole of Scotland. We are coothy characters, earthing up the potatoes, tending the red-and-pink sweet peas in the fullness of July and waiting for the dahlias and chrysanthemums to burst into bloom for the August flower shows. Well-doing local men, from modest beginnings, get knighthoods or even seats in the House of Lords, advancing like Barrie himself and the local boy in his play, *What Every Woman Knows*, who became a Member of Parliament. In his play *Mary Rose*, the young Highlander, Cameron, is a gawky youth of twenty, in the poor but honourable garb of the ghillie, and is not specially impressive until you question him about the universe. He knows French and reads Euripides and is a divinity student at Aberdeen University. In a little notebook he jots down details of his English employer's 'ferry nice manners and . . . general deportment, in all of which I haf a great deal to learn yet'. A French lassie, spending a year teaching in Kirriemuir's academy while preparing a thesis on Barrie for the University of Grenoble, told me that Barrie's description of Cameron showed great respect for the Highlanders.

To his description of the Lowland Scot, Barrie added a touch of disputatious thrawnness, a solid respect for the kirk, a fugitive gleam of poetry, and he was ready to press out his stereotype of the Scottish character. This is how a writer, once accepted, gives credence and the stamp of authority to ideas that would otherwise float around, undefined. We accommodated ourselves to Barrie's stereotype, lived up to it, believed that that was 'the way it sposed to be'. Barrie's skill in drama reinforced the impression. Making his rectorial speech, on Courage, at St Andrews University, Barrie waved a letter to him from Scott of the Antarctic that had been salvaged from Scott's tent in the polar snows. That was powerful conditioning, showing that Barrie and his ideas were at the centre of the power that controlled our attitudes and our lives.

I was surprised to find that his contemporary, A. S. Neill, who had a similar upbringing near Forfar, ten miles from Kirriemuir, was generously disposed towards Barrie. He traced Barrie's career and his own very different career back to their common, bleak upbringing in which there was little love or laughter. Barrie compensated for his deprived childhood by escaping into the dream-child world of Peter Pan, Neill by founding a school which would give children the love and encouragement and freedom which he had longed for.

Forty years after Barrie and thirty miles farther north, at Arbuthnot in the Mearns, Lewis Grassic Gibbon rejected the Barrie assumptions and melted down the stereotype, and, in a similar way (that is, by producing accepted literature), set in process a fundamental change in our way of looking at our earth journey, and at ourselves. He was outwith the literary convention which says that a writer should present a slice of life, and leave it at that. He was not content to record life in a Mearns farming community and in Aberdeen and Dundee. He asserted, more whole-heartedly than Burns, his belief in human equality. His Mearns folk grow out of the soil, like Hardy's Wessex countrymen. He felt that the place to look for wisdom to guide us was among his Kinraddie neighbours who might be the legatees inheriting insights that were becoming indistinct and insecure. He was harking back beyond Knox and Columba to commune with the ancient tenants of these fields. He was working in the dark, trying to find his way; Barrie gave the impression that he was working in the daylight and that everything was clear.

By daytime the broad coastal plain of the Mearns and Angus is a cheerful place. James Patrick's pictures record the sunshine and the red soil and tall beeches and sycamores of great girth. In winter the well-found farms, their buildings and dykes and bridges all of the old red sandstone, look comfortable and reassuring. Birds brooding on a snow-covered roof above a crow-stepped gable, warm-coated hunters returning, a blue and red farm-cart, the earth puckered into hollows and rising into platforms, give to the landscape the richness of a Dutch painting. In summer the burn sparkles, the blue sky has a few fluffy white clouds, the pieced farm-landscape and the straight, tree-lined roads and the farmer, strolling along with his two collies to have a look at the sheep, smile at us from the paintings. Angus is a rich, domesticated land. The soft contours of the Sidlaws on the south contain the territory like a garden wall.

On the coming on of the night it can feel different. On a late afternoon in November I came up through Angus. The ploughed earth, the stubble and bracken and withered beech leaves and the red canes of willow and raspberry shone in glorious sunshine and the burnt stubble was inky black. The light thickened and the trees stood out black against the residual glow in the south-west and took on a clarity of silhouetted detail. People made for their lighted houses and closed the doors. 'Light thickens and the crow makes for the rooky wood,' wrote Shakespeare in *Macbeth*. Maybe he came up this way through the Glamis country if indeed he visited Aberdeen, and felt unease at being overtaken by darkness. 'Now spurs the lated traveller apace, to gain the timely inn.' Maybe it was all phantasy, but I knew what the traveller felt, this eery sense that came with the drawing-on of the night. There's a strangeness, an uncouth quality, about these Angus place-names, Oathlaw and Conveth and Kinettles and Bogindollo and Justinhaugh; and above all Nechtansmere which suggests the swirling mists of time murking our vision. It's at Dunnichen near Forfar, a grassy field beside a burn where a battle in AD 685 decided that Scotland was not to be taken over by Northumbria but to remain an independent nation. In the dark when we may be more sensitive to such communications, are spirits abroad trying to make contact with us, wondering how we are tilling the land they bequeathed to us (bright red at Laurencekirk, a murky, brown-black round Finavon Hill), craving assurance that their sacrifice at Dunnichen wasn't just so much blood down the burn, and trying to decode for us those cryptic sculpted stones they left for us at Aberlemno overlooking the broad valley of Glenmore and troubled that we are so dense, so unreceptive? We are opening our minds to wild surmises, and some of them may be valid. (It is Edinburgh University that gave house-room to Koestler's Chair of Para-psychology.) Maybe all of us have, for example, an awareness of the presence of the past which comes to us as smells come to a dog snuffling in the undergrowth, an elusive sense of kinship but maybe only of longing and bafflement. It may be race memory or extra-sensory perception or only a will-o'-the-wisp making fun of us. Maybe it is related to the perception of natural things that Jacquetta Hawkes was on about. In *The Spoils of Time*, C. V. Wedgwood wrote that 'The Bushmen and the Pygmies have senses alive to the vibrations of nature, scent, sound, and the presence of hidden water, that civilized man has lost; they live in a tacit partnership with the earth, the air, the trees and grasses and elements. It is their only strength in a world where they have been, for generation after generation, driven back and contained.'

We should be encouraging the young to open their minds and spirits to other ways of looking at life and the universe, to loosen their attachments to the received doctrines. Western civilization atrophies our faculties. The priests don't *know*. Maybe it's all unconscionably different from what we were told. What if even the spreading beech-trees of Strathmore have (as the ancients thought) a spirit of their own, during the day putting on a show of friendliness but their real nature, the spirits that inhabit them, emerging in the dark?

Maybe it's civilization's turn to be driven back and contained. The liabilities of civilization, of being cityfied, are piling up on us disconcertingly. We begin to have a sense of the temporariness of the technological invasion of the landscape, a feeling that the pylons, the car-transporters, the electric headlights gashing the darkness, the metal sentries listening on the hilltops are on the way out. Maybe the indwelling spirits are looking morosely at the structures that deface their earth and pre-occupy their children and publish the continuing fear that hobbles humanity.

Places less than a score of miles from one another and of roughly similar terrain may have a different spirit about them. The Romans had a sixth sense that vibrated to the spirit of a place, the *genius loci* as they called it. The Carse of Gowrie (the land between Dundee and Perth, bordering the Tay) has a feeling about it different from Strathmore and the rest of Angus. This alluvial land has apple orchards. One of the Cries of London was of the apple-sellers advertising Gowrie apples, 'Flower of Monorgan, the top of the tree'. Today Dundee visitors (a pail tied round their neck so that both hands are free) pick rasps in the way that you milk a cow. There is more sunshine and more thunder in the Carse of Gowrie than in most other places in Scotland. There are several place-names containing the word 'inch' which date probably from the time when the Tay covered a wider area than now; Inchyra, Inchture and the inches at Perth. Some of the villages of the Carse remind the European visitor of the rich food-producing villages of the Jura or Côte d'Or, the red of squashed fruit on the brown earth, an economy that grudges every square metre not devoted to cultivation, houses clustering closely round the village church. The Carse has had commercial relations with Europe for centuries. In mediaeval times it sent salmon to Belgium and France and got back Bruges cloth and Bordeaux wine and Rhenish wine. In his book, *The Fair Land of Gowrie*, Melville wrote that at the end of the thirteenth century Edward I overran Scotland and brought with him trained fishermen, so that 'many a barrel of Tay salmon must have accompanied the Stone of Destiny to London'.

For centuries the people of the Carse watched cargoes going down the river from Perth, salmon, sheep, gloves, paper, and, up river, flax, 'lintseed', porter, cheese, groceries, wood, iron, lime. Some of the ships were bound for Petrograd and the Hansa towns, and Hansa merchants visited Perth. Linen from London was bleached on Perth bleachfields. Like inquisitive cats, people were prying into many of the secrets of natural substances, and seeing what they could make of them. The first mill in Scotland for crushing lintseed into linseed oil was built at Huntingtower, two miles away. The oil was used for paint and printer's ink, varnish, tableclothes and floor-cloths, glue, knife-handles and in medicine for burns. Perth foundry built the first iron ship on the east coat. When the young ask us, 'What makes Scotland tick?' some of these stories would help them to appreciate what kind of characters their grandfathers and grandmothers were long ago. They're not likely to make much of the information that James I was killed in Perth and that James III made Perth the official capital and that it was in Perth that Bonnie Prince Charlie proclaimed his father king of Scotland. They might be amused at the inconsequence of the change of trades in Perth. Once it was tobacco and snuff and ropes and gloves that they worked at; the father of Scott's Fair Maid of Perth was a glover. Now it's whisky and insurance and glass. What will it be tomorrow? They would readily envisage a scene in the Carse where the new railway ran close to the Tay and a goods train overtook a sailing ship and hooted as it passed it and maybe the exasperated captain, seeing an ancient craft coming to the end of its days, shouted at the enginedriver, 'I hope yer biler bursts!'

In the sixties I spent twelve hours at Perth Railway Station, gathering information for a radio programme. Passengers and goods were on the move all the time. I had no idea that there were so many Scots who wanted to be some place else. Perth was the hub of the wheel of Scotland, in perpetual motion. Like shipping on the Tay, the railways offered not only a service to the public but a way of life to those engaged in their operation. In the early days of steam, the Perth enginedrivers spent part of their Sundays, unpaid, instructing the apprentices in running repairs, and initiating them, in the manner of the mediaeval masters, into their craft, its lore and prides, its kenspeckle characters and the heroic and more usually humorous events that befell them, the glories of the railway races from London to Aberdeen. There was a railway culture, a soil into which the apprentices put down roots and which nourished them and gave them a pride of identity. But it's what are called the human stories that rivet the attention of the young. An Aberdeen teenager, lodged in Perth Prison, told me that when his father, an enginedriver, was driving the Aberdeen–Glasgow train, and when he came within earshot of the prison, he sounded a pre-arranged whistle. For our Scottish teenagers that communication between father and son would hold more significance than an archive of royal Jameses.

Perth was the home of Patrick Geddes (1854–1932) who has been described as 'the first town planner'. He was biologist, ecologist, philosopher, polymath. Like Leonardo and Goethe he asserted his right to take all knowledge for his province. If you go in for medicine in Scotland, it's medicine you study and no monkeying about with literature or art or history. Scottish doctors, encountering English colleagues in the 1939–45 war, were surprised at their knowledge of Indian history and recent Roman excavation. It was against this Scottish tradition that Geddes took his stand. In 1919 he was contracted by Dr Weizmann to prepare a design for the new University of Jerusalem. In his conception of the new university on the crest of Mount Scopas (continuous with the Mount of Olives) he tried to unify several things – the old buried city of David, the old buried city of David, the old Moslem, Jewish and Christian city, the vast, spreading, modern suburban area, the city's future expansion. It was to be a unity of the cosmic and human order, for lack of which, he said, Hellas failed. What does that mean, a unity of the cosmic and human order? Matthew Arnold said that we mortal millions, in the sea of life enisled, long to be part of a great continent with which we have lost touch. Geddes was longing to re-establish communication not only with a continent of human beings but with a universe of living and inanimate things. The Jewish idea of this unity, expressed in Psalm 148, was behind his plan for the new University of Jerusalem. 'Fire, and hail; snow, and vapour; stormy wind fulfilling his word; Mountains and all hills; fruitful trees, and all cedars; Beasts, and all cattle; creeping things, and flying fowl; Kings of the earth, and all people; princes, and all judges of the earth: Both young men and maidens; old men and children; Let them praise the name of the Lord.'

When that lesson is read in the kirks, people nod sagely, without comprehending. If a pupil asked, 'What does that mean? How can snow and vapour praise the Lord?' I'd find it difficult to answer. Worshipping the Lord, praising the Lord, magnifying his name, is an exaggerated, imprecise way of using words. (Most politicians slide easily into this vague language.) I think it means, Let us be glad for the gift of life and the glory of creation, and aware that we are one with all creation. Geddes tried to express this unity literally in concrete terms. Round the base of the great dome of the University of Jerusalem he built a double ambulatory. One was for the general view; the other, furnished with the instruments of all the sciences from astronomical to social, was to show the oneness of study and life. I can understand darkly what he was after but I think he over-estimated the power of symbolism over people's minds. In the Outlook Tower in Edinburgh he tried to impress on visitors that the city's life was a product of its ethics and science and art. To do that he used a periscope and revolving mirrors to reflect the panoramic view of the city, a living entity, its buildings and buses and hurrying people, on to a flat screen. But what remains in my recollection is an amazingly clear picture of a multi-coloured washing, flapping on a line.

From Jerusalem, Geddes went to Bombay and founded a chair of sociology and civics. Then to Colombo to enlarge the postal system and prepare an engineering plan to combat river flooding. Then back to plan garden villages on Mount Carmel and fight a general who wanted to use Scopas for a vast military camp. It had been the site of Titus's camp when he sent his troops to destroy Jerusalem. Geddes went to France and founded a Scots college on the outskirts of Montpellier, and the college has given its name to one of Montpellier's streets. He was in the tradition of Michael Scot and Admiral Cochrane and Lord Kames, enquiring and initiating.

Ten miles north of Perth, where Strathmore and Strathtay meet, the Romans built the headquarters for Agricola's Legion, the only legionary HQ in Scotland. The camp at Inchtuthil is a vast extent of level ground that makes the sky look an immense dome, and it was well-suited to house a legion and provide a servicing and repair depot. It was hygienic and comfortable and the baths had glass windows. There were 6000 soldiers here and a large civilian population. It was from here that they marched north through pine woodlands, mixed here and there with oak, elm, alder and willow, to fight the Caledonians at Mons Graupius which may have been anywhere between Strathmore and Aberdeenshire. Tacitus, the Roman general's son-in-law, makes the Caledonian chief, Calgacus, say that their children and kinsmen were taken to be slaves in other lands, goods were taken to pay tribute, land taken to supply corn, bodies to build roads through swamps and woods, all under blows and insults.

In modern times nearly a million nails were dug up at Inchtuthil, twelve tons of them and all sizes from one inch to sixteen inches. Three years after the Romans crucified the defeated Caledonians, orders were given to dismantle and evacuate Inchtuthil and all the forts north of the Forth–Clyde line. They buried the nails under six feet of earth. The top layer of nails rusted and fused, and kept oxygen away from the rest, and, when a recent generation dug them up, they were like new. If the spirits of the legion's centurions are free to haunt the terrain they briefly controlled, they would see an obliterated camp beside the river they knew, an outboard engine chugging away, pushing fishermen in a boat up-river, the mellow westering sun shining on golden stubble, a white house back from the river protected by a rampart of bluish firs, and then at night the lights of Perth, ten miles away, tincturing the low clouds blood-red like a soaked bandage. Terminating Strathmore, the little triangle whose sides are Tay, Isla and the Loch o' the Lowes and whose corners Perth, Dunkeld and Blairgowrie (the centurions' daily haunt two millennia ago) is friendly, cosy country of little, twisting roads, unexpected hills and brown-sandstone villages. Nothing much to show for all that earnest endeavour, the drills, the forced marches, the killings, the terror, the torturings, the road-building, the pep-talks, the citations, the food transports. And all those nails.

More of a mark on the earth's surface was left by the Romans at Ardoch, twenty miles south-west of Perth on the road to Stirling. They dug themselves in, impressively, in great earthworks. They were the mighty shovellers. These huge mounds that they piled up in millions of digging hours remain to amaze us, a long-term mark on the configuration of Scotland as earth rolls onward into space. If I were teaching a class in Braco today, I'd encourage the pupils to imagine an encounter with a legionary some moonlit night on the Roman road between Braco and Kaims Castle, in which the pupils asked him, 'Was your digging really necessary?' I guess the legion-ary would reply in the manner of a centurion's pep talk or a quality newspaper's editorial, magisterially intoning the ritual message about the onward march of civilization. If the legionary had been to a good school he would describe Rome's mission in the words of Virgil about warring down the proud and sparing the vanquished.

Strathearn and Strathallan at the heart of Scotland between Perth and Stirling is open country of white steadings and smooth farmlands bordered by the smooth outline of the Ochils to the south and offering vistas into the highlands on the north. There are still fields of rushes, relics of the end of the last ice age. It's a frontier valley, a place of base camps, rendez-vous and departures, a place to rest and regroup. Thousands of Brent geese and greylag geese take over tenancy of fields beside the River Earn. For them, too, it is a place to rest and regroup.

Stirling was the gate through which passed Picts and Scots and English and Jacobites and Hanoverians. Inevitably the great rock in the plain was crowned with a fortress which was duly upholstered (like Balmoral) with tartan and glamourized with military romance. From the battlements you can see the white flagpole of Bannockburn. Bannockburn and Burns's poem about it, *Scots wha hae* (especially when sung to the fearsome beat of the Corries' drums) have assumed a mysterious ascendancy over Scottish feel-ings. The commemorations of Bruce's army defeating the English at Bannockburn and of Scotland's football team defeating the English at Hampden Park in Glasgow are sacraments in our emotional life. We Scots are bewildered by our history. It was dreich, like January weather of rain and sleet and hail and snow, bloody, sometimes inhumanly savage. For what purpose did we dree our weird of a story drenched in blood? What was achieved by all those wars against the English, wars of Stuart and Hanoverian succession, wars of religion, imperialist wars, 'the killing time', Pinkie, Cullerlie, Falkirk, Barra, Killiecrankie, Sheriffmuir . . . the names like a dirge taken up and echoed abroad, Malplaquet, Quebec, Lucknow, Brandywine . . . ?

What is even more sinister is the feeling that all that haemorrhage is inexorable because that's what life on earth is like. We have to accept it now and for evermore. Nothing we can do about it. That's what a Scottish education does to the Scots. It makes them endure as a sheep before its shearers is dumb. It is unthinkable that the suffering could be set down at the door of stupid, blundering rulers. If I were talking to the young about it, I'd tell them, for comparison, about a period of Spanish history. In 1808 the Spanish painter, Goya, had watched from his window a Buonaparte firing squad at work, shooting Spanish rebels. He had recorded the stances of the executioners and when it was over he went to see the corpses in their pools of blood. His picture 'Scenes of the Third of May' is described by Alastair Boyd as 'perhaps the greatest *protest* painting of all time'. The faceless firing squad, the mindless killers, who will move on to the next job when this one is over; the victims who have faces, souls, and are shit-scared. 'This work . . . could only have been painted by a Spaniard sensing in his soul the fury and bewilderment and agony of a people unable to understand the antics of its rulers.'

Stirling is a food-producing centre. In the auction mart they chalk up the names of the farms from which the cattle come – Todhill, Hawkhill, Birkenwood, Bogton. It is a summary of the enduring countryside of foxes and hawks and birch-trees and boggy ground. Two hundred years ago a Stirling seedsman started improving turnip seed and the firm played their part in improving the nourishment of Scotland. They sell their seed in hundredweights to large farms and tiny packets for back gardens. Stirling markets seeds, eggs, beef, sausages. The parts of the pig that don't go into sausages are used for animal food, artificial manure and soap, and the hair goes into mattresses.

Into this background of romantic history and realistic agriculture, how do we fit the University of Stirling? There are broad expanses of emerald-green grass, a Henry Moore sculpture and a tall beech-tree that also looks like a gigantic sculpture against the mottled grey sky. A Venetian-like bridge crosses the water. Black tree-shadows fall on the pink-tinted, sunlit water as if the sun had been sited to provide this effect, accessory to architect Matthews's staging. From centre stage the players see a panoramic backdrop that takes in the Wallace Monument and the sunny, tree-covered hill in the direction of Airthrey Castle, and, at night, lights dancing on the loch surface and low-set lamps that flood the grass verges. German students sang a sentimental song, 'Ich hab' mein Herz in Heidelberg verloren.' If I had been a student in Stirling I could have lost my heart to Stirling. There is as much romance here as has been woven round Heidelberg, Stirling Castle competing with Schwetzingen, the Forth with the Neckar, Ledi and Vorlich and Schiehallion competing with the Odenwald. From the clasp of the curved seats in Stirling's coffee bar, students look out on fairyland, the sunlit slopes of beech-trees, the verdant hope of their beginnings and the fleeting splendours of their decay a panorama of the seasons. This was the local habitation given to the dreams of philosophers and architects. From the comfort of the study-bedrooms the students could organize a council, a boycott of shops overcharging on the campus or a new Scotland. The new principal, Cottrell, formerly a professor of chemistry at Edinburgh, aimed at making the Department of Education's philosophy central to the university. There was much that was amiss in the upbringing of the young but it was going to be enquired into. I thought that Scotland might be standing on the top of golden days. There was hope and goodwill in the air. In sanctioning and funding this new venture the authorities were accepting responsibility for past faults (that was new) and were going to try out a working model. We would learn what reforms were feasible and which of our ideas were moonshine.

I remember Cottrell, a slight unobtrusive figure in a red shirt, wandering through the students' common room, sitting at a table chatting easily to them over a cup of coffee, a salesman consulting his customers, a seeker, a physician bringing the analytical skills of the chemist to the diagnosis of the ills of Scottish education. The experiment was quietly on course. 'Until the work was done, it was hardly known to be a-doing,' wrote Newman about the sixth century experiment of Monte Cassino. Maybe Stirling would develop similarly. But we were over-optimistic. The opponents of reform were only holding their fire until a sufficiently newsworthy event gave them an excuse and a launching-pad for an attack on the university. They found it on the day when the Queen arrived. A widely publicized newspaper-photograph showed a student ostentatiously taking a swig out of a bottle at the moment when her car was passing. The media went gloatingly to town, and the outraged rulers of England and Scotland moved in to restore the former shape of education. Stirling became just another Scottish university. At that juncture in Scottish history success was unlikely. All Cottrell could do was to see how far he would get before they shot him down. Stirling got a considerable way.

Most of the history books describe Scottish history as a procession of events which the majority of us were powerless to influence, the story of a charismatic élite running the show. In 1913 a different kind of Scottish history was published. It was H. M. Cadell's *History of the Forth*. It gives the people who live in the region of the river a better idea of what their region was like long ago. An enterprising educational authority would have filmed the story to tell their pupils about their background, the volcanoes that thrust up the Ochils and the Pentlands, the depositing of gravel and mud and sand and limestone and marl, its firming into the honey-coloured stone of which the New Town of Edinburgh was built, the Tay and the Forth meandering across Europe, the Ochils sandpapered by the millions of tons of ice cover. And then the appearance of man on the scene. Under Blairdrummond Moss a holed piece of stag's horn was found beside whales' bones and the archaeology detectives say that it proves that Neolithic men hunted whales here. Then the sea level fell away and the water withdrew and trees appeared. The Romans felled them, not knowing much about ecology, and the area filled up with water. That was Blairdrummond Moss.

Twenty years after Culloden when 'the national awakening of Scotland was just beginning and men of brains and enterprise were everywhere turning their minds to the better development of the country', Lord Kames, aged seventy, employed hundreds of evicted Highlanders to clear the Moss. It was an epic venture. He ran a burn through the moss and each Highlander got ten acres at right angles to the burn to clear. They were ridiculed as moss lairds, undesirable aliens. They paid no rent for their first seven years on their cleared land. In the High Moss, George Meikle of Alloa and his father (who invented the threshing machine) made a large water-wheel and it was installed at the Teith's confluence with the Forth. It was constructed like the ancient Persian and Chinese wheels but Meikle probably knew nothing of them and re-invented it independently. It went on working for over fifty years. As the bog was emptied, more tenants took up residence. Men, women and children worked even by moonlight, the women making more this way than by spinning. Their ingenuity was applied to the making of their houses. A deep trench was dug round the site. Then all they had to do was to scoop the inside of the proposed house out of the peat. Cadell paints an attractive picture of these peat houses when the family had moved in. Heather and other moorland plants blossomed on the roof. For firing all they needed to do was to dig and dry peat. Peat reek rose from the lums and illicit stills were hidden in the peat stacks.

Initiatives like this land reclamation were part of the great awakening of Scotland after 1760. There was an infectious spirit of enquiry in the air. More and more people began asking questions. James Watt's father-in-law was a bleacher and Watt became interested in bleaching as well as in steam engines. Hitherto cloth had been bleached by boiling first in ashes, then in sour milk; now they sought different alkalis and acids. In 1787 bleaching with the new element chlorine was carried out commercially in Aberdeen. A new constellation of enquirers glittered in the Scottish and English skies – Watt, Boulton, Roebuck, Wedgwood, Macintosh, Gordon, Cochrane. To make a violet dye, Gordon got lichens from the West Highlands and sent people to collect human urine. As they went round the houses they found that greedy suppliers were offering a watered-down product and it was to circumvent them that the hydrometer was invented. The urine collectors carried pocket hydrometers. When the supply of West Highland lichen gave out, Macintosh went to see Gustavus Adolphus IV of Sweden and started a prosperous trade importing Swedish lichens. As a result of this enquiry into what things are made of (that is, their chemistry), there were developments in calico printing, waterproofing, and tar. Cochrane wrote a book about chemistry and agriculture (1795). In 1780 the industrial revolution's iron contributed to the agrarian revolution when James Small yoked two horses to his Carron-made iron plough. Previously two horses and four oxen were needed to draw a wooden plough.

In 1913 when he published his book, Cadell wrote that it was again 'high time for every patriotic Scot to wake up and consider how best to put an end to this reaction, and resume such beneficent schemes as our enterprising ancestors started long ago'. The peaty water had surged back, as it were, into Blairdrummond Moss. There is a comparison between the Scotland of the 1780s and the 1980s. When life is getting on not too badly, we accept. It is when things are getting desperate that we question. Material poverty pushed our forefathers into asking basic questions about the constitution of matter. Cultural poverty is driving us into asking basic questions about the constitution of our society. A livelier school and university system would show the young that the old structures have broken down and would give them the knowledge which would help them to come up with new initiatives to produce a community which had both stability and freedom. Education is for action. In an emergency similar to ours (the need to rebuild their society from the foundation), just when Kames was setting about the clearing of the Blairdrummond Moss, the American colonists were sending to Britain for books on political enquiry that would help them to answer *their* questions. Fawn M. Brodie, in her biography of Thomas Jefferson, wrote, 'The Scottish Lord Kames became, along with Locke, his master and guide to the theory of natural rights.' I wish I knew enough about Kames and Locke to judge what contribution their Old World ideas made to the Declaration of Independence of the New.

CHAPTER FIVE

Glasgow and Galloway

'The Only Countryside We've Got'
title of film about wasteland in Glasgow

When the traveller leaves behind the castle-topped clutter of grey buildings that is Stirling and makes for Glasgow, he is confused with a welter of appearances that won't fit into a pattern. There are television antennae on farmhouse chimneys, sun and shadow on the Ochils, bundles of newspapers awaiting readers or the shredding process, scattered litter, kilted schoolboys from fee-paying schools trying to resuscitate a highland tradition, a pit bing, a factory for making kitchen stoves. Then, nearer Glasgow, cooling towers, a liquefied petroleum gas plant, a deserted, small school, and the accumulated untidiness of an industrial area. A generation ago everybody used to redd up when they were expecting visitors; it was churlish not to give them a welcome. Glasgow has lost heart in the effort to make a derelict landscape look presentable or to bother about how her visitors feel. It's like picking your steps through rubbish to reach your host's front door. When we entered the tunnel beyond Cowlairs, a group of lively children, who had been watching the diesel dials and calling out the speeds from the windows just behind the driver's cabin, suddenly saw the yellow and green and red lights of the tunnel and gazed with wonder and one of them said, 'Isn't that braw!' The farther end of the tunnel was illuminated with what looked like an altar at the end of a long, dim cathedral-nave, the focus of attention. I was as puzzled and mystified as they were and waited for the uncovering of the mystery. What had seemed a lit altar turned out to be a maze of rails illuminated by the daylight at the end of the tunnel.

'Economic forces' (we are told) created the Glasgow desert – the grey, highrise flats, the lower tenements of red and brown brick, the streets of blackened sandstone, an abandon of weeds in open spaces, crowded streets that the yellow and green buses traverse on the way out of the city, advertisements for smoking and for giving up smoking. It's an ungainly builders'-yard. They do bits and pieces of tidying, of make-do-and-mend, flattening Bridgeton and the Gorbals, responding to the immediate pressure. 'Accommodation for the homeless!' barks the economic force threateningly and they run up megalithic boxes for megalopolis. 'Speed up traffic!' and they erect nightmarish overways on stilts. They certainly help us to get through the city quickly. We once timed it. From the airport in the extreme of the city, past Ibrox football ground, shipbuilding cranes, the Clyde (a narrower river than I expected, narrower than the Tay at Perth), on to the highway and then to the Stirling road, east of the city; twenty minutes. From these elevated roads Glasgow at midnight looks like a child's electric railway on a massive scale, dotted with dangerously slim skyscrapers and myriads of pinpoint lights and throbbing with busy-ness. The Scottish villages where people cling to the tradition of sleeping when it is dark belong to a different civilization. It is glamorous at night. During the day it is plain ugly. What hope have we of mitigating the savagery of greed, or the suction of dividends into some insatiable belly? Something ruthless and non-human has taken over, implacable, inexorable. The foreign traveller might have looked for some surviving enclave, like Monte Cassino in the dark ages, that would still be nurturing the humane values, tempering the wind to the fleeced sheep. What about Glasgow University? Would that be part of its function? I believe not. However reluctantly, the university opts out.

I walked round the university late at night. From Gilmorehill there is a panorama of lights, some densely crammed together, some sparsely spread out, over the city. The dry leaves of a sycamore rustled faintly. It was quiet up there beside the university buildings where James Watt devised his modification of the Newcomen engine. The university is an impressive, slightly oppressive building. Like the education it delivers, it is intended to have a daily, subliminal influence, and the students can hardly escape the cumulative effect that the builders intended. The suppliers of education are intelligent, sensitive, hospitable. More than newspaper editors they give the impression that they are determined to see themselves in the role of free seekers after the truth, fearless communicators. But a shadow hangs over them. At the end of the day most of them are not on our side. What they communicate is ultimately their masters' voice. They are the insiders. We are out there on our own.

In Glasgow you see human aspiration at its most poignant. We seek a group, a comm-unity, in which we can lose our querulous egoism, to which we can give ourselves without qualification. It could be our country. But the minority in power rejects us, alienates us, and we look elsewhere for those sheltering wings. In Glasgow they give whole-hearted allegiance to a football team, Rangers, or Celtic. The Elizabethan Sir Philip Sidney said that poetry claps wings to solid nature. That's what football does in Glasgow. When Celtic have scored a goal the massed green-and-white-barred scarves flutter horizontally with the little quick movements of insects' wings and a population takes off into a throbbing, joyous flight.

The Glaswegians are warm people, friendly, outgoing. A visitor can sense friendliness in the accent. Unlike many people in Aberdeen who try to ape the English accent, the Glaswegians feel confident and relaxed in their use of the local speech, perhaps because there are so many of them. They are unaware of any need to modify their vowels and trim their consonants, and incomers seek to defer to this homely pronunciation. Incomers, black people, Scottish lowlanders gravitating to the capital, Highland refugees from feudal landlordism, Irish Catholics quickly make an amalgam conforming to the Glasgow formula. In a discussion at a football match a skilful television programme showed how a Rangers-supporting Pakistani and a Celtic-supporting Italian had accommodated themselves to the speech and mores of the city. It is a place of condensed humanity making common cause of the restrictions under which they live.

In this moonscape jungle, people go crackers, children commit communal murder and seek refuge in heroin. Those who have run amok are imprisoned in a sullen keep called Barlinnie. The open space outwith its walls, as extensive as the space round a Johannesburg compound for black miners which allows room for armed tanks to manoeuvre, deepens the feeling of menace. Wells's novel, *The Island of Doctor Moreau*, describes an encounter with sub-men who are inaccessible to the human quality that we call pity, and are therefore capable of any cruelty. Shakespeare too was frightened at the fragility of the defence of humanity against their own committing of frightful deeds. He wrote of the stopping up of the access and passage to remorse and to the 'compunctious visitings' of our natural tenderness. He imagined wraith-like figures, 'sightless substances', that wait on nature's mischief and in crises assume control of human beings. Glasgow has pushed its luck too far in hoping that in a crisis it can depend on the intercession of human kindness. There are awful murders and awful walling-up of murderers.

We are brought up to believe that a dungeon like Barlinnie is a natural part of the landscape like a bridge or a farm steading. The unspoken menace that surrounds Barlinnie is deepened, not alleviated, by the to-and-fro in the vestibule and the front office, the busy-ness of the staff, the voices on the telephone, the presentation of passes, the conversation of warders going off duty. It is an effort to maintain the pretence that this is just another association of human beings going about their normal business. Barlinnie was built in 1880–6. Inside there is a large rectangular area and, on each floor, an open corridor all the way round from which warders can look down into this well. The secondary school in which I taught in Fife was built to the same plan and about the same time. Teachers and warders had an uninterrupted view of central hall and corridors, an essential requirement of a house of correction.

In both schools and prisons there are compassionate teacher-warders who are permitted to modify the regimen. In Barlinnie a Special Unit was set up, an oasis in a desert of hostility. I was invited for a midday meal there. I didn't know if people round the table were social workers or murderers. I discovered that both groups were there, indistinguishable from one another. There was relaxed discussion, more basic and purposeful than several university discussions in which I had taken part. One murderer told me that what was wrong in the Fife school where I worked was that there was 'no discipline'. Over the coffee a prison warder sat back, throwing in a word only occasionally, like a university lecturer encouraging his students to argue things out for themselves. Later he told me that he had been seconded for half a year to Oxford University's department of criminology.

'You'll learn a lot from them,' I said.

'They'll learn a lot from me,' he countered.

He had left school at the earliest leaving date and hammered out of his experience some new ideas on the function of a prison. His self-confidence gives grounds for hope in Scotland's future.

A prisoner took me to see his cell and those of his friends. There were pictures, record-players, radios, easy chairs, shelves of books. They were like hotel bedrooms but particularized by the tenant's choice of ornament or furnishing. Elsewhere there were craft rooms and work in progress. It was like a Benedictine monastery. An extensive mural they had made expressed savage criticism of the social system and the people who manipulate it (or maybe also are manipulated by it).

On another occasion the Special Unit put on an exhibition of prisoner art. In paint and clay there were the figures of other prisoners, representations of anger and domination and sex, and pictures of chaffinches that came in from the sky through the bars and stayed a little in the precinct and went back to the sky again. With the help and local advice of Glasgow youngsters, the association called the Third Eye put on a film protesting against a proposal to make a motorway through derelict land in the city. The film was called 'The Only Countryside We've Got' and showed, in the midst of the ugly city, broom in flower, teazles, ransoms (good for cooking), horse radish, hogweed, butterbur, comfrey, foxgloves, a tortoiseshell butterfly, a mouse's nest under discarded polystyrene, and a beautiful shot of a derelict motorcar in the snow.

But the success of the Special Unit isn't followed through. It's as if an exile from the Hebrides had sown daffodils in the Gorbals or like an industrial firm which feels that its prestige and public esteem require it to set up a research lab and thereafter refuses to take the risk of putting into large-scale production the results of its successful experiments. A Chicago professor said that the USA sets up showplace schools incorporating the latest ideas in pedagogics, thus disarming its critics, but restricts educational initiative to the showplaces. It's a recognized defence mechanism of an established order. Psychologists and criminologists and philosophers study

Barlinnie but the Scottish prison system is not thereby much
modified. The inaccessible, unidentifiable people who make the
final decisions about what goes in Scotland don't set much store on
the findings of philosophers and psychologists. They don't let academic studies influence their interpretation of reality. Glasgow
University's culture is in a different world from the principles on
which Barlinnie is run. This dissociation is another evidence of
alienation in our society. And so is the convention that it's OK
to shout your head off if you're talking about merciless, violent
criminals or the 'meaningless, senseless vandalism' of juvenile
delinquents; but you must modify your language and tone if you're
talking about the people who created or permitted the Glasgow
desert, and control our society. They must be dealt with tenderly.
The convention on civilized debate comes into operation. Glasgow
and Scotland need a more sympathetic study alike of the hard men
in the prison cells and the hard men who decree a punitive system
of society. I've seen in chief constables and judges and government
scientists and air vice marshals and other of society's warders a
steely coldness that induces a slight shiver, as if they were frightened of their repressed compassion.

Glasgow is the product of a society that doesn't know where it is
going, whose God has led it up a blind alley. Continuing his journey south to Dumfries, the visitor would find evidence of a sum
that hadn't worked out properly or that left an untidy remainder.
Old prams have been dumped on the railway banks. A sewer vents
into the sea. There is a massive power station at the edge of the sea
at Hunterston. Coal pits heal over, the earth's skin growing again
after having been gashed. There are pipes, black earth, factory
refuse. Industrial Man has been bull-dozing his way through the
landscape. Earth and rubbish have been heaped into a large con-
tainer called 'Tidysite'. On the main roads there are lorries trans-
porting calcium hydroxide, nylon salt, sulphur trioxide, caustic
soda, timber and frozen vegetables.

The country round New Cumnock and Sanquhar is a dull, dreich
landscape of reeds and bogland and few trees, of glaur and discom-
fort. Grey cement additions have been made to the backs of older
buildings, white smoke comes from two power stations and black
smoke from another tall lum. The dining-car of a railway train is a

comfortable place from which to get an overall picture of the terrain, rumpled, planed, ridged, pathed, the concavities due to
undermining, the dumps, humps and howes, and the face of the
countryside altering with the play of the sunlight upon it. An
unobtrusive message on a table-mat says that the first public
diningcar was on trains between King's Cross and Leeds in 1879,
when the food was cooked on a coal stove. I wonder what the visiting social anthropologist from New Guinea makes of the news.
Maybe he scores up a credit to British Rail for telling their customers about British social history when they might have made a
pound or two out of advertising Beelzebub's beer. Maybe the BR
educator was on to something more significant than he realized.
There is a longing, almost a yearning, in all of us to enter into the
experience of the earlier occupiers of these buffet car seats and we
seize on these fugitive pieces of evidence about the passengers
supping soup that was heated on a coal fire in the galley a hundred
years ago. It's the same unspecific longing as makes a Glasgow
father ask, 'Where will we go today?' as he gets the car out of the
garage on a Sunday morning, and the family decide between the
claims of a National Trust castle like Culzean near Ayr or the home
of Bonnie Annie Laurie or the traces of Devorguilla and the Red
Comyn and Bruce and Burns and Barrie in the red sandstone town
of Dumfries, and the opportunity to admire the Victorian sweep of
a fine parabola of rails and platforms at its railway station. We seek
to make some sort of sense out of our landscape and its configura-
tions, and the story of the people who tenanted it before us and we
are frustrated when the clues don't add up to an explanation.

Beyond Dumfries, in Galloway, the clues do hang together. It is a
land of well-found farms, well-maintained dykes round the fields,
prosperous beech-trees, fine tall oaks and sycamores and ash-trees,
bright green grass and black cattle in the Ur valley and, beyond the
river, woods of spruces and larches. It's a humpy, green countryside
of twisty roads and white farmhouses. It has a character and identity of its own, as individual as its 'doon-hamer' speech. There is a
softer air and lusher pastures than in Aberdeenshire and a different
architecture. But there are parts of Galloway where you might be in
the north-east, Deeside or Donside or Strathspey, woodlands, lochs
and water lilies, rounded hills, heathlands and bog myrtle and

crags, the ubiquitous sound of water, standing stones on top of a hill. And, like Aberdeenshire, Galloway has prosaic areas. Newton Stewart is a featureless town in spite of the fine River Cree. It has been tidied up and painted, and flowers have been planted, but it has no sparkle. People have been preserving their drystone dykes, modernizing their houses, reafforesting bare hills, warding off the nuclear scientists and trying to resuscitate an old meal mill. In Galloway the Scottish nationalists are active, confronting the other parties with probing questions, carefully prepared.

In a Galloway valley there are scattered sculptures that visitors leave their cars to stroll across to look at. What does the visitor get out of looking at them? The social anthropologist from the Third World could reasonably expect an answer. Part of the answer is that all right-thinking people are supposed to have a place in their lives for art just as television companies are supposed to have a religious slot. In an open landscape on a hillock between two or three trees there is a figure of Mary, pregnant, being told about the son she would bear. There was dignity and kindness and calm about the group, an oasis of peace in a troubled world. Handel used the Hallelujah Chorus in the *Messiah* (he said) to express the otherwise unutterable feelings he had of the power and majesty of 'the great God himself'. But Epstein's purpose was less easily comprehensible.

CHAPTER SIX

The Borders

With a tale he cometh unto you, with a tale that keepeth children from play and old men from the chimney corner.   EVERYMAN

The region called the Scottish Borders is a magic land. East of Dumfries the thoroughfare from Glasgow to Carlisle is astir with the busy-ness of the eighties. Lorries transport farm equipment, office furniture and fitted kitchens and liquid sulphur and pipes. The cross-section of a lorry-load of pipes is like a honeycomb. Pipes are as much a necessity for survival in our decade as baskets were in an earlier century. Change transforms the valley. The railway is electrified to Glasgow. The need for wood has covered the smooth face of the hillside with a ten-days' growth of fir stubble-beard. The old narrow road is redundant and looks rejected; slowly the natural world will reclaim it, will grass and weed it over, and it will become one with yesterday's seven thousand years, until an archaeologist rediscovers it and announces, 'There was a main thoroughfare here once.' A solitary sign expresses a human refusal to be bulldozed by what is called the pressure of events. It says, 'Free range eggs'. Farther east, away from the leaching effect of the main valley into England, the resistance to change is stronger. The traveller is entering one of the most amazing regions in Europe. It's the land between Edinburgh and the Cheviots, the counties of Selkirk, Roxburgh, Peebles and Berwick.

I lived for six years in this countryside and loved it. It has the spell of a woman who is not all that good-looking but has a fey quality that attracts and holds her admirers. Alexander Gray, poet from the Braes of Angus and academic economist, wrote about the unlikely qualities of his girl that caught and held captive his fancy. A friend

109

of mine from Lochinver in Sutherland visited the region and never left it. His Highland brothers couldn't understand this new-plighted troth. The region has no Highland sublimity of scenery, and most of the towns and villages have little grace of architecture. So where does the attraction lie?

The region has a unity of place; it is a kingdom on its own, inducing a tough local patriotism in its subjects. We lived on the Melrose Road outside Galashiels, looking across to Galafoot and the Tweed at Abbotsford. Near our house was a plaque in a wall recording that here Walter Scott, ill on his journey home from Italy, 'sprang up with a cry of delight' on seeing the Eildons. The inscription gave a special poignancy to his generalized poem on patriotism.

> Breathes there the man with soul so dead
> Who never to himself hath said,
>   'This is my own, my native land'?

A Galashiels woman told me that, returning from a day in Edinburgh, she felt safe when the train, having climbed up the watershed to Fala, began the descent into the valley of Gala Water. It's an atavistic feeling of being in your own territory again that the Border reivers and moss-troopers felt when, after a cattle-stealing sally, they had won clear of danger and felt bielded by their own Border hills. You don't venture outside the well-kent territory unless you have to, and then you get back as quickly as possible. 'A day out o Hawick is a day lost.' When James Hogg, the Ettrick Shepherd, was trying to make writing pay for his farming, Scott planned to help him, explaining that, to gain patronage, he would have to go to London to attend the coronation of George IV. But Hogg refused because, if he went, he would miss St Boswells Fair.

Belatedly we are discovering that Hogg chose the better part. If Scotland is to become healthy, to become whole, we should listen to him rather than Scott, because he got his priorities right. The Scott gospel that individual advantage is paramount has eroded communities outwith the Borders, crumbled their cohesion. When Melrose or Gala or Jed or Langholm or Selkirk or Hawick or any other Border club supplies a man for Scotland's rugby team, it's usually a man from Melrose or Gala or . . . , an amateur (a lover of the game), and not, as in soccer, a footloose mercenary unrelated to the community.

Just as Border wool is reinforced with long fibres that give it continuity, the local awareness of community includes those who lived in these towns long ago. The annual Border festivals keep their memories fresh. There were St Ronan and James IV and David I, moss-troopers and Cistercian monks, Thomas the Rhymer and St Cuthbert, King Arthur and Merlin, Agricola and his legion, Covenanter conventicles, all the abbeys, Mary Queen of Scots, Montrose, Walter Scott. Their ceremonies crystallize round local figures, usually on horseback, Cornets, Standard-bearers, Callants, Braw Lads, Beltane Queens. Some of the ceremonies are recent, others have a long history. The Selkirk Common Riding, they maintain, has been celebrated annually for six hundred years.

My wife and I rose early one June morning to go to the Selkirk Common Riding, six miles away. At seven the rain had stopped but the sky behind the hills was grey and uncertain. Two hundred people on horse crossed the Ettrick at a walking pace, the standard-bearer leading on a white horse. All the time that the long line crossed, singly or in twos or threes, there was the sound of hooves on the stones of the river bed, muffled by the two-feet depth of water. The scene hasn't changed much in several hundred years – sky, hills, river, and people on horseback. You could imagine, said my wife, that you were watching a band of moss-troopers setting out on a raid.

The summer festival of Galashiels is of more recent origin. A group of Gala folk, energetically supported by the doyen of the Scottish directors of education, W. D. Ritchie, set up their own programme of riding the marches and celebrating their history. Down near the rugby ground at Netherdale a raidstone marks the place where Cromwell's soldiers got a bellyache eating sour plums. Resting on a Sunday, they were annihilated by the local men, and 'Sour plums in Galashiels' was later adopted as the motto of the town, and was commemorated in the song. The will-o'-the-wisp of heraldry leads its followers in inconsequential directions. The coat of arms of Galashiels showed a fox looking up at inaccessible plums on a plum-tree. The caption might have read 'Sour plums', or, as we might more likely have said, 'Sour grapes'. But the La Fontaine fable had nothing to do with the Comwell story. The raidstone's origin is equally humorous. A pupil of mine saw it being set up.

But none of that takes away from the genuine enthusiasm with which the people of Galashiels enter into the annual celebration of their history. They commemorate the part that Ettrick Forest played in the union of James IV and his English bride. They ford the Tweed at Galafoot and are received at Scott's house at Abbotsford, thus lightly impressing on the young riders that ancient churchmen used that same ford to get across the Tweed. I don't know why the Borderers are closer to their origins than the rest of us Scots are. In that region I have been aware of the presence of the past more acutely over the whole region than elsewhere. John Buchan, who had Border roots, was sensitive to such mysteries and used phrases like 'the blanket of the dark' and 'the gap in the curtain' to suggest a tenuous border between the past and present. Border? Was there something in living in such a sensitive region that heightened awareness? I've listened to a packed gathering in a cinema in Galashiels on a June evening raising their voices in Burns's words to Haydn's music:

> But Yarrow braes nor Ettrick shaws
> Can match the lads o Gala Water,
> Braw, braw lads.

Nothing much in the words except their local habitation, but a community was soaring above an earthbound life, buoyed up by infinite longings, losing itself in a surge of generosity and happiness. At times like these we see, albeit through a glass, darkly, the potential of our country and its people. This is how we might be living much of our time and not only in brief escapes into music or poetry or fantasy or whisky. We are like gliders searching for thermals to give us a lift. The massed people of Galashiels, singing from their hearts, express a longing for a reintegration of life, a longing to live permanently on the sunny uplands.

There is a concern for music in the Borders. Ruskin told about a local man, who, as he lay dying, realized that maybe he was the only one who still knew the notes of the old tune of 'Sour plums in Galashiels' and he sent for somebody skilled in musical notation to write it down from his playing. Ruskin said, 'Is not this strange that a man, setting out on his heavenly journey should be concerned to see that the tune '*Sour plums in Galashiels* should not cease from the earth?'

Maybe the ancient minstrelsy and the modern festivals spring from the same roots, the desire to make sense of our earthly sojourn. Throughout Scotland, teachers read the ballads to their pupils and tell them that they are a vital part of our Scottish literary tradition. But usually they are a classroom chore, an exercise in literary appreciation. They are fossils that have been preserved. The mother of James Hogg, the Ettrick Shepherd, rebuked Walter Scott about his ballad collecting and publishing. 'They were made for singin an no for readin; but ye hae broken the charm an noo they'll niver be sung mair.' Tamlane gained a place in literature and folklore, and the ancient belief that the fairies paid their dues to hell at Carterhaugh on Hallowe'en was reduced to a quaint fancy. The Scottish schools sapped the ballads further because they didn't make it credible to the young that their forefathers and foremothers could have believed these things and sung about them with feeling. The beliefs and songs were a natural growth, living things, the yearning of a community of shepherds and weavers to read their experience aright, their fumbling imaginative efforts to find a satisfying explanation of the antic natural phenomena, the ferlies, that were their daily and nightly experience. The ballads reveal the speculations they were lured into in their search for meaning.

One spring evening when the moon was flitting in and out of clouds, I walked down the road from Selkirk on the south side of the Ettrick and crossed the river. That's Tamlane country. Near the road was the very place, the farm of Carterhaugh, still holding on to its magic name. I was ready to be magicked into acceptance. The setting was right. The lights of Selkirk, the capital of the fairy kingdom, were shining in the distance. Round about were green-brown softly-outlined hills. Barred strato-cumulus clouds half hid the sky and a blue-yellow moon floated behind the cloud-curtain, shining on the water when I crossed the Ettrick bridge. The soft sound of the water was clear in the evening air. Behind the walled garden a light was on in the farmhouse of Carterhaugh. Telephone wires and poles, a tractor working late, an aeroplane humming overhead were

minor intrusions that the setting was able to contain. It was not difficult to feel that a shepherd friend of James Hogg, travelling from
an outbye hirsel to Selkirk on a moonlit evening, would come
under the witchery of the scene.

It's difficult for a Border child to know where fantasy ends and
perceived truth begins. At a high point of the road between Melrose
and St Boswells there is a stone commemorating Thomas of
Ercildoune (Earlston), the Rhymer. With all the hard realism of
Roman letters cut into stone it declares that here Thomas met the
Queen of the Fairies and began Scottish literature. What is a trust-
ing youngster to make of that? Thomas Hardy's Wessex countrymen believed that at twelve o'clock on Christmas Eve the cattle
sank down to their knees, and Hardy, a sceptic, said that if a childhood friend invited him to go to the lonely barton they used to
know and see the oxen kneel, he would go with him, 'hoping it
might be so'. We would find a much fuller response from the young
if we took them fuller into our confidence, differentiating clearly
between the things we know to be true and the things we know to
be wishful fantasy and the things about which we make inspired (or
uninspired) guesses.

The story of the Romans and their camp beside the triple
Eildons, Trimontium, is fairly clear-cut. Glimpses of the reality of
their sojourn in the Borders are offered by Edinburgh's National
Museum of Antiquities. From Trimontium, archaeologists have
dug up chariot wheels, a cavalry helmet made of brass, a wooden
bucket, pieces of leather tents, horses' bits, blacksmiths' tools.
There's a cooking pot with the words 'Turma Crispi Nigri' (Black
Crispy's Squad) indented clumsily upon it, maybe by the cook. Botanists working from pollen grains, archaeologists, historians and
other detectives working over the clues dug up at the camp site,
have come up with a picture of the Tweed valley when Agricola and
the Ninth Legion were there. The heath-covered flanks of the
Eildons came down into peat and hag; there were patches of
swamp; roads were paths, higher up, twisting round boggy ground
to the villages or through deep woods; there were oak, alder, pine,
hazel, birch, mountain ash, more trees than now and therefore
more mist, a humid atmosphere; in the Tweed there were frequent
alternations of rushing water and stagnant willow or rush pools.

There were big and little insects, harsh-sounding birds that caught the fish in the river, beaver, wolf, wild boar, Caledonian bear, reindeer, elk, giant ox. Transport was by packhorse, waggon, and boats on the river.

The description of Agricola, written by his son-in-law, Tacitus, can be translated as 'He was a man lacking in force,' or equally as 'He was never aggressive.' He had lived through Nero's reign and probably had seen Nero in his amethyst toga parading through a room filled with the scent of violets and verbenas. Agricola's Rome was a city of violent contrasts, a city of narrow streets and tumbledown houses and foul-smelling alleys; and of Goering-like extravagance and luxury. The Pretorian Guard in yellow uniforms and red girdles and big earrings rode on their Numidian horses. Hindoos, Arabs and Ethiopian giants paraded the streets. In the gardens were peacocks, flamingoes, swans, ostriches, gazelles, antelopes. A crescendo of musical instruments echoed and drowned out the confusion in men's minds. The populace thought the Christians were cowardly when, confronting the specially-famished Hibernian wolfhounds bounding into the arena, they knelt down in prayer. Men with scourges drove the gladiators on, and their coffins lay ready. The Greeks set up an altar to Pity, but that was something that didn't come into Nero's scale of reckoning.

That reality gives us a loom on which to weave our imaginings of what it was like to be a legionary in the Borders when Agricola was there. The great Julius Caesar was as far from them as the Duke of Wellington is from us. A legionary might have had a grandfather who was one of Pilate's centurions and had spoken with Jesus of Nazareth. Some of his older friends might have been massacred in Boudicca's uprising against Rome and he would have recounted the story in the same tones as Boers speaking of Zulus, or Yankees speaking of Indians. 'A good Injun is a dead Injun.' Vesuvius, and the destruction of Pompeii, would be fresh in their memories.

That is the furniture of the minds of Roman soldiers serving in the border outposts. We can imagine the conversation over the evening meal as they supped their soup and looked down through the trees on the Tweed. They would be shooting a line about sexual triumphs over local girls. In the irreverent military folklore would be a story of a Balearic slinger who had yawned in the face of great Julius when he was fully launched into one of his pep-talks, or somebody would exhibit a Palestinian relic, a piece of the coat of a Palestinian construction-worker for which the crucifixion party had diced. I think Agricola would have talked easily to Black Crispy's squad round their cooking pot on an evening. I invited to Galashiels Academy, to talk to the pupils, General Christison who in retirement was growing fruit-trees near Melrose and I found him a character like Agricola. He spoke modestly about his experiences in the First World War and about his encounters with Lawrence of Arabia. I can imagine a legionary venturing a question about the forthcoming expedition against the Caledonians. 'Sir, why do we have to bring this proud people to their knees?' His reply would have been a model of compromise, the compromise of a sensitive man steeped in tradition. In justification he might have quoted poets who magnified Rome's task in the world, bringing civilization to the barbarians. It is still the function of some literary notables to validate the policy of the government. But deep in his heart he knew (as Tacitus said) that he would be creating a desert and calling it peace.

His heart wasn't in it, or at least he had reservations. That's something that history-teachers, like politicians, play down. We owe it to the young to admit to our doubts. I have always found the young tolerant when we didn't pretend to omniscience. They would fully understand the experience of Eadwine of Northumberland who in the seventh century extended his rule to the Forth and gave his name to the city which guarded that northern frontier, Eadwine's Burgh. He married his sister to the king of Kent and with her from Canterbury came one of Augustine's Christian propagandists. The Northumbrian Elders, cradled in the worship of Thor and Odin, called a meeting to consider the propaganda. One of them said:

> So seems the life of man, O King, as a sparrow's flight through the hall when you are sitting at meat in winter-tide, with the warm fire lighted on the hearth, but the icy rain-storm without. The sparrow flies in at one door and tarries for a moment in the light and heat of the hearth-fire, and then flying forth from the other, vanishes into the wintry darkness whence it came. So tarries for a moment the life of

man in our sight, but what is before it, what after it, we know not. If this new teaching tells us aught certainly of these things, let us follow it.

Thirteen centuries later we are still groping and credulous. What we can tell the young is this. When the Christian sings, 'I know that my Redeemer liveth,' he doesn't really know. Anyway, not in the sense in which we habitually use the word *know*. He is longing, like the Northumbrians, for a certainty that is not yet available. The Northumbrian Elder advised, 'If this new teaching tells aught certainly of these things, let us follow it.' The human race is only now growing out of its childhood, doing without the props of fairy stories, trying to piece together, as through a glass, darkly, the evidence available to it. It is to the advantage of the young to understand how the propaganda for some doctrines came to influence people. In the year 627, the thoughts and feelings of the Northumbrians were finely balanced, and when that happens, it doesn't need much to tilt the balance. People don't like to remain long in the limbo of indecision. Two arguments persuaded the Elders to switch their votes away from Thor and Odin, the Norse gods, in favour of the new god. One argument was that the new god could tell them with certainty what happened before they were born and what will happen to them after they die. The other argument came from a disillusioned priest of the Norse gods. He said that all his assiduous worship of the Norse gods hadn't brought him as much favour and fortune as had been given to others who had not been so fervent in their worship. These arguments prevailed and the Northumbrians were converted to Christianity.

Edwine's successor, Oswald, called in the propagandists of Iona Christianity. Boisil went to Tweed and Cuthbert to the log-shanties of Melrose. What conversations did Cuthbert have, a local man speaking with the Border burr, with the farm-workers he met trudging along the boggy tracks? He knew that they had become Christians because, for whatever self-regarding or altruistic reasons, the local thane had thrown in his lot with the Northumbrian King. When we were in the RAF in South Africa in 1942, a friend of mine asked a black lorrydriver, 'If your child were ill, would you call in the white doctor or the witch doctor?' The black man replied, 'I'd call in them both.' Like him, Cuthbert's Borders were between two worlds, bemused by warring gods.

And then by warring propagandists of the same god. Was it from Canterbury or Iona that the words of eternal life, the living water, issued? There are few teachers in Scotland who pay their teenage pupils the compliment of presenting this issue to them straight, and asking for their comments. There is a convention that the majority of people (seventh century peasants or twentieth century pupils or black lorrydrivers) are incapable of understanding these things, but no class I've ever taught would have failed to be interested in the propaganda war between Canterbury and Iona. Canterbury propagandists introduced relics of saints. A commission was set up to adjudicate between the competing gospellers, but a celestial joker might have drawn up the agenda for the conference of wise men that was going to make the decision. It concentrated on two subjects on which Canterbury and Iona disagreed, the date of Easter, and monks' hair styles. (Violent controversy on pupils' hair styles still exercises the minds of Scotland's educational priesthood.) The chairman asked who held the keys of the kingdom of heaven. Both sides agreed that it was Peter. Columba had no key. The chairman gave his casting vote to the Peter party on the grounds that if he reached heaven and the porter turned his back on him, there would be none to open.

Border pupils are puzzled by this report. How could grown men, even in the seventh century, be so naive? But no teacher confirms in them such an obvious assumption. The aura of Cuthbert's tutor, the Venerable Bede, veiled Northumbria, and no teacher is expected to encourage twentieth century pupils to ask irreverent questions of such a venerable body of early churchmen. In so far as they think about it at all, the pupils assume that the Synod of Whitby ecclesiastics were experts, endowed with some higher wisdom, outwith their ken, and they relinquish their questions. And that is the intention of the educational exercise.

The reluctance of many of the young to go along with the official line on history and culture is ascribed to dullness of intellect. A brighter child (say the men from the ministry) would be more enthusiastic about the whole canon. That is unwise of governments. The scepticism of the young is an asset and if the propagators of culture were wiser they would follow up the unspoken questions. The homely truth is usually more appealling to the young than the laundered, starched dogma. In the Melrose Abbey museum the guide was extolling the blue and pink glazes of the Roman pottery. 'It's amazing how they achieved that variation of shades on the same plate,' he said.

'Oh no it isn't,' interrupted one of the visitors who turned out to be a Doulton potter. 'The Romans didn't try to produce these effects. Insufficient oxidation. That's the reason for these colours. They had used up all the oxygen inside their kiln before the whole plate had been changed to an even colour.'

We were left with the impression not of master potters but of intelligent fumblers who would discuss their fiascos and try to do better next time. Farther along in the museum there was windswept foliage carved in stone, and the head of a grinning, toothless monk. In the nave of the abbey are capitals on which monks had cut pictures of brussels sprouts and curly kail, and high up, what was doubtless meant to be the face of an angel but it is the face of a bonny, Border lassie, smiling. The mason made a good job even of the strings of the lute she is playing because they are still there, delicately carved in stone. On what is left of the tiled floor of the dormitories there are intersecting circles and optical illusions created in tiles. That's not the picture of the monks that the history books give. They lead us to imagine a life given over to prayer and copying out manuscripts with ne'er a thought of brussels sprouts or braw lasses. The school history teacher, especially in the Borders where the veil between the past and the present is thin, should try to satisfy our children's longing to see and feel and smell and taste how it was long ago, to sit with Cuthbert's converts in their log huts where the water seeped in through the roof and cold draughts made the cat creep nearer the fire.

But finally these youngsters are realists. After all the clues about Border life in the past have been examined, they ask 'What do they all add up to? What is this Earth lark about? How do you suggest we should be spending our brief time here?' The conclusion reached by the mediaeval monks is not very encouraging. In the flaking red sandstone of Dryburgh Abbey I read the words, 'Homo est bulla', Man is a bubble. That's not a proposition that commended itself to the Border kings. Eadwine and George IV, like their present-day equivalents, were more concerned in the effect of pomp and circumstance in establishing their rule, than in the pursuit of truth. In his *Short History*, J. R. Green wrote, 'A royal standard of purple and gold floated before Eadwine as he rode through the villages; a feather-tuft attached to a spear, the Roman tufa, preceded him as he walked through the streets.' Like a Greek chorus, commenting on the antics performed on the royal stage, the monks inscribed these words on Melrose Abbey.

> The earth goeth on the earth glistring like gold.
> The earth goes to the earth sooner than it wold.
> The earth builds on the earth castles and towers.
> The earth says to the earth, 'All shall be ours.'

By the year 1500 new questions about both temporal and eternal things, given impetus by Huss and Leonardo and Columbus, were kindling the imagination of some of the Scots, and particularly of King James IV. (He was killed at Flodden, three miles south of the Border, in 1513.) G. M. Thomson's *Short History of Scotland* (one of the more imaginative of Scottish histories) sketches an appealing profile of James.

> Like his time, he stood between two ages; two sets of ideas warred within him and in the end destroyed him. On the one hand, he was the man of the new era, eager, curious, restless, unable to receive an ambassador because he was making gunpowder, endowing the thaumaturgical and aeronautical adventures of an Italian alchemist, encouraging the establishment of a printing works, sending prospectors to look for coal in Kintyre, pensioning poets, building a navy, encouraging trade and fisheries. He spoke five languages, and he loved to loiter in the arsenal where his smiths were forging cannon, in the shipyards where his new navy was being constructed, in the counting-houses of the Leith merchants. He was ambitious to play a part in the politics of Christendom such as no other Scottish king had ever done, and, in fact, he made Scotland a European power which foreign potentates were compelled to heed.

In his many-sidedness and in that touch of megalomania
he had, James was the true Renaissance prince, forceful,
thrusting, inquisitive, secular. But that is only half the man.

The other half is pure Middle Ages. He was stricken with
an intense remorse for the part he took in the fatal revolt
against his father and, in expiation, wore a belt of iron to
which a few ounces were added every year. He was liable to
fits of an almost pathological depression when he would
make lonely pilgrimages to lonely shrines, when he would
wear the habit of a friar . . . and give himself up to thoughts
of leading a crusade, for which purpose the republic of
Venice actually offered to make him general of its armies.
In conjunction with his humane and tolerant dealing with
the Lollards must be taken his punctilious observance of
the rites and festivals of the Church. He was superstitious, a
prey to astrologers and necromancers . . .

Fifty-three years after James was killed at Flodden, his impulsive
grand-daughter, Mary Queen of Scots, dressed unsuitably in Paris
clothes, rode with her lady-in-waiting, Mary Fleming, from
Jedburgh to visit her lover, Bothwell, at Hermitage. In the loneliness of the hill-recesses, 'across Swinnie Moor into the dale of Rule
Water towards Windburgh Hill where the fairies were often heard
piping and holding their revels at night', Mary rode, her black
horse's hoofs squelching into the soaking mosses. A child of her
time, she probably believed that a water kelpie haunted the black
loch where the Slitrig rises. In uncertain October weather she saw
for herself the sudden hollows in the hills, the 'beef-tubs', where her
cattle-thieving subjects hid their stolen beasts. She came to Hermitage and I daresay bedded down with Bothwell under the deer-
skins of his rough bed. And then set out again, in bad weather, for
Jedburgh. In a historical novel Agnes Mitchell recreates the chill
induced in the warm human spirit by these grey solitudes. 'The
mighty heads of Cauldcleuch and Greatmoor Hill reared themselves up like thunder against the white towering clouds.' Mary was
sodden with rain and misery and when she got to Jedburgh they
had to lift her from the saddle. She lay ill and nearly died. Later she
wished to God that she had died at Jedburgh.

On an autumn day four hundred years later I followed Mary's tracks eighteen miles over the hills from Hermitage to Jedburgh. I longed to commune with this wayward, imperious character, tall, sensuous, intelligent, speaking a fluent Scots with a French accent, impetuously seeking to live her life in her own way at the very moment when the Kirk was putting up the shutters on human nature. In this elemental land, where little has changed, I would at least see Scotland as she saw it. Peering through the fog of the centuries, I saw her clattering out of the courtyard of Hermitage and taking a last look back. A gibbet arm extended from the south wall and on the east wall there is a slight projection of the wall housing a hole through which reivers could be hauled up by a rope in a dire emergency. When she broke away from fond day-dreams of James Hepburn's embraces, she looked on hills whose outlines are as smooth as a horse's back, cinnamon-coloured bracken, fawn rushes, dark-brown heather, and probably alders and ash-trees along the burnside. (Excavation at Trimontium has shown that alders and ash-trees were common in Roxburgh even in Roman times.) The passage of the centuries is shown only in more fields cultivated, bigger cattle and sheep, vehicles moving without apparent motive power on a broad highway. Two vans, one marked *Liddesdale Egg Grading Station* and the other *Royal Mail*, would have given Mary something to think about. So would my thermos flask of coffee. She could have been doing with a hot drink on that miserable cross-country ride. But the biggest surprise would have been the feeling of ample security. Sheep wandering unguarded on the hills and a country house whose windows were a couple of feet from the ground would have appeared even to her daring spirit as signs of reckless folly. At Hermitage the windows are fifty feet above the ground.

In the Borders more than anywhere else in the world I've had this sense of the nearness and continuity of the past. At a fort on Hadrian's wall a quarter of a circle's circumference has been traced in the stone floor by a heavy door which had dropped on its hinges. I expected to hear a decurion rap out a question, 'Haven't you got those hinges repaired yet?' It was only yesterday that the Romans and the reivers and the monks were here, as large as life. Home they've gone and ta'en their wages, and now we've stepped into their shoes. The nearness of the past makes us long to snuggle up to it closer still, to commune with the previous tenants and ask them what wisdom they distilled from the welter of their experience which, filtered down through the centuries, we could benefit from. The trouble is, we Scots are sentimentalist, suckers for romance. When reality is too much for us, and it often was, particularly in the century after Mary Stuart, we hark back to the sustaining romance, the charismatic hero or heroine, the whisky bottle or the heroin jab. Potions, opiates, charms, spells have never been far from us as we sought to see life in a mellower light. We do genuinely long to know the truth about our past, how it was then; but we subsidize minstrels who tell us what we want to hear.

If we're going to help our young to benefit from our past we'll have to go into it much more deeply. What took us, in the century after Mary Stuart, that we sought felicity not in romance but in extremes of self-denial? In 1697 a Galashiels elder of the kirk was suspended from the eldership for playing football on Fastern's Even. To play on the eve of the Catholic feast of Lent was in some measure to countenance Catholicism. Three years later Robert Wilson (if it was the same Wilson) was 'loosed from the eldership' for having given ale to some people to drink in his house on the Fast-day at time of divine service. And almost a year later he was (perhaps finally) 'deposed from the eldership' for having 'played at the wheel of fortune in the public mercat'. The records of Sabbath-breaking include mending a sack, carrying grey cloth to Selkirk to sell at the fair, having a mill going beyond Saturday midnight. The man who mended the sack was given the alternatives of paying thirty shillings or sitting on the 'drucken stool' and being publicly rebuked. He immediately paid the fine. Thomas Messer and his wife, Janet Dobson, interrogated why they were walking in the fields at the time of divine service, answered that they were going to Boldside to see the said Janet's mother who was sick. Having promised to be better observers of the Sabbath day, they were dismissed.

The Asiatic visitor, studying our Scottish make-up, would ask why so many Scots uncritically subjected themselves to arrogant church-courts, and went sleep-walking through their lives, zombie-like obeying the commands of the kirk-controllers of Scotland. The answer is in the control of the media, which in those days in

Scotland meant the pulpits, and alternative opinion got short shrift. If you've been brought up to be humble, not to trust your own opinion, you are unlikely to stand up to massive pressure. The wonder was that so much independence survived. The Border records show that the kirks couldn't relax. 'Masters of families who sit up at night playing at cards to be admonished privately to desist.' 'Those who continue drinking after ten at night, or idly haunt taverns and ale-houses in daytime, tippling therein beyond the necessity of ordinary and reasonable refreshment, to be held as drunkards.'

Most people came to heel; and then gave their reluctant admiration to characters like Mary Stuart who didn't, elevating them in song to the quality of demi-gods and -goddesses. They wanted to believe that these heroes were larger than life in order to compensate for their own existence which was narrower than life. Walter Scott became one such Scottish folk-hero. His influence shaped and controlled us for centuries.

He was a generous, friendly man, 'readily recognisable from his limp, his ruddy complexion and his border accent', indomitable in spirit, hard-working, imaginative. At school I had been enchanted by *Ivanhoe* and *The Talisman*. 'With a tale he cometh to you, with a tale that keepeth children from play and old men from the chimney-corner.' On him depended such knowledge as I had of the familiar details of historical life of Borderers, Highlanders, Covenanters and the citizens of Edinburgh. He had a journalist's nose for what makes a good story. In his introduction to Froissart he wrote, 'The simple fact that a great battle was won or lost makes little impression on our mind . . . while our imagination and attention are alike excited by the detailed description of a much more trifling event . . . This must ever be the case while we prefer a knowledge of mankind to a mere acquaintance with their duties.'

When we lived at Langlee and looked across the Tweed to Abbotsford and its sheltering belts of trees that he planted, I tried to come by just such a 'detailed description' of a ferlie in the annals of Scotland. What manner of man was he? *Annandale's Modern Cyclopedia* (1903) said that 'the desire of becoming an extensive landed proprietor, and of founding a family, was a passion which apparently glowed more warmly in his bosom than even the appetite for literary fame'. When his contemporary, the seventh Earl of

Elgin, was in Athens shipping the marbles to London (having been assured by a Turkish janissary living in the shadow of the Parthenon that Greek sculpture had been used to make an excellent marble cement for building walls) Scott was looting Melrose Abbey for building stones for Abbotsford. It would have been difficult for anybody from his early years steeped in tradition to step outside his community and turn a quizzical gaze upon it. At the age of twelve Scott went to Edinburgh University and studied Latin, Greek and Logic. It was part of the Scottish academic folklore that youngsters subjected to this treatment gained in an ill-defined benefit called culture. Scott's upbringing didn't encourage him to ask questions.

When I went to Galashiels Academy I took out of the library Lockhart's Life of Scott. Although it was an old book, the pages were still uncut. Nobody had read it through. Lockhart described Scott's anger at trade unionists who had come to Galashiels to interest local textile workers in joining a union. 'Damned agitators,' Scott called them. His contemporary, Mrs Grant of Rothiemurchus, was critical of Scott's zeal in the cheer-leading for George IV's visit to Edinburgh. In her *Memoirs of a Highland Lady*, she said that 'Sir Walter Scott and the Town Council were overwhelming themselves with the preparations... The whole country went mad.' Six years after Scott died, the Scottish chartists set out to change 'the thinking habits' of working folk, the sexual repression, the authoritarian spirit of conformity and vindictiveness, and to educate women at a time when the possessing classes frowned upon it. They organized mass meetings to protest against what they called 'the Coronation humbug'.

Mrs Grant wrote that the idea of the Highlands that we get from Scott's novel, *Waverley*, was 'utterly at variance with truth'. Of *Guy Mannering*, she commented 'The scenery Dumfries and Galloway, the dialect Forfar.' Scott went out little, she said, and when he did usually sat 'very silent, looking dull and listless, unless an occasional flash lighted up his countenance. In his own house he was another character, especially if he liked his guests ... He never had the reputation in Edinburgh he had elsewhere – was not the lion, I mean.'

But he did know the Borders and loved their smooth hills and twisting burns. He was number 24 in the list of the original 38 members of Selkirk Farmers' Club, founded in 1806. Their agenda indicates the climate of thought in which these enquiring Border farmers had their being. One night they debated the highest level at which wheat should be sown in Selkirkshire and the next night they exorcised a witch's spell by putting a horse-shoe in boiling milk. Scott shared this incongruity of outlook. Like James IV three centuries before him, he was torn between the spirit of the Renaissance and the spirit of the Mediaeval world. One day he was putting gas lighting into Abbotsford; another day he came out, 'white as a sheet', from the tiny cottage beside Manor Water where the Black Dwarf had pointed to his cat and said to Scott, 'Have you poo'er? *He* has poo'er.'

When a character like Scott becomes a national legend, his influence, like a wall, holds up traffic in ideas. The most we can hope for is to be like him. He is the glass of fashion and the mould of form. G. M. Thomson said that Scott was 'a rounder, sounder man' than Burns. He was probably unaware that he was propagating a political value and narrowing the range of qualities which we Scots ought to regard as estimable. (By implication he was saying that in some way or other Burns was 'unsound'. Was that because of politics or sex, or what?) Scott's influence is clearly seen in John Buchan, also a Borderer. Buchan repeatedly avowed his allegiance and in 1932, the centenary of Scott's death, brought out a book about him. Like Scott he was a Tory ('for the glamour of it', as a Highland writer put it), he had a hankering after the landed gentry and patronized ordinary folk. Both of them were students of history and writers of verse and well-paid writers of historical novels. Both of them were religious, both avoided women characters, both of them liked the outdoor life and were 'scenery' writers. It is a limiting package in which Buchan allowed himself to be trussed up.

Buchan had great gifts. He could be magic. There was sorcery in his uncanny gift of imbuing a line of Goethe or of a revivalist hymn with a spine-chilling significance in a spy story. *Greenmantle* and *Prester John* compelled my admiration when I was a child even more than *Ivanhoe* and *The Talisman*. A Highland writer summarized his gifts:

> He was a magician in atmosphere. He sweeps us off our
> feet in the first page and carries us forward rapidly to the

last, in a dream of adventure, high spirits, daring enterprise, heroic romance. And all this in a style limpid, rapid, easy. If there is a better writer of English than Buchan, I have yet to meet him . . . His feeling for place is always present – an English garden, a Scottish moor, the white peaks of the Drakensberg, the steaming African bush, the blue ice of the north . . . We at least are proud that Scotland, so often called dour and hard, bred Robert Louis Stevenson and John Buchan – two men who in a harsh world still spun the thin gold thread of poetry and romance, and with it drew us lightly into the youthful regions of out-door adventure – to generous triumph or more noble failure.

The Buchan story has often been repeated in the annals of Scotland. His upbringing and early experience marshalled him in the direction of advancement in England. He was brought up in a Presbyterian manse, second only in size to the 'big hoose' of the laird. The ministers were constantly tempted to seek liaison with the gentility. After Culloden some of the kirk minsters, following the example of the lairds, sought to assimilate to the English pattern, modelling their children's education on the lifestyle of the Church of England vicars. Like the manses, the vicarages were second only in size (as Jane Austen said) to the manor-houses but, unlike the ministers, the vicars were often themselves of the gentility. The university was the ladder by which the ambitious sons of Scottish ministers could ascend the ladder to the gentry's heaven. It wasn't enough to have a Glasgow University degree; you could go on from Glasgow to Oxford as an English aristocrat could go from Eton to Oxford, a nice usage which put Glasgow University in its place. Buchan made the grade, he received the accolade of acceptability and went on to the next stage of his career; he became one of 'Lord Milner's young men' in South Africa.

During the First World War a little more than a decade later another minister's son, John Reith, who was ascending by the army ladder, clattered into his father's kirk in Glasgow, resplendent in officer's uniform, his sword clanking noisily by his side in the hush that preceded the opening hymn.

In the veldt John Buchan felt himself strangely at home. The Boer upbringing was almost identical with his own Calvinist upbringing. But the Boers were resisting the political and cultural colonization that Buchan was being railroaded into accepting. I imagined that for the rest of his life he was pulled both ways and he tried to reconcile the two forces. In *Greenmantle* he made the Afrikaner recruit to the Royal Flying Corps, Peter Pienaar, an admirer of John Buchan. Peter Pienaar was proving that he could square his new-found loyalties with the values of his Calvinist upbringing. The Earl of Montrose was one of Buchan's heroes. Montrose had Covenanter roots but ended up on the king's side. In *Witchwood* Buchan makes Montrose, travelling incognito through Covenanter territory, sound like a well-spoken SAS man in IRA territory in Northern Ireland. Buchan was trying to dispel his own doubts by throwing over them the mellow light of Montrose's romantic daring. But the doubts about the values he had sacrificed remained. In *Sick Heart River* he tried to expiate his faults by sending one of his characters into the bleakness of the Canadian Arctic to try and find redemption.

Buchan must have felt reassured by the post-Boer-War history of South Africa. Boer-War hero Jan Smuts took service with Oxford and Westminster and the British army, and like Buchan tried to graft his political-military-scholarly philosophy on to the gnarled rootstock of uncompromising Boer Calvinism. Deneys Reitz, the author of *Commando*, a magnanimous and honest man, went into exile in Madagascar after the Boer War but was ultimately persuaded by Smuts and his wife to make his peace with the British victors and take office with the pro-British South African government. Later the career of the soldier-scholar Col. Laurens van der Post followed the same direction. This theme is common to Scottish and Afrikaner history and perhaps to all subjugated minorities. Ambitious Caledonians who did exceptionally well in the Roman civil service and got a senior job in Pannonia or Egypt might aspire to marry into the Senate, assuming the in-idiom with the toga. Dr Johnson in the eighteenth century remarked on the number of Scots heading south lured by the noble prospects. People cut their losses and throw their lot in with the winning side. If you can't beat them, join them. Maybe these Scots just wanted more out of life than a cold climate, a disapproving god and rural and industrial poverty had to offer. Like the Children of Israel, they were pulled both ways, by the fleshpots of Egypt and by an inner voice recalling them to a diet of locusts and wild honey in a craggy wilderness.

The rulers of Scotland (and maybe all rulers) don't present the choice to the young fairly. They try to make the young believe that there is only one choice that any right-thinking human being will make. The story of Scottish education shows that from the establishment of the Presbyterian Kirk and the publication of Knox's *Book of Discipline* in 1560, its purpose was to dominate the minds of the young, to make them feel that any alternative to Presbyterianism was unthinkable. Donald Campbell's play, *The Jesuit* (1976), suggested that in the newly Presbyterian Scotland of 1614 there were many converts who had their doubts and asked themselves if after all they had done the right thing in forsaking the Catholic faith. Maybe it was a closer-run thing than the Presbyterian winners led us to believe. Whichever side emerges on top tries to persuade the rest of us that there was never the slightest doubt about the outcome and the rightness, and therefore the continuing success, of their cause. Last century and this century, capitalism, a protégé of Calvinism, elbowed out its senior partner and now the emphasis is on making the young believe that any alternative to capitalism is unthinkable. But life (we should tell the young) isn't like that. It is much more tentative, insecure, open to enquiry, its axioms subject to reversal. The issues are not nearly as clear-cut as they are presented to be. It was Scotland's grievous loss that Buchan never had the choice (the fleshpots or the wild locusts and honey) evenly presented to him. I think he realized too late the nature of the values he had relinquished, borne away by the stream of consensus in which he was caught up. That consensus taught him to undervalue the majority of his fellow-countrymen, to write us off too easily. One day we'll win, but every apostasy postpones our deliverance.

When Buchan under-rated us, seeing us as largely of a piece, unremarkable, undifferentiated, he was forgetting our history, our cosmopolitan origins. One day in Galashiels Academy an art teacher, surveying his class of fifteen-year-old girls, tried to identify for me their racial characteristics. The pupils were busily engaged in mixing colours to reproduce on paper the pinks, greens and browns of the whinstone wall of the playground, unaware of our scrutiny. He said, 'Take that first row. It starts with the gypsy type. Then there is the Nordic and after that the Irish colleen. I don't know about the next two; they're mixtures. But the girl beside them is as Spanish as a Goya picture and she came from Aberdeenshire. Beyond her is the Slav – those cheekbones. And the last one, her names makes her Irish and she's a Catholic, but she doesn't look Irish at all. She looks Jewish, doesn't she?' The study in ethnology was interrupted by a question. 'Please, sir, how do you get that funny, purply colour?' The teacher deftly mixed some paint and she said, 'Thank you. I would never have could dae that masel.' The Border idiom (in which the verb *can* is not a defective verb) and the Border lilt (the rising inflection at the end of the sentence). A visitor would have described her as a native Borderer, but both her parents came from Lombardy.

The Purveses and Elliotts and Scotts in the school register are intermingled with Polish names from the forties. And much of the foreign blood in Border veins is of earlier transfusion. The Roman troops at Trimontium were cosmopolitan. French masons took part in the buiding of Melrose, French courtiers accompanied Mary, prisoners of war from Napoleon's armies were employed to alter the course of the Tweed near Innerleithen. Children are con-formists, desperately keen to belong, to be subsumed in the accepted pattern, to adapt to the climate of speech and attitudes and values. In one generation most of the offspring of these unions would have become patriotic Borderers, sharing in Walter Scott's pride of place, his love of the terrain. One of the constituent parts of love of country is children's love of the natural world. Most parents and schoolteachers are capricious and always chivvying them but there is an abiding consistency in nature, the same yesterday, today and forever. It wraps them round with a sense of security and peace.

The Borders had a sheep economy, as Aberdeenshire had a cattle economy. Maybe that's one of the reasons for the difference between the people of these regions; maybe the animals they tend make shepherds different from cattlemen. I suppose it is the young we'd have to ask if we wanted to know why the Scottish metrical psalm 'The Lord's my shepherd' has ringed the world and nobody sings (as far as I know) 'The Lord's my cowherd'. Perhaps the

Indians extend their veneration for cows to hymns and endearments. It is strange, the emotive ties that bind us to the animals on whom we depend. The Eskimos speak of God's little seal. Is it the warmth of the wool, the innocence and vulnerability of the sheep, our dependence on sheep, that has woven them into our everyday language? The Lamb of God, the sheep hear his voice, spinning a yarn, the warp and woof of life, heckling, all these word-usages speak of sheep-life inextricably bound into human life, of human beings who speak their thoughts in metaphors derived from sheep. 'Ma wee lamb,' says the mother to her baby. That's a coothie part of our history. Less comforting is the story of the sacrificial lamb.

Even a confident community like the Borders was unable to stop London closing down its railway. It was a major Scottish asset, this scenic route south from Edinburgh by Melrose and Hawick, Teviotdale and Liddesdale, past Newcastleton and Hermitage where the roads don't go, across the 'debatable land' to Carlisle. It was called the Waverley route. Where you can see its track it looks like another derelict Roman road, a line of communication withdrawn. It was for a century a unifying force, integrating the community. The decision to shut it down was initiated by experts ignorant of all save the economic consequences of their deeds and often even of these. The rape of the Waverley route is one more argument for taking power out of the hands of an élite and giving it to the people.

CHAPTER SEVEN

The Capital

Historians . . . conceive of cultures as chaotic and
morally neutral swamps from which 'great men'
carve out plantations.

MARILYN FRENCH, *Beyond Power*

In describing Edinburgh I am mindful of the foreign visitor at my
elbow, asking about its influence on Scotland. Edinburgh is a city
of museums and gowns and institutions, a place of checks and
balances that slow down Scottish life, coldly formal, east-windy,
unfeeling. Its public buildings look like Greek temples. Its gaze is
firmly fixed on ancient Athens and its aborted buildings on the
Calton Hill were intended to earn for Edinburgh the title of the
Athens of the North. Its lawyers, kirk ministers, dominies are
preoccupied with precedents and ikons. The eighteenth-century
buckles on the shoes of the Moderator of the Church of Scotland
are a sign of where the kirk's thoughts lie. A liberal writer who had
been critical of Scottish law-courts was blackballed by the lawyers
when he sought to join a prestigious Edinburgh golf club. Edinburgh's Merchant Company schools, the rampaging dinosaurs of
the Scottish educational desert, confirm the children in the ideas of
their fathers, and the proletarian comprehensives have no alternative but to fall in and follow their leaders, deadening the creative
imagination. The Enlightenment was not a beacon illuminating all
Scottish life. It left much of Scotland unlit. Edinburgh's old town
was as awful as Dickens's London but the intelligentsia, Scott and
Jefferies and Cockburn, found no major questions with which to
confront the indignity to which an élite subjected the majority of
their fellow citizens. In finely symmetrical crescents of honey-
coloured Inverleith stone, the elegant houses of the New Town
were built to the specifications of apartheid, the patterns of

132

'Upstairs, Downstairs'. They were designed to build social division into Scottish society. Scotland's intellectuals, mounting the impressive front steps, allowed their attention to be directed away from the basement windows below-stairs behind which the ranked menials (scullerymaids, kitchenmaids, parlourmaids, tablemaids, lady's maids, housekeepers, cooks, footmen, valets, butlers) ettled to get an eyeful of daylight while they performed their appointed duties, cleaning the knives, washing the earth from the turnips, trimming the lamps, airing the clothes, sewing on emergency buttons, answering the imperious bells, dumbly accepting rebuke, waking the ladies and putting them to bed, servicing the gentry. How could intelligent people become so calloused that they accepted without demur a system of apartheid? For example, how could imaginative architects be persuaded to employ their talents on the design of beautiful buildings to house such separation?

We in remote, rural Aberdeenshire were foxed by Edinburgh's enlightenment. There is a figure of speech called synecdoche (e.g. 'All hands on deck') in which the part, to which the attention is directed, is taken to represent the whole. For many generations we had been brought up to reverence intellect. By an easy synecdoche we were accustomed to reverence those who were deemed to possess intellect. It took me a long time reluctantly to concede that I had been naïve. I had believed that the intellectuals were not of common clay. Ruefully, I realized that they are more vulnerable to praise and flattery and the temptations of titles and degrees, readier to be put on the waiting-list for honours, than I would have credited. At first it amazed me that these gifted Scots, scientists and theologians and academics, should have such a preponderance of common clay in their constitution. Nowadays I am more amazed that we Scots should have been taken in by them for so long. That is the basic, traditional error propagated by Scottish education and a Scottish upbringing. Only now is Scotland escaping from its educational folklore and learning the lesson, 'Put not your trust in the academics.'

A chapter on Edinburgh is the appropriate place in which to insert an outline of Scottish education, the wayward process which helped to shape us. A recent book on Scottish education and culture details the paradoxes of the Scottish character.

Forthright speech, and subservient conduct.
Aggressive masculinity, and maudlin sentimentality.
Contempt for, and envy of, most things English.
Moral righteousness, and guilt.
The democratic myth, and the corruption of power.

Jim Sillars of the Scottish National Party said that we Scots are like sheep, lying on our backs bleating. An editorial on the devolution plebiscite said that we Scots are 'feart'. How were these paradoxes and this fear produced? The story of what Scotland taught its children during the last fifteen hundred years helps to answer that question.

James Scotland's *The History of Scottish Education* starts off with the statements that 'education is primarily training in literacy' and that therefore the landing of St Columba in 563 marks the beginning of 'effective Scottish education'. Although the author realized that education is 'the passing on of a social and cultural heritage', the whole of his history is devoted to book education and a strange, inconsequential tale it is, like a novel without a plot, going off erratically over the hills on tracks that lead nowhere. The Scottish people, the beneficiaries of this system, had little say in where they wanted to go. They were like passengers fogbound in an international airport, standing around in bourachies or singly, disconsolate, and at the disposal of the traffic controllers. It's like a tale told by an emotionally disturbed character who had lucid intervals. I tried to reduce it to some consecutive sense so that young Scots, whom I was addressing, should be aware of where we had been and how we might plot our farther course.

Columba taught ordinary people the alphabet for the first time in Scottish history. Some of his protégés learned to read and even to write. In the following centuries monks wrote manuscripts in Latin and Greek and Gaelic. As Christianity spread and dioceses were divided up for better administration into parishes, parish schools began, teaching singing and masses for the dead and grammar, but, by the time of Bruce and Bannockburn, the nobles had progressed only as far as signing documents with their initials. Paper replaced parchment and hornbooks were the vehicle of education. They were inscribed with capital and small letters, numerals, the Lord's prayer and exorcisms, and, to protect the expensive paper, were covered by transparent horn as today's AA manuals are covered by cellophane. Latin, the necessary medium for learning and church services and law and diplomacy, was so dominant that it became a synonym for education. Latin was education. If you had Latin, you were regarded as educated; if you hadn't Latin, you weren't educated. The medium became the message. That mystical belief survived in Scotland to AD 1950 and thereafter began to fade.

In St Andrews University (founded 1411) the students studied logic, physics, metaphysics, ethics, philosophy and a book of Solomon. Its governing body said, 'Especially we forbid any female to enter our college except the common laundress, who shall be not less than fifty years old.' In 1451 the pope allowed a university to be founded in Glasgow 'that there the Catholic faith may be spread'. Aberdeen came in 1494. Two years later James IV introduced one of the first education acts in Europe. All barons and freeholders were to put their eldest sons to school from the age of eight or nine until they acquired 'perfect Latin', and thereafter for three or four years at arts and law, so that 'justice may universally reign through all the realm'. Even the most gifted of kings can't get round to asking questions about everything and has to base his legislation on the orthodoxy of the current experts. There is an appeal and a pathos in his stated belief that from a college education would flow justice through all the realm. These mediaeval universities were like secondary schools today and the principal dealt out corporal punishment to defaulters.

The student-children of the Reformation began their day by kneeling before statues of Christ, and studied Virgil and Cicero and had evening disputation and prayers. They could get the rod for lateness, running in the corridors, talking in class, lingering too long in the lavatory, using the common tongue instead of Latin, and, finally, 'mischief', a blanket term which was defined as 'conduct prejudicial to good order and scholastic discipline'. Nobody asked why these youngsters were less than enthusiastic about Horace, Cicero and Erasmus. Four hundred years after the Reformation, Scottish schools are still run on these principles. Children are to be moulded into the shape approved by those in power.

The dominies were doing what they considered best in the

interests of the children and of Scotland. In spite of his strange, Dr Paisley-like prejudices, John Knox was one of the outstanding characters in Scottish history. Nobody can emerge unscathed from the whippings endured by a galley-slave and we should forgive his angers when we consider his utter fearlessness, not a common commodity in twentieth-century Scotland, and the energy with which he sought to provide a school in every parish in the land. Within the limits of sixteenth-century ideas, he was searching for a better Scotland and so, I believe, was Mary Stuart who lived just up the High Street from him. They were both valuable people, the tolerant queen, experimental, venturesome, and the apostate priest, energetic and fearless. But for their loyalty to the voice of their upbringing and religion they could have brought about a better Scotland. But bleak, cruel theologies, or diabologies, have held the Scots in their grip down the centuries and neither John Knox nor Mary Stuart could surmount their prejudices to acknowledge their common humanity. If only one or other of them, escaping from their upbringing and clinging to the shadows of the street to avoid scandalizing Scotland, could have made a secret rendezvous in the house of the other for a private discussion in which, forsaking all indoctrination, they reached out for fellowship and an uninhibited revelation of what, in the depth of their being, they felt about their brief tenure of life and power and about how they could unite to suture their torn country. But neither could be free from the effect of the searing marks that their religious education had branded them with, any more than could Mary's grandfather, James IV.

It was not Knox's fault that progress in school-building was slow. The property-owners (the 'heritors') were reluctant to pay for schools. In Stirlingshire when they failed for repairs, money was taken from fornicators' fines. In Knox's Scotland the lairds didn't have to sit on the stool of repentance for fornication. That indignity was reserved for working-class and middle-class sinners. The dominies ate porridge and kail and cabbage and lived in houses where there were mice and rats and insects, their life's ambition to tutor a lad o pairts who would go straight from the parish school to the university to build on the sound Latin foundation he had received. If there was such a thing as the Scottish character, the dominies for three centuries after the Reformation provided some marks for its identification. There was a psychiatric compulsiveness in their dour drive for perfection in the Latin language. A youngster in the Aberdeen Grammar School had used the phrase *humanum genus*. Melvin, the rector, corrected it to *genus humanum*. The boy quoted Sallust in defence of his own usage. The headmaster pardoned him but warned him in future to take Cicero and not Sallust for his guide.

In his Latin grammar, Melvin quoted the writings of Celsus, Priscian, Probus, Caesar, Charisius, Phocas, Cato, Pliny, Mela, Serenus and some of the ancient glossaries to indicate to fourteen-year-old Aberdonians that the gender of the word *pollen* was uncertain. Lord Cockburn, one of the torches of the Edinburgh Enlightenment, lamented that 'there was only one great classical school in Edinburgh, and this one placed under the Town Council, and lowered perhaps necessarily so as to suit the wants of a class of boys to more than two-thirds of whom classical accomplishment is foreseen to be useless'. He helped to set up Edinburgh Academy where young boys had three and a half hours of Latin and Greek daily. The headmaster was always an English clergyman and usually an Oxford graduate. Cockburn didn't enquire what enlightenment these favoured children got out of Thucydides, Aristophanes, Euripides, Homer and Horace. He was a total subscriber to the dominies' creed that Latin and Greek are good for children.

In 1833 the rule was relaxed and students in the medical faculty of the university could opt to take their academic examinations in their own tongue instead of Latin. Seven years later the last thesis in Latin was submitted – by a Jamaican.

The 1872 Education Act made school attendance compulsory for all children between the ages of five and thirteen, took control out of the hands of the church and charged the ratepayers for education (and parents for a contribution direct to the teachers). It was a creditable effort to let in some light on a singularly unenlightened culture but the religious obscurity persisted. Twelve-year-olds had to know the history of Judah from Hezekiah to the Captivity, the Acts of the Apostles, the doctrine of the Resurrection and parts of the Shorter Catechism. ('How do we escape the wrath and curse of God due to us for sin?')

All of this determined obscurity has been consistently played down in Scottish history. I was brought up in the comforting belief that if somebody proved clearly how a motor engine or a medical treatment or a school curriculum could be improved, the improvement would automatically follow without obdurate resistance, broadening down from precedent to precedent. Scottish history shows that it is not so. We are not living on the sunny uplands of a rational society, founded on free discussion. The professional world is a much more dangerous, unpredictable world than I thought. Dark forces materialize out of the gloom, sabotaging change, diverting the stream of irrigation into the sand. Just as the Enlightenment never got to intellectual grips with Latin, so twentieth-century Scotland never got to grips with school education. A report called for sweeping changes in the presentation of history and a 1957 schoolbook, *A Scottish History for Today*, got so far round to the interests of the pupils that it reported that Queen Margaret fed nine orphans with the same spoon as she put in her own mouth and that a sixteenth-century English visitor to Edinburgh said that 'the cobwebs above his bed were so thick, they might have been blankets'. But that was as far as concessions to realism went. Much of the rest of the book was formal history, the abstract conceptions that pupils don't comprehend. In a bluebook on secondary education the Scottish Education Department said yes, we do need sweeping changes, and the second part of the book said that the best way to introduce these changes was by depending on the old usages. In Scottish religion and education and law, the theory is sometimes unexceptionable; the practice is something else. That is Scotland's main malady, the alienation between theory and practice.

The Scottish Education Department, or its masters, are not above trickery. In *Scottish Culture and Scottish Education 1800–1980*, Humes and Paterson (on whom there are fewer flies than on most chroniclers of Scottish education) reported on the background of the people appointed to committees producing reports on Scottish education in the mid-fifties. We all believed that they represented a cross-section of Scottish opinion. Not so, as Humes and Paterson discovered. They were largely of a type, the generally accepted stereotype of Scotsman (few women amongst them) believing in egalitarianism, respect for the intellect, abstract argument,

discipline, 'stretching' the pupils, and a mildly reformist national-
ism. It was a compound of Scott, Barrie, Buchan, Bridie, Elliott,
Johnston and Hetherington. (In 1960 Hetherington, principal of
Glasgow University, said that student grants should be kept low so
that incentive to academic excellence should not be weakened.)
Most of those selected for these advisory committees had followed
what one writer called 'the Kirriemuir career'. They were the
characters that Barrie found admirable. Few of them came from
Glasgow and few of the ills of industrialism were studied.

It came as a surprise to me that the stereotype of the typical Scot
was a deliberate creation. This was how our rulers wanted us to
think of ourselves. A *persona* is dangled before us for our admiration. The word derives from the mask worn by an actor in ancient
Greece. Our voices and personalities will sound through these
masks, suitably modified. This was the personality, the model of
Scotsman, that I had to try and live up to, the prevailing Edinburgh
orthodoxy to which I had to accommodate my view of what life on
earth is about, the model of those who entered whole-heartedly
into the prosecution of the Scottish purpose. The pressure to con-
form is everywhere to submit our private decisions to the ruling of
the judges.

The history of Scottish education forces questions upon us. Did
Columba have a consistent view of the character of the future Scottish nation that would be moulded by the education that he was
initiating; or did he just think that it would be a good thing if more
people could read and write? I think he hadn't given it much
thought. Like religious priests, the very similar educational priests
assume that their product is to be of inestimable advantage to the
people in darkness to whom they are offering it. Missionaries cross
the sea, and land in what they consider to be a backward community and set about proselytizing it. St Columba's mission to the
Picts can be compared with the English mission that landed in
Nigeria in AD 1840 to convert the Yoruba tribesmen. In 1970 the
vice-chancellor of Lagos University looked back on the upbringing
which had been replaced. Previously, youngsters had gone hunting, fishing, farming with their fathers, learned from their elders
their people's history and traditions, participated in religious festivals of drama and art and dancing. After 1840 'the children learned

to read and write and to yearn for white-collar jobs'. Their role was to service the traders who arrived in the wake of the church missionaries. Latin became as potent a magic in Africa as it became in post-Columban Scotland all those centuries earlier.

The lesson to be learned from the history of Scottish education is that the whole process needs to be looked at again. It is not a carefully thought out and consistent philosophy of life designed to give fulfilment to pupils and prosperity to the state. It lacks reverence for the young. The Scottish dominie quells his children. The Educational Institute of Scotland, participating in a book on world education, illustrated its contribution with a drawing of a Scottish classroom in which the whole class had their hands up in answer to a question. No drones or rebels in this hive of busy bees.

In theory the course of Scottish contemporary history is charted out of the advice given in many committee rooms in St Andrew's House, up the hill from the east end of Princes Street. Experts and administrators and provosts, in conclave in wood-pannelled rooms, have their coffee, and a lassie clears away the coffee cups and they settle down to a two- or three-hour session. The conduct of the meetings and the wording of the reports are in harmony with the brown furnishings. The Asiatic visitor could easily believe that he was seeing liberal democracy in action. But he would be mistaken. 'Consultation' means that the administrators select from the proffered advice what suits them or what they can't avoid adopting even by the most sophisticated delaying action. At one meeting in which I took part, one of the administrators' representatives, called euphemistically an 'assessor', confronted with a radical proposal from one of the members of the committee, said, 'Oh, they'd never accept that.' Once in St Andrew's House I heard a subversive say, 'You don't get pupils to develop awareness by feeding them information on a nature trail. This transmission of information doesn't produce the end that the education system assumed it would produce. Well, what will produce these ends? That is the question on which the whole vast university-and-school structure may shortly founder.' But the Scottish administrators have been taught by their English public schools to listen courteously and then to isolate the subversive, making him feel uncouth, and the discussion resumes its bland course. At another committee meeting, an exasperated headmaster asked if, at their next meeting, he could introduce a pupil. Permission was readily given. At an appropriate juncture at the next meeting he was asked to bring in the pupil, whom he had left sitting outside the door. He brought him in and said, 'Mr Chairman, this is a pupil.' And while the committee prepared to follow a routine of question and answer, he took the pupil out of the meeting and resumed his seat.

The culture propagated by Edinburgh, on which the administrators were brought up, is equally remote from Scottish daily life. At a graduation ceremony, the degree of Doctor Honoris Causa for Magnus Magnusson, BA, Knight of the Icelandic Order of the Falcon, Rector of the University of Edinburgh, was proposed by the vice-chancellor of the university. Few recipients of the honour could have been so worthy. There were his tact and his gift of peace-making between students and senatus, his scholarship in Icelandic literature and Palestinian archaeology, his regular appearance on 'Good morning, Scotland' on BBC radio. And then came the ritual deference to classical literature. In one of his letters, Cicero said that, in a play popular in the Roman theatre at the time of Pompey the Great, Pompeius Magnus (the smarter members of the audience guessed what was coming), one line was so popular that it had to be thrice repeated. It said that it was to Great Pompey that the Romans owed their unhappiness. The vice-chancellor said that by a transposition of words they could make the line applicable to present-day Edinburgh. It was to Magnus that the university owed its happiness.

I had encountered the same classical phenomenon at the end of a week's conference at Oxford. The headmaster of one of the English public schools combined his vote of thanks to the chairman, whose name was Eden, with his farewells to those from all over the country who had participated in the conference, and he wrapped it all up in the approved manner by quoting the last five lines of *Paradise Lost*.

> Som natural fears they drop'd, but wip'd them soon;
> The World was all before them, where to choose
> Thir place of rest, and Providence thir guide,
> They hand in hand with wandring steps and slow,
> Through EDEN took their solitarie way.

The stranger to western civilization would be intrigued at the way in which the high priests of education in Scotland and England bludgeon and distort a passage from their holy books into serving their purpose. Scriptural quotation is an essential component of ritual and ceremony.

Graduations at Edinburgh University were picturesque ceremonies. Wall space climbing up to the roof was filled with pictures of Greek or Roman figures sitting or standing on steps leading to classical buildings and engaged in intellectual discussion. The organist played *Il Penseroso*-like music on the pealing organ while the parents and their friends assembled. There were parents accustomed to the occasion and at ease, approvingly seeing their children tread successfully the paths they themselves trod a generation ago. There were other parents in their Sunday best, proud of their children who had made the grade into a socially approved status. Some of these latter parents were identical with a group in Germany described by Hermann Hesse – well-off, seeking to look down on the administrator (beamter) class who made less money than they did, but nevertheless proud that their children had made the entrée into that professional group.

The procession began, the entry of the priests. The Dean of the Faculty of Divinity said a prayer. The words were beautifully chosen and appropriate and rang true. Almost I was persuaded that this was not ritual but reality. The capping of the doctors of philosophy drew attention to the programme which listed the subjects of their research. They had completed theses on textual and hermeneutical aspects of Paul's use of the Old Testament in 1 and 2 Corinthians, on the Targum and Peshitta texts in the Book of Chronicles, on social concern in British preaching, on urbanization in Zambia, on the diseases of chickens and cattle and lambs and pigs, on the geology of the Tweed, friendship, job design, middle-class parents, paranormal abilities, African business managers in Kenya, ward sisters in hospitals, the meaning of work and leisure in the lives of players and gardeners. (But on that occasion no thesis on the effect of cultural theses on the lives of the people of Scotland.)

The other graduands were capped, received a word from the acting vice-chancellor and walked across to accept from a girl in a beautiful summery hat the red cylinder containing their Latin-worded degree certificate. The acting vice-chancellor addressed the new graduates. The organ struck up, the procession re-formed and filed out. The sun shone beautifully. Cameras recorded the scene. Graduates posed against the monument in the gardens, or the hall, or the more distant Salisbury Crags, happily. Parents greeted unknown parents, sharing a success, wondering about a future. Then they drifted away to restaurants to mark the occasion, laughing with the waiter in Denzil's, ordering salmon or lamb, drinking toasts in sherry or Bordeaux or champagne.

It was an occasion and it was right that it should be presented with ceremonial and recorded in Scotland's annals. But it must abide our question. I enjoy the music, the ceremony, the black gowns, the gold braid, the hoods of red and green and the subdued gold. The acting vice-chancellor said it was a happy occasion which should not be dimmed by cataclysmic references. Was he saying that some doubts have crept into our hereditary esteem for our universities? We feel honoured to share in an occasion like this, beautifully staged, celebrated with the pageantry of a mediaeval guild. We are proud of those children of ours because they have been given the skills to heal and reconcile and blaze new trails and increase understanding, maybe even to bring democracy to Scotland. But we are uneasy. Whose side are the Scottish universities on?

Scottish culture in the twentieth century, however hard it tries to declare its independence, finally depends on the patronage of the powerful as Italian culture did on Medici Florence. Novelist William McIlvanney speaks from experience and the heart when he tells the story of a mining community in Ayrshire. He is angry about the apartheid to which working-class folk, his own family and their neighbours and friends, are relegated. The hero of the novel *Docherty* (published in 1975), almost inarticulate with anger, explodes, 'The bastards don't think we're folk! They think we're somethin' . . . less than that.' But McIlvanney's intention was lost on some of the reviewers. By assessing the book on a literary canon, 'a work of art', they isolated it from any political infection. They praised it appropriately. A beautifully wrought novel. His phrases hammer against you like a collier's pick. A human history is mined with humour. It was as if an aspiring Scotsman had entered the book for a literary competition. Its influence was contained within the frontiers of belles-lettres. That suited the purpose of the patrons of the quality press.

The story of Scotland's history and law and art and literature and religion and politics is of restricted experiments. The initiators are liable to be pulled in at any time from their flirtation with libertarian ideas. Nevertheless there was much fertilization of ideas.

The ancient city of Edinburgh maintains a metropolitan air. There is a baronial dignity about these strongly-built high houses, the pink building in Lady Stair's Close and the turreted country-house between the Lawnmarket and the Waverley Station from where you can look across to the blaze of lights on Princes Street. They have endured slumdom and, dignified, have survived into better times. Imaginative architects have built into the new Grassmarket the lure of its lurid past, dating back to 1477 when James III gave it a charter as Edinburgh's marketplace, and to the Porteous riots, hangings, martyred Covenanters, Burke and Hare the body-snatchers. In the alleys there is a thriving trade in the furnishings and utensils of past centuries, jewellery and china, leather cases, spoons, brass lampstands, old clothes, grandfather clocks.

From a low-flying aeroplane the new town of Edinburgh is incredibly beautiful. Its crescents have the grace and symmetry of an aerial view of an ancient Greek theatre like Epidauros. From the ground, on a late winter afternoon every tuft and hook and feather of the sycamores and elms and birches is silhouetted clearly against the opalescent sky above the setting sun, and in that sky there is just a touch of pink like the inside of a mussel shell. In the east the full moon, rising, is like a Chinese lantern suspended against a pale blue sky. Over at the Forth a prodigal ellipse of orange lights traces out the form of the road bridge. The lights of Rosyth and other little towns receding along the estuary are like coloured pins denoting centres of habitation on a map.

In spite of its richness of history, its beauty, its Festival, Edinburgh is a failed capital. It has never managed to assimilate the disparate forces that struggle within it, into a homogeneous whole. It didn't really try, being intent on exhibiting the Upstairs image. Neither the Heart of Midlothian nor the Hibernian football ground gives the impression that the city is as concerned about the comfort and entertainment of its citizens as it is about its Festival patrons. This is what happens in modern times to a city that is hung up on a heraldic view of its past and capitalizes on it by presenting to tourists a culture unrelated to the lives of most of its citizens. The culture propagated by Edinburgh is of a piece with the literature taught in Scottish schools. Football crowds are beyond the fringe. The Hearts ground at Tynecastle is like a proletarian enclave in a metropolis of classical architecture, and it has its own advantages. It has the intimacy of Shakespeare's Globe Theatre, being enclosed on four sides by the grandstand, a block of tenements, a brewery wall and a school. Spectators have a sense of being nearer to the players than at Pittodrie in Aberdeen and people watch the game from the tenement windows.

Edinburgh's Craigmillar is a proletarian enclave well organized and supported, a prototype for communities beginning to take the direction of their lives out of the patronizing minority, and with an earthy realism. A community member complained about the dinner her daughter was offered at school. But she short-circuited the proper channels. She took the pudding and a spoon to the education office, insisted on seeing the director of education, and laid pudding and spoon on his desk with the injunction, 'Taste that!' The school dinners improved.

CHAPTER EIGHT

The Kingdom of Fife

To become totally reduced through mindless work
is the fate of the great majority of the people in all
progressive countries.
ADAM SMITH, *The Wealth of Nations*

For centuries, Fife was a self-contained peninsula. Its isthmus-connection to the Scottish mainland is blocked by the Ochils and it was encouraged to look seawards in the direction of Europe. Its ugliness and beauty, its landed gentry and communists, ancient monuments and computers, mines, industry, shipping, fishing and farmlands have made it a microcosm of Scotland. Fife presents to us in small book, in manageable, more easily comprehensible form, the influences that mould us, that make and mar us. In giving an account of what it was like to live in Fife in the second half of the twentieth century, the accountant has to try and set down in debtor and creditor columns the commerce of ideas that were being transacted in the minds of men and women and children, ancient prejudices, new fears, changing attitudes, waxing expectations, the influence of climate and landscape and buildings, making people choose this road rather than that, stay quiet or erupt, elect for sweet content or the excitement of going for bust on money and prestige.

Maybe places do exert a subtle, long-term influence on the people brought up in them. The houses of Kirkcaldy are solid, reliable, unromantic. Most of the people who have lived all their lives there are solid, unromantic, reliable, brisk, brash, they have a no-nonsense kindness and a delight in puncturing fantasy. A Gaelic-speaking headmaster in Kirkcaldy said one day, thinking nostalgically about Lochaber, 'I came to Fife for my sins.' His local-born deputy said, 'You came to Fife for more pay.' I'm not sure, though, of the validity of generalizations based on these stories. Maybe Kirkcaldy nurses more poets than Lochaber.

We are all artists, cherishing a flickering inner light even if all we can do is to sow a packet of nasturtiums in a windowbox in a desolate street. In Kirkcaldy and industrial Fife there were gathering signs after the mid-century that folk were clearing up, planting rose-bushes in neuks of streets where previously laurel had hidden litter, rebuilding, hurrying on change, eager to get into a new house and remove torn cement sacks and planking and make the encircling desert into a garden. The author of a contemporary book, *The Greening of America*, wrote of green shoots pushing up through the ferro-concrete of an industrialized society. That was happening in Scotland too. A senior pupil suddenly rushed out of a Kirkcaldy classroom one day and disappeared into the country hinterland. Later he was asked the cause of such an irrational outburst. He said, 'I just wanted to see green things growing.' People were becoming aware of deep needs as of vitamins.

Like glimpses of sunshine, glints of beautiful landscape raise the spirits and give balm to hurt minds in the same way as music or poetry or comeliness of human appearance or action. Fife has rich seams of such resources. When there is snow on the high ground between the Beinn Inn and the Eden valley, the West Lomond stands out like the dome of St Peter's above the level white rampart of rock which is broken by an ancient lava-flow or a recent fall. From the Fife end of the Tay road bridge, Dundee's skyscrapers at night are transmuted by random lightning into fairy towers. On the southern frontier of the Kingdom on a winter night, low black rocks stand out of the moonlit sea, a dense constellation of orange and primrose lights identifies Edinburgh and the moonlight is filtered on to the earth through soft mops of cottonwool cloud. Where the cottonwool has come apart, the blue darkness of the night sky shows through. There are other scatters of light on the Lothian coast. There is a sharp east wind and, unceasingly, the low roar of the sea.

Inland from Largo on a late-January day, children slide and skate across the ice of a crater-pool. Beech-trees surround the circle where a long-extinct volcano erupted, and the trees scale the rocks up the slope to the snow of a level field. Rough water-eroded clefts in the hillside are roofed with shelter-giving trees. Ten thousand snowdrops and many aconites are in flower. Another week, and under the trees near Sir Andrew Wood's canal at Upper Largo, there are holes in the snow where water has fallen from the branches, and the movement of the dry grass stems has chafed round each stem a vertical tunnel of the same diameter as that made by the falling water-drops. Against the snow, the sixteenth-century tower and the eighteenth-century buildings and the boughs and delicate tracery of the trees look black as in a Bruegel picture, and crow-stepped gables reinforce the likeness to Flanders. Gulls look whiter against the greyish-white sky. There is an expectant hush in the air, broken by attempts at spring song made by sparrows and starlings. A low-flying yellow helicopter disappears into the damp haze. A triangle of wild geese fly east at a low level, an occasional quiet honk reassuring the company that they are on course and safe, and they too disappear into the haze.

On a March evening, under the power of a snell north-east wind, the dark wall of an oncoming wave, darker even than the aquamarine of the sky overhead, breaks into a white line racing along the top of the wave and briefly a curtain of spray is blown off this white top into a continuous band above the wave. The dark blue overhead thins to a light blue on the horizon. The turf of the hummocky golf links feels springy. The Lothian coast's galaxies blur into a confused light like the Milky Way but the nearer lights of Leven and Methil and Buckhaven are amethyst and orange. The equinoctial tide is far out on Shell Bay and we walked a long way over the pools, shifting stones and watching communities of buckies and small crabs scurrying away as the coal-black water cleared. There were hermit crabs, red weed, a shag, a dead eider-duck, empty tins, a tomato-sauce bottle and, washed well up the beach, an oil drum, still watertight, seaweed torn from its moorings, pieces of wood and a primus stove. Inland, an owl flew so softly and effortlessly that the silence arrested attention; it is as if somebody beside you is speaking but not a word comes out of his mouth. The owl did a skilfully executed banking turn and sat motionless on a post as if it were part of it.

In spring on Kilconquhar Loch are great crested grebes, pochards, shelduck, swans, moorhen, reed bunting, teal, black-headed gulls, coot. Round about there are hawks and grouse and a barn owl is being chased by seagulls. Every spring we waited for the return of a corn bunting to utter his dry and jangling notes from the same section of the telephone wires on the Hatton road near the wood above Keil's Den. All these things and April sunshine, escaping fitfully from white clouds and black clouds, sometimes blink-bonny, are like tunes and poems and familiar faces that beguile our pilgrimage. In the summer, oystercatchers bury their orange-red beaks in the sand where the lugworm are. Streamlined terns fly with delicate, elegant manoeuvres, as good at aerobatics as swallows; they have long streamers projecting from their tails like those of the swallows. At night there is an incessant excited piping of the seabirds on the crags beyond the sands. The water thumps through the rock corridors like the thumping of ship pistons. Green-brown and dark-brown seaweed, bladder wrack and fern-green enteromorpha weed is thrown up on to the sands. A seal may be biting its way out of the salmon nets. In the shore pools there are dahlia anemones and periwinkles holding on to seaweed, and starfish.

I was a schoolteacher in Fife for sixteen years and tried to communicate to the pupils (sons and daughters of miners, factory workers, forge workers, linoleum workers, motor mechanics, shopkeepers) an awareness of this parcel of earth on which they had found themselves. In the summer term the school chaplain, the Rev. Robin Mitchell, who was the BBC's bird-man, took the pupils on country walks through Keil's Den and over to Pitscottie. For the first ten minutes they listened to him as he drew their attention to wood anemones and the pink-tinted samaras of the elm and the song of the robin redbreast ('a wee trickle of notes'), and then they assumed independence and began to ferret things out for themselves. They once discovered a dozen pheasant's eggs cooked in the ashes of a tinker's fire that the tinker had covered over and forgotten or disowned. They were enjoying the freedom of the countryside. Freedom is a noble thing, said Barbour, the father of Scottish poetry. 'Freedom makes man to have liking.' The pupils, freed from classroom pressures, became different people, relaxed, smiling, reacting more sensuously to the natural world. Sometimes in their exuberance they hardly noticed Mitchell but it was he who had noiselessly pulled back this gauzy curtain and let them into a new world. He was unobtrusive, an enabler.

The pupils had been out in the Forth catching mackerel. They had seen a lobster-creel being made at St Monans and sugar juice being squeezed out of beet at Cupar. Some of them had been down a coal-mine. They had climbed the Lomonds and been aboard a cruiser at Rosyth and visited factories and farms. The cameras with which they were equipped sharpened their vision as they looked for significant or memorable scenes, or a humorous juxtaposition, to record. We decided to send them on a figure-of-eight flight over Fife which would integrate the separate snapshot images they had already gained. They would see Fife as a coherent whole, the yellow whins on the hill-slopes, the edging of brown sands on the East Neuk, and they would get size into perspective. Most of us find even large-scale maps misleading. We don't have an imagination powerful enough to look at an inch and see it as a mile.

From Scone airfield near Perth the aircraft followed the Tay. It was slightly alarming for them to see the green earth sinking away below them and to look down, like a seagull that has come in from the Fife coast, on streets and traffic and smoke from houses and then fields. If you have never in your life been higher than the top of a swing in one of the big wheels in Kirkcaldy's springtime Links Market, it takes some getting accustomed to, to see Fife gradually coming into view a quarter of a mile below you, Newburgh, the twists of the Tay and the Eden, and the lush meadowlands of the Howe of Fife. From the air it is easier to envisage the digging of ditches to let water escape from boggy fields into the River Eden so that the fields could grow rich crops of wheat, oats and potatoes. At Falkland they looked down on the ancient palace and an ugly linoleum factory, almost side by side. They compared the old, unplanned town of Auchtermuchty, its houses sprawling out along the main roads, with the new, planned town of Glenrothes which has crescents and trees and grassy patches and bright colours. And then Kirkcaldy, the pupils' home town. There was the harbour, and a ship or two unloading cork from Portugal and wood-flour from Denmark which would be stirred into linseed oil to make the magma of linoleum. From the harbour they traced Kirkcaldy's long High Street. Then they were lost in a conglomeration of buildings until they could pick out the school and its playing-fields and from there begin to get their bearings and home in on the avenue where they lived and yes, sure enough, that was their house and somebody waving a white tablecloth from the back garden. And then it receded as the aeroplane did a circuit and they were over the Beveridge Park and when they looked back, Kirkcaldy was fading into the distance and they were already past Burntisland and almost on top of the girders of the Forth Railway Bridge. 'It looks not very strong,' wrote a pupil later. They were seeing the earth in a new perspective, toy houses, dinky motor cars, flimsy loops of road, railway lines like pieces of thin string. If the prophet Isaiah had been there with them, he would have said, 'That's as I imagined it. The nations are like the small dust of a balance and the isles are a very little thing.'

The plane flew north past Dunfermline and industrial West Fife to Loch Leven where Mary was a prisoner. The Lomonds looked less striking when we looked down on their foreshortened tops, flattened like a roly-poly, than when we had looked up to them from their base. We flew east along the River Leven over paper-mills to the town of Leven at its mouth. 'Towns are easily known from the ground but from the air one has to think a bit,' wrote a pupil. We crossed Largo Bay and saw the string of fishing villages of the East Neuk. On the way back towards the northern confines of Fife, the pilot climbed to 8000 feet to let the pupils see the whole of the county spread out before them from the Forth to the Tay, but the Forth became indistinct before the Tay came into view. Nevertheless, they did get an idea of what an extensive area Fife is, a kingdom.

It was not so easy for the pupils to visualize their position in time. I scrabbled through the history-books trying to assemble a serial story that would put them in the picture. There were Fife's raised beaches at the twenty-five, fifty and hundred feet marks where people lived when the glaciers retreated in 8000 BC. I watched an archaeologist as he delicately stroked away with a paintbrush the sand from the skull of an Iron Age figure unearthed from the sands of Largo Bay, and I tried to visualize these sea-sand burials and a stooping mourner from whose cloak a metal cloak-pin was the only other material evidence of the nature of their lives. And to recreate the circumstances of the emergency in which Vikings stashed away treasure of silver, scale armour, shield, sword-hilt and part of a sword. In 1817 a tinker found them on Norrie's Law and sold some of the silver to a Cupar watchmaker. Pitscottie's diaries tell about James III's and James IV's Scotland and the battle in the Forth, 'terrible to see'. 'All the woods of Fife' were felled to build the three-feet-thick walls of James IV's ship, the *Great Michael*. The pupils showed a flicker of interest in James's admiral, Sir Andrew Wood, a romantic hero who fought the English and defeated them. At Largo the tower of his house survives, like a fat, brown pencil topped with a weathercock, and so does the canal that he dug so that prisoners of war could pull him, a lordly figure, in his barge to Largo Kirk on Sundays.

Fife is littered with history as the late-spring roadsides with the rich sweepings of apple blossom and chestnut flowers. Culross on the Forth and Balmerino on the Tay were daughter abbeys of Cistercian Melrose. Balmerino was especially liked by Madeleine, the French wife of James V. Its view is across a wide estuary to the even skyline of the Sidlaws. A Spanish chestnut, believed to date to the abbey's founding, lingers on superannuated, propped up and waterproofed by cement. Even today the chapterhouse is an attractive building. There are relics of cloister and church and sleeping-place and sewer, and the abbot's house. We found semi-precious stones on the shore but the intertidal stones were treacled with an oil slick.

Near Largo is Pitcruvie Castle, an unredeemed ruin. Squelchy mud prevented us from entering the ground floor, the home of pigs. On the first floor was a fireplace big enough to contain half a tree under its funnelled chimney. The flat arch over a window space remained precariously and crazily in position. Ash-trees grew out of the five-feet-thick walls and two bourtree bushes from the floor. The ancient keep, dated 1200, had been quarried to provide sandstone for the present farm-building. Why sweat to cut stones when an earlier generation has done it for you? There was a Henryson-like, unimproved simplicity about the place. It was mud and pigs and sheep and grain; undirected burns made marshland and one of them had scraped out a deep cleft. There were alders and elms. On one side it looked down over the Keil Burn, on the other up to the cloven Largo Law. It was here that on his return, Alexander Selkirk (Robinson Crusoe) wandered about, lamenting his lost island paradise.

Beyond what is now Victoria Street in Kirkcaldy was the burgh muir where folk grazed their cattle and cut their peat, and where some of our pupils lived. When Cromwell destroyed ships and storms seriously damaged the harbour, the town had to sell the burgh muir to raise money to repair the harbour. I told the pupils about the reek from the saltpans, especially obnoxious on washing-days, the nail-making, the whaling, the linseed oil, the flax from Russia. A pupil brought to school a metal seal which had been dug up in his garden. It had Russian lettering and had arrived in Fife probably tagged on to a consignment of flax. But there was more interest in the trial and burning of a witch accused of putting a spell on a Kirkcaldy seaman.

East Fife remembers the Dutch connection. The clearinghouse for Scottish cargoes at Campveere wasn't any farther away than London. Fife merchants, striding through the streets of Campveere and Middelburg on Walcheren Island, had their horizons widened. They admired, maybe, the beautifully white linen headdresses of the women (still shining in the Dutch paintings) and compared them with the flaxen-grey cloth of Fife and enquired into the Dutch expertise in bleaching. Certainly wood ash was one of the cargoes they brought back to Fife, along with the red pantiles that continue to this day to give their distinctive charm to the roofs of the East Neuk. Among the fishing villages, pulley arms stretch out for lifting goods to upstairs floors and lofts as in Holland and there is a Dutch tower in Crail. Unconsciously we imitate the people we admire, assimilating their customs and attitudes and architecture and growing into their speech patterns. To the Dutch we may owe our pronunciation of the letter 'i' as in 'fire' and we pronounce, in the same way as they do, their words uit and huis and laan and meester and meisje ('missie' – a wee lassie). Where they say gerookt we say reeked, and where they say hoog we say hich ('high'). There is a coothiness in Scottish speech as in manners that may be due to the Dutch connection.

In the past, Pittenweem exported salt and malt as well as fish, and imported silk, wine and timber. Anstruther shipped potatoes, and a passenger boat sailed to Leith. St Monans exported coal. Elie exported potatoes and grain from the granary at the harbour. These items have disappeared from their economy. And so have local industries such as extracting salt from sea-water, brewing, making soap, making leather, making nets, making oilcake. The way of earning a living changes all the time. New ideas are tried out – furniture, plastic waterproofing, a potato-lifting machine, making golf clubs. Elie, its busy days over, nostalgically recalls them with pub displays of sextants and binnacles and tables with raised edges as in a ship. Its crow-stepped gable houses and outside stone stairs, a gargoyle figure in a 1628 doorway, its nemesia and petunias, make it the most beautiful village in Scotland. It has a superannuated air and at one time forbade fish-and-chips. The other towns are still in the fishing business. Pittenweem has a fishermen's mutual and there is an air of independence and do-it-yourself, an absence of relying on outside big business. After landing from a night's trip in a fishing-boat I asked the fish-salesman when they would start auctioning the catch. 'As soon as we can get folk to come and buy.' Vans drew up and the bidding started. That was in the fifties, before metrication. 'How much for this lot? Four shillings. Four shillings. No? Well, name a price to start me, name a price. Two and six, two and six, two and six, two and nine, three bob, three and three, three and six, three and nine, four shillings, four shillings, sold at four shillings to Willie Reid.' There was a demur.

'I didna bid four shillings.'

'You did. You noddit your heid.'

'I didna. Well, I maybe noddit my heid, but it wasna tae you.'

'All right, three and nine, three and nine to Jimmie here.' That was the price per stone for flat fish and cod. Another boat came in with plaice and cod and catfish from seventeen miles off the May Isle.

The village of Crail specialized in lobsters. In winter the fishermen left the harbour early with the tide and lay outside to wait for the dawn since their lines had to be shot at first light. They lived in the daily presence of the sometimes fantastic adaptations of sea life. Four-foot squid suck a lobster dry without leaving any outward sign of injury. The lobsters walk across the deck like big aircraft taxi-ing. They have a black or near-black tapering body, a blue tailplane and monstrous vice-like claws. When lobsters moult, they pull themselves out of their old shell-casing as a fisherman extricates himself from his tight blue jersey. They don't like light and they wilt in the wind. The boat deck was littered with the refuse of the lobster creels, starfish, sea urchins, crabs, buckies, seaweed, delicately adapted to their medium. The fishermen's outlook is different from that of their landlocked neighbours. 'They that go down to the sea in ships, that occupy their business in great waters; such men see the works of the Lord, and his wonders in the deep.' When the sun shines, the unbroken surface of the sea is thick inlaid with patinas of bright gold glowing with a clear steady light like planets, and the smooth wavelets make patterns of barred shadows on the water. Like the Viking *Seafarer* the Fife fisherman has for companion the yellow-breasted gannet that has an eye for the fish-shoals and crash-dives into the water with fearsome speed. The fisherman, like the airman, has the feeling of having escaped from the land and its earthbound community, floating venturesomely, precariously, in a new medium. He has the delight and the occasional flashes of fear of a young boy's brief truancy from school. He has the freedom of the sea, the temporary illusion of being emancipated from the land. St Andrews looks different from the sea, as from the air. From the sea its grey towers and clock steeple are frontier outposts. North of Arbroath the Angus coast is sometimes hidden by a grey mist. Here are the contours of Scotland that met the eyes of the Viking longboatmen.

From here it's easier to focus on the basics of our existence, the terms on which we have tenure of the earth. Just like the sea creatures that he hunts, the Fife fisherman has to adapt to his environment or perish, and he too has made subtle adaptations. 'Kutch' or 'bark', a foreign tree-gum, was used to preserve lobster creels because it killed sea-organisms and washed out the salt which would have drawn in moisture and rotted the cords. When we landed back at Crail about one p.m. the fishermen switched on their radio to see if the current rail strike in France was over and they could resume their lobster exports to the restaurants of Paris.

Farther west on Largo Bay, Buckhaven too had been a fishing village but those days were over. It wasn't often that the pupils were able to follow in clear detail the steps by which the present has emerged from the past, how a human community adapts to a changed environment in order to survive, switching over to a different way of life, the biology of the metamorphosis of a fishing village into a coal town. It was like studying the succession of movements by which a lobster jettisons its old shell and grows another. The Town Clerk of Buckhaven and Methil lent the school a model of the new sea-town that was to take the place of the derelict fishing village. Only a generation earlier, the foreshore was covered with golden sands and the houses, picturesque as a Cornish village, enclosed it and clambered up the slope beyond. Between the school and the edge of the slope down to the sea there was a grassy patch called 'the verandah' from which our forebears looked out beyond the red tiles and white and red and black walls of the fishermen's houses to the sweep of the Fife coast from Leven to Macduff's Castle to the Wemyss Caves and the sparkle of the sea and, on a clear day, to the Lothian coast twelve miles away. But there came a day in the Industrial Revolution when the local council let the mineowners sink a coal shaft close to the sea. As the pit bing of refuse grew, the tides of the Forth swept it out into the estuary and back towards the shore, distributing the black silt over the golden sands, filling up an open-air swimming pool and separating the lifeboat station by a pile of refuse from even the highest turmoil of the waves. Scraps of discarded metal and a pile of horse-dung lay on the black beach. The old houses of the fishermen looked the uglier for the glimpses of architecture which persisted in squalor.

A teacher scrapped his programme for the morning and discussed with his pupils the model of the new sea-town. Up to that time they hadn't been much interested in the history of the Fife coast. It mattered nothing to them that their village was founded by Dutch settlers. Their unspoken comment was 'So what?' But that morning it was different. Their imaginations leapt the chasm from the drab reality to the bright dream and the teacher filled in the stone-and-lime of the dream. The new blocks of flats would be staggered to give everybody a share of the sunlight and a view over the Firth. They would have dream kitchens and modern furniture. Lifts would be available to anybody who wanted to go from the high ground to the beach. The black beach would be earthed over and grass would be sown and there would be flowerbeds.

'Where would they hang their washing?' asked a practical girl, anchored in the year of the discussion, 1959. The teacher said that there would be spin-dryers. 'Will there be boats on the shore?' another pupil asked. It was a significant question. The fishermen had gone to work in the pits but many of them still had their roots in the sea. The teacher hoped there would still be boats. 'If they plant grass, how will they keep high tides from covering the grass and killing it?' The teacher said they would build a sea wall. 'But if there is a sea wall, how will you get to your boat?'

The discussion splayed out in different directions. There was a tug of the heart between the lure of the sea and of the dream kitchen. A new age required new houses. You used the materials and ideas of your day and age. The fishermen had gone and there was no point in rebuilding houses to fishermen's specifications. For example, in some of the old houses there were built-in hidey-holes where the fishermen hid when the press-gangs were about; but miners living in modern flats have no need of a place to hide in. They discussed the heart-searching, or was it the bribing, of the council that gave the go-ahead to the coalowners to dig the pit-shaft. Fife's education convener said, 'All your benefits come from the point of the miner's pick at the coal-face.' The golden sands had disappeared; were the compensations worth it? The pupils talked about the bing, the villain of the piece, and about erosion and geology and they realized that the obliteration of the golden sands was a tiny incident in the story of the changes on the face of the earth. And the coal-mining itself was only a short chapter in the geological story.

In the new town of Glenrothes in the fifties there was the same sense of acceleration applied to the leisurely pace of tradition. Gardens were left unenclosed, there was a Dutch-like variety of architecture, and the traditional brown and dark greens of doors and windows were replaced by pale blue, mustard, red, royal blue, light green, magenta, sand-colour, pink. The tradition of fixed ways of furnishing a living-room lost its hold. We talk much about freedom in politics and religion and economics, but freedom of taste is important, too. We awoke to the possibility of alternative ways of doing things. We accepted people of several European countries as neighbours and from them learned about edible fungi that had been growing unheeded in our fields and hedgerows all these centuries. Sauerkraut appeared on the table and vodka on the pub shelf. And there was something else that contributed to a new outlook. Those European neighbours of ours felt that they were in at the beginning of something new, equally with those who had flitted from the next village or the next county; it was their show, too, and they were taking part in running local societies. They were not 'incomers' in the way they would have been in a Highland or Border town or village. They were part of the community in the way that a Bulgarian shoemaker or a Scottish joiner was, in a pioneering Canadian settlement at the turn of the century. We were members one of another. One Hogmanay an old Fife woman in our street was dismayed to find that her radio had stopped working. A neighbour from Latvia spent two hours repairing it. These folk gave us a new slant on things. Some of them spent much time listening to news bulletins from Berlin and Warsaw and Moscow and Oslo, and our insularity melted. A German told me, 'When I first went to work in this country the foreman showed me round the machines and said, "Ye'll no hae machines like this whaur ye come frae", and there, right in front of us, were the words "Made in Czecho-Slovakia".' The same Hogmanay we were sitting at our German neighbour's fire, waiting to welcome the new year. There was a knock at the door and he went to see who it was. A few minutes later he came back along. 'That was Charlie,' he said. 'He's a Pole. He works with me at the coal face. He's got one of the finest tenor voices I've ever heard. No, I couldn't get him to come in. He said, "I was just passing and I thought I'd tell you that the 'cello is the best musical instrument in the world and that Schumann's 'cello concerto is wonderful music." And away he went up the street.'

There was gainful interchange, too, between Scots hitherto unaccustomed to living side by side. On a Saturday morning the professional man suggested to his neighbour that he should consider the planting of Jerusalem artichokes, and his craftsman neighbour told him that he didn't have to go to the expense of buying a lawn roller since all he had to do was to fill a small dustbin with cement, leaving a hole through the middle for an axle to fit the handle to. I doubt if there was ever in Scottish history such a free exchange of ideas, such a willingness to suspend final judgements on colour schemes and political opinions and on the bringing up of children. The Community Council's newsletter had a drawing of the chief architect, flower in buttonhole and plan under his arm, chatting amicably to two youngsters whom he'd come across tearing up new plants. The plan under his arm might have been inscribed 'The new Jerusalem'.

But rough winds shook these darling buds of May and the springtime hopes were only meagrely fulfilled. The administrators were the first to drive a horse and cart through their own plan. The idea of Glenrothes was that lawyers and motor mechanics and railway porters and postmen and policemen and teachers should live next door to one another. But already the architects had created a special area a short distance outwith the town in which they built distinctive houses for senior officials of the development corporation. In Keith Ferguson's *A History of Glenrothes*, there is a photograph of Fife's Labour Lord Lieutenant welcoming Princess Anne to the official opening of the Fife Institute of Physical and Recreational Education in 1971. The Lord Lieutenant is wearing a military-style uniform, a peaked hat, a bright, broad sash from which hang two long tassels, and he carries a sword. He looks like a colonel of the Grenadier Guards in full-dress uniform.

A Labour miner who was provost of Buckhaven and Methil, told me wryly about Labour disillusion in Fife.

> In the old days of the Tories we would be standing about talking, waiting for the county council meeting to begin, and the Earl of Elgin would say, 'Well, gentlemen, maybe we should make a start.' But now we have a Labour convener, and an official comes smartly into the room and orders us, 'Be upstanding for the County Convener.' We stand up beside our seats round the table and the County Convener strides in and says, 'Be seated, gentlemen,' and we all sit down and the meeting begins.

It happened that way in Russia, too. A Russian novel told of a working-class father advising his Communist son, who had risen to power. 'You must be seen to be a master. You must buy suits of the very best serge.'

One function of a school is to tell the young, as fairly as possible, the story of their forebears. There could be a panoramic quality in the sweep and continuity of the Fife drama. Not so long ago the miners were serfs working in narrow, dripping-wet coal tunnels and, when they died, not permitted to be buried in what was called consecrated ground. (Right down to 1968 in the Balgonie pit, miners were still working in these cramped tunnels. Their arms, scraping the tunnel surface as they shovelled coal along, were permanently marked with subcutaneous specks of coal.) In the cottages two centuries ago the clack of weavers' looms was heard for twenty hours out of the twenty-four and life was, in the words of one historian, 'a mere permission to breathe'. There were hunger riots. Fifers were punished savagely for trying to escape from the ecclesiastical, educational, political ideas of their upbringing, and a quiet man like James Clunie, Dunfermline MP, friend of John Maclean, whom I talked to in his retirement in Windygates, was imprisoned for conscientious objection to war service and for 'sedition'. That's one side of the story. But equally Fife history records the submission of rebels, the communist agitator who accepts a knighthood, the militants who come to heel. And there is the lighter, humorous side of the Fife story. A Milton-of-Balgonie schoolteacher told me about his grandfather who was a fireman on a railway engine. After taking the engine from Cardenden to Lochgelly, he and the engine-driver went into a pub for a quick drink, but they had left the brake off and, when they emerged, the engine was nowhere to be seen. What action should resourceful human beings take in such an emergency? They went straight to Perth and enlisted in the Black Watch and were posted overseas. Another day an inspector came up in a light engine from Thornton to see why the signalman in the Cardenden signalbox wasn't answering the bells. He found a trio in the signalbox playing a violin, a cornet and a melodeon, and sacked them.

The pupils don't feel that the actions of their forebears (miners, weavers, musical railwaymen, agitators, accepters, all kinds of characters, humorous, ingenious, disillusioned, tenacious) are as much part of their own life-story as their own foetal development, flesh of their flesh and bone of their bone. History is seen as the transactions of remote characters in parliaments and council chambers and development corporations, a spectacle they are occasionally invited to watch, an unintelligible performance in which they and their parents have no say. Another device intended to prevent them from thinking that they counted in the Scottish scheme of things is the use of abstract terms. A phrase like 'Kirkcaldy's water supply', if unilluminated by reference to physical things, is a metaphysical use of words. In examinations they gain the marks for manipulating the appropriate words that describe the municipal development and improving hygiene of last century but they don't visualize the accompanying physical machinery, the ingathering of the water from the hills, the purification, the strange power of water to rise to the level it started from, the repair manholes, the frost prevention, the time and ingenuity that went into the invention of scouring valves, the cunning taps at its journey's end. For that reason they don't appreciate what they owe to their forebears, clever chiels who did as much as the physicians to help us to live longer. We bussed a class of Kirkcaldy pupils to the hollow in the hill where their water supply is collected and then they walked back many miles above the pipes, across the Howe of Fife and past the Rothes colliery to their own kitchen taps. It was a hot day and they became thirsty and one joker lay down on the ground in the attitude of a French Foreign Legionary caught in the Sahara and gasped, 'Water! Water!' Next morning he turned on the kitchen tap with a clearer understanding and maybe some gratitude, aware of the human achievement and initiative that produced one of the mundane miracles of our society.

It was an accident in the school that led me to discover about the overflowing energy and initiative of the pupils. A boy, charging round a corner, had banged into two girls carrying records for the school's weekly dance and broken three of them. I was discussing with a class how much restitution he should make. Sympathy with him dried up when I said he got no pocket-money. 'He could go out and earn some money,' said one boy. It was when I asked how, that I learned how resourceful they were. They weeded gardens, cut hedges, gathered potatoes, rose hips and brambles, delivered milk, morning rolls and newspapers, took racing dogs for walks, creosoted fences.

'How do you land yourself with a job creosoting fences?' I asked one of them.

'Well, you see a man working in his garden and you say to him, "Your fence could do with creosoting", and he'll say "Yes", and sometimes he'll have a brush, but if he hasn't, I know where to get one.'

Another pupil said 'lemonade bottles' and explained that his pal and he had spent all their money at a funfair in a nearby town and, to get money for the bus home, they collected on the prom empty lemonade bottles, making enough money to pay also for a fish supper at the other end of the bus journey. Several pupils worked at the football ground, selling programmes and potato crisps and clearing up afterwards. Two boys kicked in the ball when it went outside the pitch and they got a bonus for a win. One pupil went round with the man who bought rags, exchanging them for balloons, and his job was to play a trumpet, made out of the handlebars of an old bicycle, to announce his arrival. One pupil collected driftwood from the shore, beams from condemned houses, fishboxes from fish-shops, and cut it up and sold it or firewood. With this money he equipped his football team with jerseys.

All this enterprise confirmed our guess that it was the school curriculum that was inadequate and not the pupils. We sought to discover what were the things that caught and held their attention. An unlikely character, an English government spy who wrote a history of Scotland's 1707 union with England, made a contribution to this research. He had hit on some of the things that capture and hold the interest of the young of all ages. About the year 1715 in a London coffee house he met the Fifer, Alexander Selkirk, and got his story out of him, the devices and ingenuity by which he survived on a desert island. He elaborated on it and embroidered it in *Robinson Crusoe*, a book whose popularity testifies to humanity's hunger for comprehension of the simple terms under which we hold tenure of the earth and to our desire to measure ourselves against real requirements, our ability to cope with life on the frontier. Crusoe succeeded in measuring time and in reckoning seed-time, he made baskets, cured food, invented a cooking-pot, learned how to cut stones and winnow grain, he made charcoal and an anchor and a potter's wheel, clothes, butter, cheese. He failed to make ink or a wooden cask that held water or an umbrella that came down, and the boat he built was so heavy that he couldn't move it into the sea.

Crusoe spent twenty-eight years on his desert island. The real Alexander Selkirk from Lower Largo in Fife was on his island for four years and four months. The successes of the real Selkirk were making goatskins into clothes, for which he used a nail as a needle, he ground down iron hoops to make a knife, he made shirts. His failures were, surprisingly, that he couldn't eat fish because he had no salt (yet he must have coughed in the reek of the Buckhaven saltpans that made salt out of sea-water); and that he couldn't make shoes (yet he must have seen his father, a tanner and shoemaker, make them). But maybe the lack of shoes was no handicap to a sea-man who as a youngster had spent all his summers walking barfit round Lower Largo.

These are the basic things, the elements of survival, that young-sters enjoy discussing. Crusoe said that if it hadn't been for the luck of salvaging gunpowder and tools from his ship, he'd have had to use his teeth and claws, like a beast, to eat a goat or a bird. Once in a lesson on Early Man and how he fenced in a plot of ground, I asked the pupils how he would have driven in the fence-posts. I offered them a metre-stick and a wooden-backed blackboard duster and a length of string, and challenged them to tie this equivalent of a stone hammer-head securely to the piece of wood. Their first efforts were poor; the hammer-head was dislodged by a single blow. But with a terrier-like determination they tore away at the problem and invented a figure-of-eight fastening that resisted my hardest efforts to dislodge the head. This appeal to human ingenu-ity captures the imagination of our pupils. They enter into the spirit of the Iron Age people, such as those buried in the Leven sands, who smelted iron in fires using bellows made out of goatskin. At Skara Brae our forebears used the shoulder-bone of a cow for a shovel. The Beaker people of Fife, as the Colessie excavations showed, made drinking-vessels in layers of pottery without the benefit of a pottery-wheel. Their ingenuity has been handed down to the young Fifers of today.

There is a common belief that we Scots have traditionally gone back to the basics, exhaustively questioning everything. I got the impression that the Scottish democrat intellect fearlessly probed the foundations of our civilization. It was not so. It did ask ques-tions about many things but the permissible ground in which first principles could be investigated was restricted. Here is an example of that restriction. Schumacher, author of *Small is Beautiful*, quoted Kirkcaldy's Adam Smith:

> By that which a person does all day long, he is formed. His work forms him. And if you give him mindless work, he becomes a mindless person. And he cannot become a good citizen, he cannot be a good father in the family, or mother for that matter.

Schumacher added, 'And then surprisingly – or not surprisingly – Adam Smith went on:

> But to become totally reduced through mindless work is the fate of the great majority of the people in all the progressive countries.'

And then Schumacher comments: 'He did not say, "This is terrible, they must not do it." No, he had much the same mentality: "Well, that is just too bad, but that is the price we have to pay." And we all know that the human being has a marvellous fortitude in tolerating the suffering of others.'

Most of Fife's Labour councillors accepted, and propagated in their schools, the doctrine that the enduring of mindless work by the majority is the inevitable price of the wealth of nations. They accepted the academic opinion that the majority of Fife children are of limited intellectual ability. They accepted that there must therefore be a minority of decision-makers, and a majority of people on whom the decisions are to be imposed. They felt that the ambition of all right-thinking working-class people was to escape from their community and *rise* in the world and if possible join the worshipful company of decision-makers. The mindless work was to be done by the mindless people. Fife children were to be brought up, in the words of their education policy, 'with the right attitudes to work'. That might require force. Harold Wilson spoke with relish of 'the smack of firm government' and Fife Labour councillors supported corporal punishment in their schools. Little in their upbringing had given them an opportunity to envisage an alternative order of society. These were the political ideas circulating in people's heads in Fife in the second half of the twentieth century.

CHAPTER NINE

The Central Highlands

I am not yet born, provide me
With water to dandle me, grass to grow for me,
    trees to talk
To me, sky to sing to me, birds and a white light
In the back of my mind
To guide me.   LOUIS MACNEICE

The Fife pupils got a god's-eye view of their kingdom, they saw it as
a whole, by flying over it. It's very much more difficult to see the
Highlands as a whole, to get a grasp of this tumultuously variegated
territory. But if we Scots are to take in hand the running of our
country, we have to begin by taking a grasp of it as a whole. To hold
it in our minds, we impose a pattern on it, a grid. If we draw on a
map a semi-circle centred on Inverness and mark on it four radii, to
Perth and Oban and the Butt of Lewis and John o' Groats, we have
divided the Highlands into four manageable regions: the Eastern
Highlands (east of the Inverness to Perth railway); the Central
Highlands (between that line and the great trench of lochs, Ness,
Oich, Lochy and Linnhe linked into the Caledonian Canal); the
Western Highlands and the Islands; and the Northern Highlands.
We draw maps to find our way through these complicated
wildernesses so that we can the better grasp our environment, and
feel at home in it as a frontiersman stakes out his claim and
establishes himself within it.

   Having inspected these regions from the air, the pupils should
fill in the details by ground exploration, walking, pony-trekking,
sailing or on skis. On these journeys they become acquainted with
the local history, the rise and fall of a pulp mill, an oil-rig
construction yard, a scheme for social reconstruction, a dam over
an island burn. They become aware of the ebb and flow of ideas by

which people regulated their lives, the siege laid to their minds by the emissaries of Jesus and Mammon, the philosophies that became irrelevant as new entrepreneurs and their ideologies took over. Human beings hunger and thirst for an integrated view of their background, this parcel of the earth's crust on which their lives are to be enacted. They want to know what's round the next bend of the valley and how it all hangs together, its present with its past and this valley with other valleys. Each new glen traversed, its identifiable personality discovered, is another clue to the crossword, another blank filled in. It's like making sense of a page of print.

From Fife we frequently took the pupils to the Highlands. The Forestry Commission (who saw their Scottish remit as not limited to trees) leased us a hut beside Loch Rannoch which became a base camp for journeys farther afield. One spring morning I joined a group which was going for a week's stay at Rannoch. We crossed the Howe of Fife to Perth and followed the Tay north through an area where the first larch-trees in Scotland had been planted two centuries earlier, making a beautiful landscape more beautiful. It's an area of fine wrought-iron gateways and there will be a story there, of a skilful blacksmith, improving his valley. The field of Killiecrankie raises the ghost of 'Bonnie Dundee' who hunted down the Covenanters. Their belief, that only a silver bullet would kill him, has entered the mythology of Scotland. What was Claverhouse really like? Sombre and sinister like a Hollywood gangster? What did his troops talk about as they walked along the Perthshire roads from one assignment with death to another? Always the reality is just that little bit outwith our reach, tantalizing us, our knowledge too scrappy to be nourishing. South of Killiecrankie we turned west off the Inverness road and followed the Road to the Isles towards Tummel and Schiehallion. Beside the river we stopped for a break. A cuckoo was shouting away, close at hand. 'That's the first cuckoo I've heard this year,' said the woman teacher in charge of the group. 'It's the first cuckoo I've ever heard,' said a girl pupil.

At Trinafour near the other end of Loch Tummel the grass is still green because thousands of cattle spent the night there going to the Falkirk trysts. But we didn't ask the pupils to memorize the fact.

The twenty-one-year-old uncertificated teacher wrote a report on the week they spent at Rannoch. Until then few of the group of fifteen-year-old girls had been farther north than Perth. The Highlands were a new world to them; it wouldn't be over-romanticizing to call it a fairyland. They looked for resinous sticks to start the fire with in the morning; collected rain-water to wash their hair in and enjoyed the easy lather, the feel of the water and the shine on their hair next morning; they learned to move quietly while watching a peewit patrol the area round its nest; they watched ants and lost their aversion to creepy-crawlies; they learned that mosses keep meat and milk cool. The Scottish school tradition of dictating to the pupils the answers to questions they haven't asked was stood on its head. It was when pupils had asked the questions that the answers were given. Trees struck by lightning prompted questions about what lightning is.

Schiehallion is near by, a beautiful three and a half thousand feet quartzite cone of a mountain. We missed the opportunity of helping our pupils to use it to experiment the weight of the earth, repeating astronomer-royal Maskelyne's experiment of 1777. It is a good mountain for the experiment because it is such a clear-cut, uncomplicated cone. He measured the extent to which a pendulum is deflected from the vertical by the mass of the mountain. The pupils, who respect cunning, would have been intrigued by the baffling power of a mass of mountain-rock to pull a freely-suspended pendulum towards itself and by Maskelyne's ingenuity. During their stay at Rannoch the pupils must have asked questions to which the Schiehallion experiment would have provided the answer.

Some of us teachers take a long time to learn the lesson of questions first. Later we took another group of girls along the road on the north side of Loch Rannoch and explained that this was the Road to the Isles. 'By Tummel and Loch Rannoch and Lochaber I will go.' They weren't interested. I told them about a seventh-century monk called Chad who lived in a cell here and afterwards became Bishop of Lichfield; I showed them a ruined clachan and the track by which a hostile group from Ericht had come over the hills to wipe out the people of the clachan some centuries earlier; opposite us across the loch was Glen Sassun which got its name from the English (Saxons) who fled over the hills to escape from Robert the Bruce. But what was Saint Chad or a ruined clachan or even Bannockburn to them? Even a nearby house called 'Chemistry Cottage' where birch charcoal had been used to make gunpowder raised no interest, but they did gather round eagerly when I showed them the very branch of an ancient oak-tree from which had been hanged the last man to be condemned to death in Rannoch for sheep-stealing. On the way back I said they hadn't much enjoyed the walk. They said no, too much walking. I asked did they like being in Rannoch, and they answered spontaneously that they did. I said well, what was it they liked? They found difficulty in putting together an answer. And then one of them blurted out venomously, 'At home they're nag-nag-nagging at you all the time, do this, don't do that, hurry up. Never a minute's peace. They're at you at school and they're at you at home. Up here you get peace.'

There were setbacks. A boy annoyed animals, destroyed a cane chair and blew up a petrol drum. With some misgivings I went to see the head forester in charge. But he said, 'That's all right. Chaps like that are the very ones you want to send up here. They most need the kind of life they get here in the forests. We can cope with them.' I wish he had been appointed head of the Scottish Education Department.

We found the Nature Conservancy as generous in coping with our pupils as the Forestry Commission. Pupils whom we sent to the May Isle in the Firth of Forth entered into an orgy of smashing seagulls' eggs. The tabloid newspapers attacked us. This is what was to be expected of a school lacking in discipline. But the Nature Conservancy defended us, aware that good citizenship is not produced by continuous public vituperation of the young. The National Coal Board also felt a responsibility to the young and supported us, particularly in our efforts to take more pupils to the Highlands and for longer periods. People who had developed patience and initiative in dealing with the recalcitrance of materials and natural things were unlikely to get uptight about the recalcitrance of teenagers. It was just another problem to be solved. An experiment is made; even if it fails, we learn from it and try something else. But amongst the professional educationists of St Andrew's House there is little of this accessibility to new ways of thought. Their cultural training is in past answers, not in present-day questions. They KNOW the answers; if the teenagers don't come up to specifications, we must remould the teenagers.

In industrial Fife the teenagers stole shotguns, climbed roofs to steal lead, stole butchers' knives to use as darts, using a tree as a dartboard. Schoolgirls, sitting in cafés listening to interminable records, tattooed the singers' names with safety-pins on their arms and then went to the seashore and fought one another in a series of single combats, scratching and tearing. The educationists and leader-writers lamented about it endlessly, asking, 'Who sinned, these children or their parents, that they were born delinquent?' From Scotland's fragmented history, from Burghers and Anti-Burghers, Auld Lichts and New Lichts, from the Reformed Presbyterian Church and the Original Secession Church, from the Free Presbyterians, from the United Secession and the United Presbyterian and the Free Church and the United Free Church and the United Free Church Continuing, from the Established Church and the Episcopalians and the Catholics, from all of these, shadows of sin and guilt have clouded the horizon of Scotland's young. In Rannoch I have seen the vision of Isaiah explode into reality. The mountains and the hills broke forth before them into singing and all the trees of the field clapped their hands. The young found what a contemporary pioneer called 'respite from pressure'. They found security in their kinship with nature, and an absence of guilt. In the Highlands, in the absence of timekeeping, and rush, the twenty-four hours stretches into an eternity.

When we sleep outside we waken from time to time and see that the stilts of the Plough have swung through a segment of sky like the long hand of a one-hand clock. The dawn chorus and then the red streaks in the sky herald the sun, and the light broadens into boundless day. With some practice we get over the urge to be up and doing. The rewards begin to accrue. We see the clouds form and advance and dissolve and take shape again. There's an ominous silence and then a wee flutter of air stirring and we get some raindrops but it mostly passes us, and blue-black clouds range over the mountains. The incense of birches and honeysuckle comes to us. There's a larch-tree like a brown gypsy girl in a cinnamon shawl.

There are fir cones lying about, stripped by crossbills foraging for the seed that lies at their core. There is a friendly silence except for the wind soughing in the Caledonian pines of the Black Wood of Rannoch, and, at long intervals, the twitter of birds. You light the wood under the kettle and, when it is boiling, put on the porridge and relish the luxury of supping it 'christened' with dry oatmeal lightly sprinkled, and garnished with creamy milk. Through the trees you get a glimpse of the loch, violet-coloured. If you stir yourself and go for a walk you hear the baa-ing of sheep and the crowing of a cock on the other side of the loch as clear as if they had been two fields away but the lapping of the water against the shore is almost inaudible. The sound of a railway train breaks through, the low roar of the wheels pent up probably in a cutting and opening out as it emerges, still far out of sight, somewhere between Rannoch Station and Corrour. A curlew, frightened for its nest, flies overhead threateningly. Quietness again for a long time. Then the peace of the morning is dramatically broken by a heavy crashing against the tall deer-fence, and a young deer, velvety-brown, rushes past, panicking to find a place where a good leap would land it back on its own side of the boundary.

Blue wood-smoke rises from a house. Ducks scattering waterdrops rise from the loch. If you listen carefully you'll hear the song of goldcrests in the pines, 'like needle-points of sound'. There are two chaffinches with slightly different endings to their call-signs. There's a sound that is something between the coo of a pigeon and the bark of a dog; it might be a raven. The air is rich with the smell of the sawmill. The postman's van passes. Back beside the dead embers of the campfire the old Adam reasserts himself and you look up the varieties of orchids you saw at the roadside but the multitudinous variety confuses you and you easily fall back into inactivity.

The day is endless. Lying on your back looking up at the sky you feel yourself one with the community of the earth, the scurrying beetles and ants, fungi and grasses, and agrimony and bog asphodel, thrushes and blackbirds, tree-creepers and the fugitive capercailzie, foxes, trout, even the mica-schist and granite of the bens. You feel one in a long, long procession; 'no man knows through what wild centuries roves back the rose'.

Three thousand years ago the sons of Korah sang, 'Be still and know that I am God.' At Rannoch on a long summer's day you get an inkling of what the voices and the twanging of the psalteries and the clashing of the cymbals were trying to express.

Clouds hide the sun and then it re-emerges. The willow warbler's song falls away in a cadence, an anti-climax, as if to imply, 'I'm not trying to say something dramatic.' There are quiet voices of people, distant but clear. Random chains of thought stir memories into activity. The Black Wood of Rannoch once covered the whole strath and the bones of old tree-roots are to be found high up in the mountains above the present tree-line. Some energetic characters felled the trees and floated them down the loch to the Tummel and then down the Tay past Perth to Dundee. But many of them got past Dundee and made their landfall in Denmark and the enterprise was abandoned . . . You go and collect wood for the evening's fire and chanterelles for the morrow's breakfast. Prompted by some unidentified excitation, the Telford story swims into your ken. Maybe it was the birch-trees. He built harbours and bridges and roads, and along the roads he sent birch wood so that the coopers of Fife and other places could make hoops for their fish barrels in which the herring caught by Scotland's newly employed fishermen could be exported to Russia and Germany. I doubt if anybody so powerfully influenced Scottish life.

The sun moves on, the clouds dissipate and regroup. There is an evening chorus of birds and it is still warm at nine p.m. Imperceptibly the daylight fades into twilight. There is no movement in the top branches and twigs of the birches. The darkness comes on, and the cool of midnight.

After even two or three days at Rannoch, the Fife youngsters became different people. Loud-mouthed, sex-experienced, cigarette-smoking fifteen-year-old girls lay on the ground, propping their chins in their hands, and watched looping caterpillars. They watched the milking of the cows. They saw how the Coire Carie had been scraped out by glaciers. Briefly the age of innocence re-entered their lives, and they became unrecognizably different. Teachers spoke with surprise of friendliness during a trek, good humour and the endurance of blisters and snow and rain with fortitude. As they fitted conformably into their natural habitat, we began to get glimpses of how a Scottish cultural revolution might be set in motion. It would begin in the country places.

One April day we walked up the Inverhadden Burn from Kinloch Rannoch towards Glen Lyon. Under dark, overhanging banks, blue-glowing ice stalagmites remained immune to the sun and one pupil lingered among them and chose to walk through the boulders of the burn rather than follow the easier way. Lower down we had seen the lyre-like curl of the tail of a blackcock, and water-beetles and water spiders and frog-spawn. Beyond the ice the burn opened into a wider glen, where white sands made a beach at the side of a loch. This was Glen Sassun, the Glen of the Saxons, the English. I told them the story. These were the soldiers of Edward II ('The Anvil of the Scots'), up there hunting Robert the Bruce. I wonder what these Sassunachs made of this remote glen six and a half centuries ago. Probably the scene that faced us was identical with the glen as it appeared to them. A herd of forty deer on the mountain slope, the spear of Schiehallion to the east, specks of snow shining like diamonds in the crevices of the hills, the soft brown of the heather, everywhere the sound of water flowing; that was the scene. Were they frightened of the loneliness of the Scottish wilderness and did they long for the water-meadows of Hampshire? Did they, like us, walk in the direction of the col at the head of the glen and come down into the valley of the Carie Burn where four centuries later Robertson of Struan, a Jacobite, hid from English soldiers, this time Hanoverian? And were there already in the fourteenth century summer shealings like those whose ruins remain, near the highest points of the pass? Maybe from details like these the pupils begin to let the past recreate itself in their imaginings and mingle with the present.

We point out to them the frequent use of the word 'annat' in the Ordnance Survey maps – in Inverness and Perth and Appin and Dunvegan and Rannoch. It was a parent church or a patron saint's church or a church containing the relics of its founder, or just a church. Where there is an annat there are traces of an ancient chapel and/or cemetery. We point to the extravagantly thick walls of ruined castles, the Kinloch Rannoch bridge built after Culloden with the money from the forfeited estates, the smoothly lined water-courses that British Aluminium dug to divert water to their

Fort William smelters, the hum of the power station near the loch and the pipes rising up the mountainside, diatomite from Skye to make car-polish at Rannoch, bigger panes of glass in old farm-houses, a small electric water-heater in a lavatory outside a roadside pub, the closing of a village school. But having lightly mentioned these things, we leave it at that. When they're interested, they'll pursue with questions. Mostly they don't. Some are more interested in the hard, step-like tree-flap fungus on tree trunks, the sharp glitter of mica crystals in granite, or waterfalls.

Sometimes I wondered about the mass of observed detail that I thrust upon the pupils and upon our own family. What are the benefits of drawing attention to the pillarbox red of blaeberry leaves in September, the crimson of the poisonous Fly Agaric, the silver bark of the birches, the interior of old cottages dark even in a summer noon, the blues and greens and browns on trout, the larch posts driven into the ground that maintain their rigid strength even when corroded to a one-inch diameter? I was comforted by an American anthropologist's account of the skill in navigation of some of the Trukese Pacific Islanders. In canoes they navigate long stretches of featureless ocean relying on 'the cumulative product of the adding together of a great number of discrete bits of data'. In his essay on 'Culture and logical process' reprinted in the Penguin Education's *Tinker, tailor . . .* , Thomas Gladwin describes a night voyage.

> Between stars, or when the stars are not visible due to day-light or storm, the course is held constant by noting the direction of the wind and the waves. A good navigator can tell by observing wave patterns when the wind is shifting its direction or speed, and by how much. In a dark and starless night the navigator can even tell these things from the sound of the waves as they lap upon the sides of the canoe's hull, and the feel of the boat as it travels through the water. All of these complex perceptions – visual, auditory, kinesthetic – are combined with vast amounts of data stored in memory, and the whole is integrated into a slight increase or decrease in pressure on the steering paddle, or a grunted instruction to slack off the sail a trifle.

In the same way I hope that all the detail casually observed in a

Highland glen may slot into the computer of the human brain, available for recall like the data on which the Trukese navigator depends.

From Dalwhinnie, farther north on the Killiecrankie to Inverness road, another track goes over the hills to Laggan. It starts in the U valley of Loch Ericht. On a summer day the alders and beech bushes near the loch were storm-tossed, the beech leaves toughened and thickened, but on the sheltered side the eroded wrinkles down to the water were more richly vegetated than I had expected. There were the usual flowers of the wetland, asphodel, tormentil, buttercup and foxglove. Until recently, foxglove leaves were crushed to make a digitalis paste and a Welsh doctor described the use that Welsh people make of foxgloves. Out in the open, in Benalder Forest, we came on a battalion of stags ranged on the slope opposite, two hundred of them, and they had sentinels posted singly on the higher ground. It's a wilderness of grass and black lines of peat, and heather. The mountain tops were in fog. Beyond Loch Pattock, butterwort grew thickly on the path. We stopped to listen and identify what small sounds there might be. There were only the thin chirpings of birds. The soft wind was so slight that the only way to tell its direction was to walk in different directions and feel the fluchter of air in your face. We followed the Pattock, a fair burn where it leaves the loch. This is a bare, lonely place where a solitary shed we came to was marked on the Ordnance Survey by a dot. Beside it was a strip of trees. In an emergency they would offer cover, shelter, and travellers would feel a sense of relief that they would not be utterly exposed to the elements in a wilderness. This is where youngsters ask basic questions like 'Why is it so level?' These plateaux are common in the Highlands. Maybe they were for aeons the bed of a loch.

The river valley grew more friendly where it cut down through the plateau. Occasionally there was an opulent Douglas fir and the river flowed and broke shallow over stones. Then suddenly a wooded gorge and the thunder of falling water. A white rose grew beside an elm close to the river. There were small blue moths and larger bright brown speckled moths. Bell heather was out. There were deep pools in the water, black as peat, and more waterfalls. A rowan grew out of a rock above the river, and, near it, a big alder.

Beside the clachan of Ballovie there were several clumps of white foxgloves and then we emerged, near Laggan, on the Newtonmore to Fort William road.

We enter on a geological fantasia as if in this region the god

> Wha biggit the bens
> And shovellt oot the glens

had been determined to put on an extra-extravagant show. At Laggan a sloping table of grey rock is crossed by a broad four-and-a-half-foot band, red and white, that stretches for twenty-five yards. A myriad mica crystals glitter in it. A lava flow pushed into crannies and collected on the level rock. On the dark rock there are twisty markings, wavy patterns. The young want to know about these ancient runes, the hieroglyphics of the rocks. They have an ear for the clang of Vulcan's hammer long long ago, and an eye for the smoke belching from his smiddy. It is on the rocks of Badenoch and Lochaber that they sympathize most feelingly with the imaginings of ancient peoples, their hypotheses about how things began. What gave Creag a Chuir such a distinctive knobbled shape so that it looks like a rock bun? Where did these huge, solitary boulders, called 'erratics', wander in here from? And above all there was the mystery of 'the parallel roads'. Throughout the area but particularly in Glen Roy, level lines cross the hillsides and if you are in a valley like Glen Roy you see clearly that they encircle the hillsides, maintaining the same levels. The highest of them indicate the highest level at which the loch stood; that was the loch shore, smoothed out by its waves. Then the pressure of the water drove a cataclysmic break in the retaining rocks and the level of water in Glen Roy and throughout the region fell for another few thousand years, during which another loch shore was ground and moulded. And then another.

A youngster, to whom I explained this story, asked why the parallel roads had breaks in them, missing pieces, and answered his own question by saying that at these places the rocks and earth would have been eroded by rain and wind and frost. In the following days he applied this new key to the geology of Glen Spean and discovered parallel roads in the glen and its recesses that I hadn't noticed, for example across the slope of Creag Chonochair, and began to visualize the glen when it was full of water and to see Scotland in the fourth dimension of time. Against this background we didn't bother to listen to the radio news and we had no newspapers, contenting ourselves with asking the random visitor about who won the Big Fight or the by-election. Our interest was more immediate events. I stood still and watched a hedgehog walking briskly up the path and turning in at the front door of the house. Sometimes a buzzard planed overhead. There were many wagtails, and wheatears living up to their name, 'white arse', displayed their white rump. In the Spean gorge the rock strata were upended and had a chewed look like plywood sawn unskilfully against the grain. Beside the water a solitary dipper bobbed up and down. In Loch Treig near by, in a dry summer you could make out a crannog. At the side of the loch, after Culloden the redcoats caught up with fleeing Highlanders and took them away for torture under the instructions of Handel's conquering hero, the Duke of Cumberland. At the side of the road was an ancient millstone still marking the site of 'Angus's mill'. There were Highland cattle the colour of larches or dry bracken. Hoodie crows croaked as they looked for carrion.

On a late evening in July the well-spaced beeches, oaks, birches and conifers transmuted the light of the setting sun as if by the interposing of a green filter. You could imagine you were within a spacious grass-floored marquee. The turf, of grass and moss, was soft and springy. Very faintly a susurration of air wafted through the branches, stirring them slightly and caressing the cheek.

In one of the soft grassy knolls, they told me, seven headless bodies were dug up. A seventeenth-century clan chief at Invergarry on Loch Oich sent his men to exact retribution on a Lochaber family. They killed seven of them and cut off their heads and carried them back with them. At the Well of the Seven Heads beside Loch Oich a grisly monument marks the place where they washed the blood off the heads before presenting them to their chief. On the monument, set up in 1812, the event is recorded in four languages, Gaelic, English, French and Latin. The 1812 chief took his dynastic responsibilities seriously.

Near the Spean there are many such grassy knolls. Sometimes the knoll dips into a cosy dell and rises again into another knoll so that the dell is like the depression between a woman's breasts. Sometimes they descend into deep hollows, natural amphitheatres where the acoustics are as clear as in the hill-set theatre at Epidauros.

An old shooting lodge, partitioned into guests' quarters and servants' quarters, is in a setting of banks of red rhododendrons and a copper beech tree whose leaves shine like dulse at low tide. A barred ground-floor window marks the place where Rudolf Hess is said to have spent part of his Scottish captivity. While our pupils tenanted the lodge, a craftsman discovered a supplementary water-tank, which had a capacity of nearly nine hundred gallons and which had been installed by the army during the war when commandos were trained here. The tank was situated on the farther side of a hill at a considerable distance from the lodge, and connected by pipes to a lower cistern near the lodge. The connecting pipes had eroded. The craftsman employed the pupils to help him put in a new line of pipes. To find a straight line between the two cisterns they would use the same methods as the Romans used to fix the line of a road across rough, hilly country. They would use torches at night.

On a June morning we left the road near Moy Lodge where a fisherman, all the way from Airdrie, was standing, midge-bitten, holding a beer can. He had fished since eight the previous night. He had seen the fish but it was too smooth for them, he said, and there had not been a single bite. He'd fish another two hours, and then the bus would come. Looking north towards Creag Meagaidh we saw the same very light-green light playing on the mountains as we had seen the previous night at eleven o'clock on Loch Treig. Beside Lochan na H-Earba there were bedstraw, heather, heartsease, cottongrass, and orange splashes of lichen on rock faces. The critic says, 'So what? You saw a dragonfly which had yellow round its eyes, a scimitar-winged bird which uttered staccato calls like a morse message, bleached trees on the grassy flank of the mountain. You noted that the only sounds breaking the silence were the ripple of the water, the plop of a fish, the humming of a fly and thin bird-notes. Horses stood unusually inside an open shed, perhaps finding it cooler there. Along the track there were smoothly rounded stones. You came to the richer, wooded area of Ardverikie where there were huge Douglas firs and bright red rhododendrons, and a youngster said that Queen Victoria would have been better advised to settle for this area, which was on her list, than Balmoral which was her final choice. You bathed in the warm water of Loch Laggan. On the way back the sun shone even more brightly, limelighting individual trees and bleaching the mown hay whiter than usual. What does all this observation add up to?'

I think it's like inheriting a house and going through a succession of cupboards to see what treasures or curiosities they may hold and make an inventory, the better to cope with it and feel at home in it and know our way about. At the march-dyke between Lochaber and Badenoch there is a signpost saying that this is the beginning of Badenoch. Badenoch becomes a defined, perceptible reality and we have the satisfaction of coming face to face with reality that Wordsworth expressed in his Scottish journeys. 'So this is Yarrow.'

Sometimes it's difficult to know why we make these trips. 'What went ye out for to see?' Jesus of Nazareth is reported to have asked the crowds mobbing John the Baptist in the Judaean highlands. Like our Sunday crowds they probably found it difficult to give an answer. We want to make sense of the welter of experience that washes up against us. We go to museums and nature trails and distilleries, we read guide-books and look up family trees, hoping it will all add up to something. We want to put it all together, scraps of the geology of the Highlands, the flora and fauna, the history and geography, gratified if we have a ferlie to report when we get home, Highland cattle the colour of autumn larches or winter bracken, salmon leaping, a herd of deer, maybe even a wild cat or an osprey or a capercailzie. The experts have provided the analyses; we want to extract the essence of all that analysis, the nourishing principle that they contain; the sensuous not separated from the rational. 'I want to know the kinds of things,' a young child once put it to me, making the words he knew express this idea at the back of his mind, the desire fully to understand and feel at home in his world (and showing an uncanny awareness of the depth of meaning of the word *kind* which the dictionary defines as 'species, nature, quality, offspring').

The Glasgow people who emigrated to Fort William in the sixties to work in the pulp mills found additional reason to bide here when they found pleasure in the changing face of Ben Nevis and in looking at a mist floating like gossamer clear of the ground on Lagganside, at the snow protected in the clefts of Creag Meagaidh, at the glitter and greenery of the Spean valley hidden by snow as a girl's charms under a nun's white cloak, the bands of the frost forcing ice-blocks up above the surface of the loch, glaucous frozen reeds in the frozen water of a marsh, the brightness of with-ered bracken in the rain, the green moss on the maroon-coloured birches. But together with that sensuous satisfaction we seek the rational satisfaction of comprehending why the pulp mill closed down in 1980 and there was 'marital break-up, alcoholism, glue-sniffing, drug abuse, mental illness and all the other unlovely symptoms of a society in crisis'. The houses built in a hurry in the 1960s are decaying, being structurally unsound, and the shops, insulated from ordinary local life, are, as James Hunter wrote, 'heaped high with the knitwear, tinned shortbread, tweeds, handcrafted pottery and whisky-flavoured marmalade which are the staples of the Highland tourist trade'.

The same spirit which lures the young into asking questions about geology and crannogs and ospreys and Thomas Telford spills over into human biology, economics. They discover that econom-ics isn't a gauzy, impalpable philosophy. The decline and fall of an industry can be comprehended, grasped in concrete terms, like the drop in the level of the water in Glen Roy. Aluminium-making failed away up north in Invergordon. What is its future at Fort William? To make a ton of aluminium you need four tons of bauxite, two tons of coal, four hundredweight of caustic soda, half a ton of carbon and 20,000 units of hydro-electricity. The *hydro* is readily available here. The annual rainfall in the area varies from 41 inches at Laggan to 161 inches at the top of Ben Nevis. The longest water tunnel in the world, fifteen miles, takes water from the Laggan basin to Fort William. Which of the links in that chain might be in danger of giving?

The young cast around for clues. They begin to see the museums as resource centres from which they take what they want and ignore the rest. The Fort William museum offers tangible assistance to those who want to get Highland history into perspective. A burial cist, dug up in Morar, contains the bones of a pre-Celtic Iberian of the time of Confucius and Darius. The aluminium works is on the site of Montrose's victory at Inverlochy. The railway goods yard is beside where the Hanoverian fort stood, and in the museum the governor's room is reproduced. When he was tired of looking at the dispositions of his occupying forces, his eyes could rest on fine china.

CHAPTER TEN

West from Fort William

Degged with dew, dappled with dew
Are the groins of the braes that the brook treads
    through,
Wiry heathpacks, flitches of fern,
And the beadbonny ash that sits over the burn.
                                        G. M. HOPKINS

The geography that made Fort William a good military centre makes it a good tourist centre. The remote peninsulas of Knoydart and Moidart and Morvern are accessible through the lochside valleys. To reach Knoydart you go north along the Caledonian Canal and turn west along Loch Garry. Glengarry is sheltered by tall lime-trees and oaks. Bonnie Prince Charlie came this way to the west after his defeat at Culloden, and fifty years later the local folk were emigrating to Canada. Beyond the opener country in which Loch Quoich is set, you come to Knoydart and the sea-loch Hourn, 'the Loch of Hell'. On a June day it is like an earthly paradise. Yellow-gold seaweed lines the loch. There is a memorable quietness that slows down your step to the rhythm of the valley and hillside. There was the quiet gossip of a hen prosaically chuntering away. A farmer guided a plough drawn by a Land-Rover at a horse's pace. A farm-steading was built of differently sized granite blocks round a quadrangle floored with round stones. The dykes round the field were of the same granite, sparkling with mica, as the rocks on the slope. The burn slid over slightly sloping tables of stone. Holly and a rowan-tree grew side by side, the rowan blossom giving off a sweetish smell. The dusty-white lochside path led through Caledonian pines, the sun lighting up their brown, almost-red trunks and the wind making a soft sound as it floated through their branches. The rock strata had been contorted into a wavy pattern. There was a ruined clachan of twelve houses. A big

181

shining white boat appeared, showing tourists the loch and Knoydart, and disappeared into the Sound of Sleat seaward. There was peace here and beauty and the sunlit serenity that Keats described in his poem about the Grecian urn. It was a happy valley that sunlit morn. But if you are even superficially aware of the dimension of time, there is a tinge of sadness in the air, the feel that Neil Gunn communicates about a liveliness that has departed from a Highland community. At Kinloch Hourn there is a sense that the vigorous young have emigrated and that their parents are making the best of it, cheerily going about their business. It was no function of the people who administer Scotland to encourage me to take much stock of the story of Knoydart's crofters and in these depopulated valleys of my native land I feel like an ignorant intruder.

Twenty miles south of Glengarry and parallel to it the railway line from Fort William follows Loch Eil and Lochailort, skirting Moidart, to Morar and the terminus at Mallaig. On the way you pass the tall monument at Glenfinnan, marking the place where Charlie unfurled his flag in 1745; a few miles farther along we pitched our tents near Loch nan Uamh where he embarked for France, five months after Culloden. The Jacobite episode was a romantic irrelevance in Scottish history. Like other races, we Scots have a history of letting ourselves be caught up in causes not of our own, unable to perceive when we are being used. Twenty-eight years after Charlie sailed from Loch nan Uamh there was a sudden drop in the price of black cattle; and Charlie's protector Flora MacDonald and her family, finding difficulty in making ends meet at Kingsburgh in Skye, emigrated to North Carolina. A year later her husband raised a force to fight for the Hanoverian George III against the colonists who wanted independence. He and his son were captured and the family suffered privations. They had risked their lives for the Jacobites against the Hanoverians. They had risked their lives for the Hanoverians against the American colonists. Did the family ever ask questions about the conflict of causes to which they had devoted themselves and their clansmen and clanswomen? There is an unreality about the scene as if it had been scripted, produced and directed by Metro-Goldwyn-Mayer. The floodlights bring into startling clarity the parts of the scene they want to illumine, and leave the rest in utter darkness. The Hollywood production (David Niven in the leading role) was in the selective tradition of the eighteenth-century producers and directors. Both groups of propagandists hire writers and artists and musicians to make their story persuasive and catch the imagination of the viewers. The Jacobite songs are among the loveliest in Scotland's repertoire. There is no doubting the depth of their feeling. But when you wander through the region, floodlit with the tales of armies on the move, of escapes and hurried journeys, you feel you are wandering through film studios where the stage has been dismantled and the props lodged in museums. To this day there is a plaintive air about Mallaig which neither the richness of broom and whitethorn nor the harbour activity of hoisting aboard food and mailbags and furniture for the Outer Hebrides, can dispel. It is the feeling that Wordsworth described in the Gaelic tune that he heard the solitary reaper singing. He wondered if she was singing about old, unhappy, far-off things, and battles long ago or some familiar matter of today, either way a melancholy strain.

Another score of miles farther south from the West Highland Line to Mallaig a road makes the third crossing of the Knoydart, Moidart, Morvern peninsula to the Scottish mainland's westernmost point, Ardnamurchan. You cross Loch Linnhe at the Corran Ferry, leaving behind the country of the Red Fox and Stevenson's *Kidnapped*. Stevenson is magic at giving the feel of terrain, a friendly man and a spell-binding teller of tales. He was not the high Tory that Johnson was, viewing the western Highlands through the spectacles of his classical education. The full Stevenson story is not told in Scottish schools. He is presented to us as the genial offshoot of Edinburgh burghal stock who spun a good yarn. We're not told about his angry political action in aid of the South Sea Islanders.

When you cross Loch Linnhe and reach the seaweed-gold shores of Loch Sunart, you are in the desolate kind of country of wildness and wet that made an impression on Gerard Manley Hopkins. He was attuned to such background of rock-and-heather monochrome and recorded the details, the burn roaring down his rollrock highroad, the bonnet of froth twindling round a black pool.

183

Picking away deep in the hills above the lochside village of Strontian, lead-miners from the lowlands discovered a substance to which the name of Strontianite was given. From it was isolated the element Strontium, the only element to be named after a place in the British Isles. The progress of earthy enquiry is as random as a snipe's flight. Strontium was found to be useful in paints and plastics and it produced the crimson glow in fireworks. And then physicists discovered that radioactive fall-out contained much Strontium 90 which is the same as the substance extracted from the Strontianite of the Highland hills but radioactive. The development of religion was as subject to unexpected twists and turns as physics. When half of Scotland walked out of the state kirk in 1843, the local laird refused to give the Strontian heretics land on which to build a new kirk and they worshipped their god in a boat moored offshore.

To complete the survey of this alien region, a strange country to most of us from the deep-delved earth of eastern Scotland, we took a boat from Oban to the Outer Hebrides. It took us along the southern coast of Morvern to Tobermory in Mull. We discovered how little our school geography had told us about this region. If we had been visiting the New Hebrides they could hardly have presented a more unexpected image. As the sun rose above Oban we glided along the shore of Mull and saw haycocks with little caps on them to keep their heads dry. A fisherman sat at his nets among brightly coloured buoys. Behind were the concave tops of extinct volcanoes. Beside Tobermory there was a gelatine-smooth sea where a Spanish galleon had sunk four centuries earlier. We bought the morning newspapers that had come up from Glasgow and resumed the journey round towards the grey shape of Calgary Bay and stopped at Coll. It was a grey-green island, much bigger than I expected. The details began filling in the void of ignorance. They were a big church, a hotel, fourteen motor cars, a pier where cakes and rolls and fruit and bread were being landed as well as two car tyres and a brown barrel. Purple and brown and grey jellyfish swam under the piles that supported the pier. Passengers in the stern of the boat chatted with a crew member in Gaelic. Then we drew away and passed a sandy beach and came to the white sands of Tiree. Again I was surprised at the huge size of the island and the number

of people on it. We were an hour there and some of the crew fished
from the stern. In the clear deep water we saw fish swimming near
the bottom and an unusual whip-like seaweed. The air was soft and
the voices quiet, not having to rise to be heard.

It's nearly fifty miles to Castlebay in Barra at the tail of the Outer
Hebrides. We saw an occasional solitary gannet, the black outer
part of its wings dramatic as it made a banked turn. We came up
through a succession of islands carpeted with green through which
rocks appeared, and inhabited by sheep. The viscous, leaden sea
shone a dull black. We docked at Castlebay at four-thirty in the
afternoon. I walked through the village and looked at Barra as
Ulysses looked at Scheria. It was all new and incongruous. In the
church of 'Our Lady, Star of the Sea' there were candles and the
stations of the cross. In the green-painted cooperative there were
tea-towels and pennants celebrating the Glasgow Celtic. There
were large quantities of long-life milk. It was like coming on a
Buddhist enclave in Buchan. I understood deeply the religious
yearnings of the Aberdeenshire fishermen, central to their lives.
They were devoted to 'The Saviour' and all they had been
taught that he stood for. The equally devout Catholic fishermen
of Barra worshipped Our Lady, Star of the Sea. Did that make
them different people? I longed to talk with them to see if this alien
Celtic Scotland, to which by heredity I belong, were really all that
different from the apparently more prosaic, apparently more
rationalist Scotland in which I had been brought up.

The boat was filling with sheep driven up the gangway. Seals
were moving about in the water, only their heads, like periscopes,
visible above the surface. We came out into the open sea, and the
bailiwick of the proud Macneils receded. We came abreast of
Eriskay and saw, beyond it, the soft, irregular outline of other
islands. Then we drew into the wide bay of Loch Boisdale and
landed at the harbour of the same name, in South Uist. When we
left, hours later, the boat had filled up. Many of the passengers were
young people, going to the mainland for work. Their parents and
friends were seeing them off, and there was a pathos about the parting, a realization that their ties with the Hebrides and their
upbringing were being weakened.

As the Hebrideans flocked to the mainland for work and the

bright lights of the industrial areas, youngsters from the industrial areas were flocking to the Hebrides to seek for the things that the bright lights didn't have on offer. On one occasion I joined a group of our Fife pupils in their journey to Rhum. At Mallaig a pupil stole postcards and a sheath knife and was showing them to his pals. One of them said, 'Ach, ye dinna dae that here. They're *nice* folk.' The boy went and replaced the goods he had stolen. The pupils were drawing a distinction between the commercial jungle of industrial Scotland, where anything is fair game, and the Highlands, where older values survived.

At the harbour they were loading oil, methylated spirits, sausages, mailbags, newspapers, a plastic rubbish bin, for the islands. The boat pushed into the Sound of Sleat and the pupils sat down and ate slices of bread and jam and viewed Scotland, for the first time, from the sea. We stopped off the island of Muck and in the boat that came alongside was the local schoolmistress, a girl from Bridgwater in Somerset. She was standing in the stern, as the boat pitched in heavy seas, as if she had spent all her life sailing between Hebridean islands. 'I'm a schoolteacher too,' I shouted to her; 'how do you like it here?'

She laughed. 'I love it.'

Three islands shared the doctor. He was making his rounds on our boat and he told us about the difficulties of responding to urgent calls. In the late afternoon we berthed at the end of Loch Scresort in Rhum. For our pupils, Rhum was as foreign as Andorra or Liechtenstein. It is full of curiosities. There is a site inhabited by hunters and fishermen 8500 years ago; it is twice as old as Skara Brae. They dated it from burnt hazelnut shells. Seabirds, the Manx shearwaters (a hundred thousand of them on Rhum), nest at 2000 feet up the mountains in burrows, like rabbits. Our guide thrust his arm into a burrow and extracted a sitting shearwater. On summer nights their gossipping can be heard down in the creeks, and the Vikings, settling down to sleep beside their longboats, thought it was the trolls talking. They called one of the mountains Trollaval.

This small island, seven miles long by seven miles broad, has beautiful mountains and a picturesque history and its challenging, sometimes harsh, environment has caused some of the economists who manipulate our lives to regard it as expendable. The British railways supremo, Dr Beeching, drawing on his ICI experience, didn't think that the Scottish railways were a paying concern and gave it as his considered verdict that the railways north of London should terminate at Newcastle. Rhum's history has been subject to just such wayward economic judgements. The crofters, said the economists, were living at the margin of existence. They carried soil on to barren rocks and established the 'lazy beds' on which they grew potatoes. To make a living each crofter had to dig daily, with a spade (there were only two ploughs on Rhum) an area fifteen yards square. What were the controllers of our society saying when they laid it down that that was uneconomic? In 1786 a visitor was fed with cream, eggs, milk, oatcakes and Lisbon wine salvaged from a wreck. The population rose to almost 500. It would have been, at the end of the eighteenth century, a good life for youngsters. We looked at ruined cottages, one of them nine feet by six and a half. Building it would have been a community activity and an educational project. The young would be set to gathering suitably shaped stones from the hillside, triangular stones for the gable, for example. When the first fire was lit, they would have watched anxiously to see if the chimney 'drew' or if the house filled with reek. As in Skara Brae, one of the houses had stone cupboards built into the wall. Life was about surviving as comfortably as ingenuity let you. We came on a ruined clachan criss-crossed with otter runs and littered with shellfish shells and otter spraint. The fate of the community had been decreed by remote and apparently irrelevant happenings. When Napoleon was despatched to St Helena, imports increased and the price of Rhum cattle dropped. When the lairds began to have big ideas about cutting a dash in the English metropolis, they needed more money than the crofters could pay in rent. Gaming houses and Hanoverian commissions and ambitious marriages forced them to clear their lands to make room for the much better paying sheep. The crofters had a love for their island. The visitor does not need any help to understand why.

From the summit of Hallival we looked down on a vast extent of calm blue sea ringed by islands, all the way from the neighbouring island of Canna across the Minch to the mountains of Uist, Skye (two gems of snow set in recesses of the Cuillins), Soay, Eigg, Muck, the white sands of Morar. Far below and all around, the sea was like a vast water-bowl in which pieces of land had been arranged like ornaments. Then out of the calm we saw a change of weather coming in over the Atlantic, approaching Scotland like a flotilla at ten knots, gathering cloud and roughing the sea's surface. It was an Olympian view and before us nature was putting on one of her spectaculars. The front approaching Scotland from over the Atlantic followed clearly understood natural laws. But the human theatricals played for the past few centuries on the stage below us followed no such understood pattern, had no plot, observed no limiting necessities. When the Mackinnons and Macleans and Mackays and Macmillans and others were driven from their homes and herded into the emigrants' ships, an eye-witness said that 'the wild outcries of the men and the heartbreaking wails of the women and children filled all the air between the mountainous shores'.

The Aberdeen zoologist who conducted us over Rhum took us to see a dam that had been built to produce enough depth of water in a burn to encourage sea-trout to swim upstream. But the men who planned it underestimated the power of a Rhum burn in spate, and it collapsed. All that hopeful work, perhaps talking late into the night planning the dam, foreseeing the difficulties, seeking to circumvent nature, then the carrying of sacks of cement up to the hills and long hours of work in the heat of the day building the dam. Then success. Then a spate after heavy rain and the collapse of the dam, and no renewal of the attempt to encourage the sea-trout. We became more intimately aware of the terms of survival on the earth and the forces that counter our best efforts. Gravity pulls down the walls of our houses, water-power breaks our dams, fatigue breaks our spirits. But then we start off optimistically on some other ploy. Up at the top of Hallival the warden told us about a fall of rock that had made some birds homeless. They came out at night to feed and couldn't get back in and didn't know what to do. A capricious fate attends alike the Manx shearwater, the sea-trout and homo sapiens.

Against these inscrutable elements of our earth journey we would draw the attention of the pupils to the things that beguiled, as with song, the pilgrimage of the Rhum crofters, the golden voice of the cuckoo down beside Loch Scresort and the morse-code twittering of the sandpipers (diddit-dah dah-dit), shaggy, long-haired, white-tailed wild goats and their kids looking out from caves on the mountainside, lady's alpine mantle, purple saxifrage and mountain sorrel on the summit.

CHAPTER ELEVEN

The Isle of Lewis

A crofting community is a way of living and cannot
be judged in terms of a profit and loss account.
1919 report on land settlement

At the other side of the island from Stornoway, looking out over the
Atlantic, the standing stones of Callanish throw in the face of the
people of AD 2000 the riddle of interpreting the lives of their forefathers of 2000 BC. That was the era of the great days of Knossos,
before there were pyramids in Egypt and before there was peat in
Lewis. In a booklet published in Stornoway in 1977 two archaeologists, Gerald and Margaret Ponting, lay out the riddle of what those
lives may have been like. The guesswork of how maybe as few as
thirty workers split local Lewisian gneiss into five-ton megaliths
and transported them to Callanish and set them up is arresting like
an Ancient Mariner's tale. These men of the New Stone Age built
sledges and pulled the megaliths on the sledges over tree-trunk
rollers with ropes made of leather or heather stems and then were
confronted by the problem of how to lever them into the holes prepared for them. They partly lined the hole with stakes to prevent its
erosion and levered up the distal end with successive platforms of
logs. Then gangs pulled the stone into position in the hole with
ropes attached to its top and held it there while the hole was filled
with packing stones. 'The stone is now capable of withstanding
Lewis gales for 4000 years, despite the fact that little of it is beneath
the surface.'

But why were the stones erected? A barrier against evil spirits, a
Druid temple, a temple to Apollo, a temple for serpent worship or
fertility rites, a king's burial place, a court of justice or a parliament,
an astronomical observatory, a focus of ley lines, or a navigation
beacon for flying saucers? What happened in this place apart? Was

it unspeakable things as in the Eleusinian mysteries of ancient Greece, blood and sex and violence, or was it as cold and formal as a Wee Free sacrament? Maybe they were sophisticated people like their contemporaries in the great days of Knossos and maybe they did align their megaliths on where Antares rose in 1880 BC or Capella in 1800 or the Pleiades in 1750. The museum-tearoom tries to compensate by imaginative photography for what the bleak stones on a rainy afternoon failed to communicate. There are pictures of these stones in fantastic settings, in snow, and in spring, and against the sunset.

Nor do we know much about the broch at Carloway, five miles from Callanish, double-walled like a thermos flask and open to the sky. I hadn't realized that there are such gaping ignorances in our history. Lewis is a gaunt island of unanswered questions and sudden dramatic responses. A Lewis artist told me that when war broke out in 1939 his father, a crofter near Shawbost who had hitherto been an unenthusiastic attender at the kirk, laid down his Bible and separated himself from the kirk and never had anything further to do with it. It was a heroic assertion. The same persistence of questioning will one day compel a richer way of living, a fuller humanity, out of Lewis religion. We should set free the imagination of our children to speculate on Callanish and brochs and kirks and all such things, to enquire for example if the first chapter of Ezekiel is about an encounter with an Unidentified Flying Object round about 600 BC. When the sky is the limit for them, they will begin to get Scottish existence into the framework and perspective of space and time.

You're aware of the sky in Lewis. There is the lifting of the threatening thunderclouds, the blue-sky intervals of hope, the Valkyrie-like wraiths and scuds and wisps and hurrying veils of raincloud chasing one another across the lower air. A century ago, in the first chapter of *The Return of the Native*, Thomas Hardy predicted the appeal of wild moorland country and some of Lewis's natives, as well as outsiders, have responded to the appeal. It's part of the quest, deciding what kind of a place you really want to live in.

The European community is taking an interest in this island on its periphery, providing money for severely functional houses. On the road south we saw many of these bungalows. Sometimes there is an oasis of mown, emerald grass and red and yellow flowers in the midst of this rocky, peaty, bleak, inhospitable wilderness, like a smile edging its way on to a forbidding, austere face. There are recent tree-plantations, channels for the acidic water, grids over the burns, new roads scraped out of the hillside, cottages where a thriving industry advertises its tweeds. Great water-trenches harness and domesticate the untamed country round Loch Seaforth.

There is a feeling of the impermanence of man's efforts to convert this untamed land into his back-garden. At Ardvourlie on the west coast the whalers set up a station, but they went away. In 1917 Lord Leverhulme bought Lewis for £143,000 in order to bring it into the twentieth century. He wanted to set up canneries and fish processing factories. But the Lewismen opposed him, unwilling to accept the restrictions of factory work, and he left in 1921, hoping to set up a large fishing port at Obbe in Harris which he renamed Leverburgh. We passed through it in the rain, a dismantled, derelict operation. It is nature, indifferent to man, that predominates.

A lacework of grey stone and ochre seaweed decorates the sea-inlets, there are little jetties where they let their boats into the sea-lochs, straight lines of white foam cross a loch, farther out in the bay are the white tops of waves and there was always in our ears the *hush* sound of the waves and, intermittently, the rising breath of the wind. Forlorn tracks disappear over the hillside, grey-white boulders are like sheep on the long, grassy slopes, the grass on the rocky hillside is now light-green, now dark, as it pleases the sun to make it, and in the distance are the glowering mountains. Hay dries on small racks. We scraped the lichen, crotal, off the rocks. It is made into one of the dyes used in the production of Harris tweed. Man occupies this outpost fitfully, uncertainly. There is an air of impermanence in all outposts of empire but nature's cold indifference to man's dream is sharper here. More at home in this environment are the grey seals, the curlews, the plovers, better adapted to the caprices of the sky, cloudy, shining blue, stormy, letby glints of sunshine, and of the grey, blue and green sea. The glowing purple heather has struck up a better symbiosis with the contorted folds of the rocks.

We camped at Drinashadder on a Saturday evening. Somebody suggested that we should pay then because a Harris man would be embarrassed to accept money on the Sabbath. The severe face of the site owner broke into a smile. 'I can't see any Harris man refusing money, whatever the day.' In the Sunday morning peace we strolled by an ancient track to Scadabay past a bank of lilac-coloured marsh woundwort, yellow gems of tormentil or cinquefoil dotted the grass inconspicuously and the roadside banks were upholstered with silverweed.

We drove along the twisting road round the lochs Grosebay, Stockinish and Flodabay towards Rodel at the south point of Harris. Water-lilies were in flower. The ubiquitous seaweed, orange-gold, ornamented the rocks at water-level, seals swam, and climbed on the rocks, a curlew piped overhead in its fugitive flight, a cormorant standing on a grass-carpeted small boulder near the water spread out its wings to drip-dry, a plover endured our inspection for a long time unfrightened. I'd no idea that peewits were so richly coloured. It had metallic-green wings, blacks, whites, purples, chestnuts, orange; more in common with the peacock than I had thought. Sitting in a van at a Harris roadside close to an unconcerned peewit we achieved vaguely a feeling of community with the animate and inanimate furniture of our parcel of earth – fitful glints of sunshine, the changing clouds, the standingstones, the shiny black coal-like mussels and other shells, yarrow, heather, seals and cormorants and curlews. We entered into the spirit of St Francis, acknowledging as brothers and sisters all these things that happened to synchronize with our tenancy of the Scottish islands and mainland.

The ancient church of St Clement's at Rodel has tombs ornamented with figures which gave us a faint idea of the cast of countenance of our forebears in this place. Beyond Leverburgh in the café at Scarista, open on Sundays, we gazed at replicas of ancient chessmen, the wrinkles and contours of their faces giving us a blurred sketch-impression of how wind and tide and strife and poor soil and their standingstones and the imaginings of primitive theology affected their lives. Outside, a lamb sheltering from the wind in the insufficient lee of a shallow peaty and grassy overhang, was a symbol of their lives. Later we saw the pictures of Lewis artist Donald Smith who is struggling to present how he sees the earthly sojourn of fishermen, big hands deftly mending nets, a grey, hard life and the primary colours of their boats and the magnificent variety of their tackle and trim, the expression on their faces like those of the Rodel tombs and the ancient Chessmen.

We'd have liked to camp beside those glorious and ample white sands of south-west Harris but rain drove us back through a murky twilight and darkness to Drinashadder, and next morning we came to Tarbert again. To replenish our store of whisky and wine we had to go to the back door of a hotel and ring a bell. Farther north we looked out over a sea-loch to a castle where a rich incomer has been weaving silken patterns into the furnishings. It was this castle that gave hospitality to Barrie and here that he wove his wispy dream of *Mary Rose*. In this romantic western seascape, dream-populated with the seal maidens of Hebridean literature, Barrie felt freer to let his fancy roam than in the dry-breid east of Scotlnd. In Kirriemuir he sometimes struggled for air, pleading for recognition of 'the poetry in the soul of a weaver' and escaping into the English fantasy of *Peter Pan* and the Gaelic fantasy of *Mary Rose*. Like the rest of us, he was a victim of the divisive stereotyping of his time which separated us Scots into two nations, the realistic east and the romantic west.

Farther along the coast we went into a 'black house', the name for the traditional dwelling in Lewis which housed people and farm animals in one building. This one has been preserved, the peat fire burning and the smoke escaping through the straw roof, since there was no chimney-hole. I was surprised at how commodious it was, draught-proof and cosy. The pictures of black houses I had been brought up with implied a rural slum.. Were they comfortable but unhygienic? Did people feel cramped in them, did children's health suffer for lack of fresh air? When I was at school in Aberdeenshire the Hebrideans were as remote from us as the people who culti-vated the hill-pastures of Nepal. We never felt what it was like to be bedded down in their island-civilization.

In Lewis the issues are stark and plainly presented. James Hun-ter's book, *The Making of the Crofting Community* (1976) should be available in every secondary school in Scotland because it tells the story of what happens to local people fighting for their rights. Bitter experience obliterated the Lewismen's simple trust that 'if our landlord knew our circumstances well, he would give us justice'.

They had imgined that a reference to the Mosaic Law on land distribution would help their case. The Lewismen in the west, like us in the east of Scotland, had been brought up to believe that social relationships in Britain were founded on such rational axioms and on simple justice, the product of centuries of Christianity and western civilization. But they were learning that economic law was no respecter of civilization's theories. When finally the Liberals were forced to pass the necessary legislation to help cottars in 1907 and 1908, the Lords turned it down. The well-intentioned government tried to buy land for the cottars but the proprietors asked inflated prices. In 1910 the Lords' legislative veto was abolished, and the Scottish Land Court and the Board of Agriculture were set up (1911). But the Board's funds were small and its procedures complex and it was generous to landowners and sheep-farmers.

We should be sober realists about the nature of governments. But we shouldn't give up hope. The 1919 report on land settlement said, 'A crofting community is a way of living and cannot be judged in terms of a profit and loss account.' The Biblical statement that man does not live by bread alone was surfacing in British politics. We should encourage the young to welcome every sign of generosity and of caring, every offer of reconciliation, that emerges from the councils of the rulers. But to keep their eyes open.

CHAPTER TWELVE

Skye

. . . on behalf of the crofters of Gaeldom
inscription on monument commemorating the
Battle of the Braes

We returned to Ullapool and from there the road to Skye took us between the glowering land-masses of Dundonnell and An Teallach, and close to the little grassed-over island of Gruinard, its forlorn jetty stretching out an inviting hand hopelessly to the mainland which has estranged it from its community. If we Scots had been consulted about the anthrax experiments which contaminated a beautiful island, we would have given a resounding veto. I've never been sure what the word *sin* means but I think that was a sinful thing to do. Any country which lets a minority make the decisions is taking an awful risk. There is hope in the extension of us Scots' knowledge of our country. Getting to know the alleys and byways of the Highlands brings us smack up against our troubles and feelingly persuades us that we'll have to take a hand in the management of this our heritage. More and more of us are being enticed into following the Ordnance Survey's coloured-in tracks from Aultbea and Poolewe northward along the shores of Loch Ewe. Like absentee landlords we are becoming aware of the variety of our heritage and charting a course to repossess it, to reverse the Clearances. An Aberdeen teacher and his wife who for many years have been introducing pupils to the community of a Highland valley told me that one of the pupils had returned there for his honeymoon. He was lifting his bride over the lintel of their joint inheritance. The spirit of enquiry grows big within them. Their potential for sussing things out and asking questions and supplementary questions develops within them. Brought up as ignorant about the

Highlands as they are, I can understand how the novel experience affects them. It's like discovering that Chimborazo and Cotopaxi and Popocatopetl are within a hundred and fifty miles of sober Aberdeen. 'Rubha nan Sasan', says the name on the Ordnance Survey map. What's the story behind that name, the headland of the Saxons? Farther down I saw 'Sron Meallan a' Ghamnha'. The OS map takes on the compulsion to investigate of the chart of Stevenson's Treasure Island. Beside both of these ciphers I found the words, Hydrographic Survey Pillar. Like the pupils I want to know what a hydrographic survey is and how they go about it. Every stone we upturn uncovers a wealth of activity that we never suspected. Why didn't our servants the schoolteachers, like factors, not tell us more about the unexpected assets of our property? And about the idiosyncracies of the characters we inherited it from?

The following morning we set off from Gairloch and travelled through Kerrydale to Loch Maree. The fresh, bright morning threw its light on the firs and the rowan berries. An ingenious exterior decorator had hit on an unusual green for the rowan leaves, setting off the red of the berries. Between the road and the mountain, before we emerged on Slattadale, flew a bird that might have been an osprey. The rocks at the base of a shallow valley shone in the sun. The heather was out, the birches shone and a shaft of sunlight beamed on the loch, and giant steps of rock led down to its surface. At Kinloche we took the minor road to the right towards Torridon. Even driving in a car through these valleys, the traveller feels the peace in which they are enveloped. Yeats said of his own similar countryside that peace came dropping from the veils of the morning.

There is peace, and a refreshing beauty on the back road from Shieldaig to Kishorn. There, from the moorland, we dropped into a rich, moist, sheltered, sappy valley of deciduous trees and came to Loch Carron and its white houses reflected in the water. The closing of the Strome ferry added half a dozen miles round the loch. We climbed steeply and came down on the main road to Lochalsh, and Skye.

From Broadford in Skye, where the outspoken *West Highland Free Press* is published, we took the road to Elgol, past ruins, a chambered cairn, a graveyard, a stone circle. In the distance are the lion-toothed Cuillins and from above Elgol there is a panoramic view of Soay where Gavin Maxwell set up a whaling station, and Canna and Rhum and Eigg, and Muck hiding behind it, and Ardnamurchan, westernmost point of the mainland. The mind's eye struggles to fill in the panorama with its ancient sea-traffic of coracles and long boats.

And to repopulate this storied landscape between here and Broadford. One of the best ways to bring alive in the minds of the young our forebears of the last two centuries is to show them their technology, moulds for horn spoons and mutton-fat candles, stones shaped into querns for grinding oatmeal, variously shaped peat spades, foot ploughs and salmon spears, milk pails and meal kegs made of wood. The imagination of the young is readily engaged in the ingenuity with which they bent the available materials of their civilization into their purpose of making life easier and more comfortable. There were cruisie lamps, and the *fleerish*, a curved piece of metal that goes round the knuckle and was used for striking sparks off flint to ignite tinder. (Its origin in an old German word meaning *fire-iron* spotlights a dark recess in our history.) Other ingenuities were whisks contrived out of a wooden handle twisted with cowhair to thicken boiled milk, ropes made of straw and besoms made of heather stems and an oatmeal sieve which was an animal skin full of holes and stretched over a circular frame. Most of these things the young feel that, up against it, they could have re-invented themselves. They would settle down with gusto to spend a year digging peat and baking bannocks over its red embers, making light and fire and understanding why Prometheus figures so largely in the human story, carding wool, twisting ropes that wouldn't disintegrate, building and thatching houses, using their artistry to imprint designs on the butter for the evening meal, reliving their history.

From Broadford we crossed Skye to Glendale and went to the museum. In the busy restaurant next door, which serves local food, we relaxed. We needed time to fit what we had seen into our understanding of Scotland, what the museum had told us. We'd smelt the peat-smoke acrid in the semi-darkness of a but-and-ben, crept into a drinking shebeen and seen its accoutrements, the bottles, the jam-jar, the utensils for making whisky. We'd looked at the furnishings of crofter living, the hand-barrow, the thatching of the roofs, the peats that the pupils had to donate to the school, the buoys for the fishing-nets. We'd read the story of the oppression of working folk in Glendale. The museum attacked the religious auto-crats of Skye and the influence they have exerted in banishing the island's traditional music and social life.

On the following morning we visited Dunvegan Castle, a museum telling a totally different story of Skye's past. This is the Metro-Goldwyn-Mayer version, the high romance. Its emblem is the 'fairy flag', a flimsy grey-green silk tissue framed on the wall, for which an exotic, eastern provenance is claimed. There is the gar-ment of an early Christian saint brought from Syria by a Viking ancestor of the MacLeods. Here are the MacCrimmon bagpipes played by the Paganinis of pibroch; on them are pieces of embroi-dery called elf spots. There is the drinking horn of a chief called Rory Mor. This is the dungeon where the MacLeod chiefs put the dissidents. This is Bonnie Prince Charlie's waistcoat and a curl of his hair cut by Flora Macdonald. Here are letters from Dr Johnson and Sir Walter Scott saying thank you for the hospitality they received at Dunvegan. Here is Scott's *The Lord of the Isles* and his let-ter to the MacLeod chief about it. Scott was entering with zest into his function of chronicler and PRO to the court and the aristocracy, enjoying their patronage. He was in the tradition of the courtly chronicler whom he admired. Froissart organized his life so that he should be acceptable to a succession of patrons; it's still called play-ing the system and Froissart got a comfortable and interesting career out of it. Edward III's wife, Philippa of Hainault, paid him to chronicle the wars of his time and write poetry. He travelled to Kildrummy Castle in Aberdeenshire and then to Brussels, Bor-deaux, Bologna, Ferrara and Rome, and then to Germany; he went to royal weddings, and diplomatic treaty-makings and knew the best people such as the Black Prince. Like a *Times* foreign corre-spondent, he wrote up the wars of Spain and Portugal. I envy him the richness of his experience. But I want to point out to my pupils the price he had to pay for it, the acknowledgement that the aristos ran the show. Johnson's and Scott's attitude to the chief of MacLeod was like Froissart's attitude to Guy de Blois and the Duke of Brabant.

Later in the day, having walked through sodden grass to visit a broch and watched the making of pottery, we came to Portree and took a side road past Ollach to the Braes, on the Sound of Raasay, where the battle was fought between the crofters and the police, whose function was to defend the cause of the landowners. On a steep, grassy rise above the narrow road and the sea there is a tablet in Gaelic and English commemorating the April 1882 battle which, it said, the people of the Braes fought 'on behalf of the crofters of Gaeldom'. The events have been chronicled in a novel, *The Battle of the Braes* by the grand-daughter of the local schoolmaster. She says that it was wrong of him to try and stop the people from fighting the battle. On the mainland just across from Skye is the village of Applecross. It sounds as if it were in Surrey. Thus do English-speakers convert the ancient Gaelic name of Aporcrosan (or Abercrossan), the mouth of the Crossan, into a shape and sound they can feel comfortable with. Round it there is a lush growth of ash-trees and sycamores but the eastern approach to it by the Bealach na Ba, the Pass of the Cattle, is a steep hairpinning road across wild country. It leaves Loch Carron at Kishorn, where they made oil-rigs, and climbs steeply past bare rocks where grass hasn't found a root, other rocks bedecked with blue and green lichens, and wet rocks where verdigris-green grass flourishes. The ancient rock, weathered grey, is a fresh, youthful pink where it has been recently fractured. On the summit it is cold in June. One or two sheep crop the grass. Ahead lies the narrow finger of Raasay and, behind it, Skye, and, to the north, the outline of the coast up Shieldaig way. A burn flows through black peaty earth to the sea.

South of Applecross is a hamlet with the inconvertible name of Coille Ghillie. It is almost deserted today. There are roofless two-storey houses and a slipway to the sea. They built their houses and outhouses simply and sturdily of the old red sandstone. It was a fulltime job feeding a family. Plenty of fish and beef but the ground unyielding, needing much attention. It can be a monotonous job, turning over the earth. You straighten your back from the digging and listen to the cuckoo or the low wind, or the white-laced waves slurring through the pebbles. Prolonging the break before you get stuck into the next drill, you rest your eyes on the springy turf carpeting the ground, the black rock and orange seaweed between high-water and low-water marks, a clump of yellow irises and a boat in the Inner Sound, all of it refreshing to the body and the spirit. But maybe no. Wordsworth has a poem about a country-man who never felt the witchery of the soft blue sky. Toil can blunt the edges of perception. Economic forces may discourage the crofter from crouching behind a tussock of grass to identify a Slavonian grebe diving in the Sound. Religion may confine his thoughts to the treadmill of local controversy on sharp points of Covenanting doctrine.

But in a quiet place like this they did live in awareness of sun and moon and tides and weather. Like Stone Age folk they expended their ingenuity in making durable shelters from rough weather, experimenting with lintels and roans and gutters and water-barrels and sailing into the wind and inventing feasible interpretations of the thunder. They enjoyed the comforting regularity of the nightly star procession, the quiet glow of the peat and the crackling of wood in the ingle. Driving a rough cart over the track to Applecross, would they have delighted in the rich colouring of lousewort, tormentil, ladies' bedstraw, the elegant butterfly orchis and in the sweet-smelling bog myrtle? Did they notice, on the smooth, sloping rock-face, a pattern of lichens – daubs of yellow and grey-blue, a sprinkling of coarse cinnamon and splotches of grey-white, and green patches that are pasture for snails – all of it like an old, col-oured map of the shires of Scotland? There are niches in the hillside where boulders have been eased out by the rain and frost and, when we dropped a perpendicular from them, sure enough the boulders had come to rest beside the track. A big one had toppled into a nar-row inlet of the sea and, over the centuries, dust and bird droppings had mulched it and laid enough depth of soil to nourish a rowan tree. Where the inlet terminated, the crofters had built a causeway to carry the track solidly over the soft ground. A little farther along there were rows of stones on the grass but we couldn't come up with an explanation of how they came to be there.

One day we left the Applecross track and walked along Toscaig Glen, looking at sundews, red rattle, red bartsia, lousewort, eye-bright, hazels, oaks. A man and his wife were turning hay with a fork. Accompanying us was a schoolteacher who had an omnivo-rous appetite for knowledge about homo sapiens. He had been an engineer, an architect, he had written a botany of Perthshire, canoed across the North Sea, built boats, and delved into history. Through the binoculars looking down on Toscaig and listening to his commentary, we saw the clachan's history. The houses could be relatively dated by the sizes of their windows; there had been a law specifying that the window area must be a tenth of the floor space. Toascaig was a Scandinavian name. A new jetty was being constructed for the boat that goes to Kyle. Every step of the way down to the sea was rich in things to take note of. Rainbow-coloured oildrops bore witness to the natural oil. There is acid in peat (you can test it in the sap squeezed from a blade of grass) and alkali in limestone. The cross section of reeds is triangular and of rushes circular. The quivering of the aspen keeps off flies, and one leaf's perpetual quivering makes a curved mark on its neighbour leaf. It's cheaper to harl sandstone houses (that is, cover them with pebble-dash) than to point them every year. That is one of the ways in which an increased value put on labour has altered the appearance of a clachan. This was a different furniture of the spirit from that provided by industrial Scotland.

We followed the narrow road south to its terminus at a sea-inlet at Toscaig, and followed a track into the hills overlooking Kyle, a land of wildness and wet, where you can see a golden eagle if you are lucky. We did see a golden plover. The track goes through a rich carpet of the vivid blue of the butterwort flower rising on a tall stalk above its sticky, insect-trapping leaves, the shy blue of the milkwort, the orange star of the bog asphodel, white bog-cotton like the scut of a rabbit, pink heath and sundew, and beside the loch there are bog beans and water lilies. The thin bird-sounds of the hills come unobtrusively to our ears, the single 'peeit' of the golden plover, the 'sizzit' of the meadow pipit.

In the high ground above Applecross an eighth century monk is buried. What was he doing here? I suspect he became a hermit believing that mortifying the flesh would clarify his view of the path to Heaven. Seated on a rock of Torridonian sandstone slightly greyed by oxidization, he would have looked out over Applecross and the string of islands, Shapinsay, Raasay, South Rona, and the Inner Sound partly darkened by cloud patterns and partly shimmering in sunlight, to the Cuillins of Skye. Did he take pleasure in the earthly view or did he, like the monk described in the Cambridge Modern History, walking along the shore of Lac Leman, pull his cowl closer about his face so that his thoughts of Heaven should not be disturbed by the beauty of the earthly lake? Views of what life is about vary dramatically down the ages.

A young London banker escaped to this region. He lived in a corrugated iron structure which the navy put up to replace a house of Torridonian sandstone which one of their shells had damaged. But he hadn't a boat and he didn't cut peat and he hadn't included in his calculations the isolation and the short hours of daylight in winter, and he left after eighteen months.

At Sandaig, fifteen miles down the coast, another refugee had taken up his abode. In the *Ring of Bright Water*, Gavin Maxwell tempted his readers with the Circe charms of this west Highland shore. Strap-hanging in the Piccadilly tube, they dreamed dreams of this wild terrain, its eels and otters and salmon and serene human beings. Thousands of Londoners, hearing the doors open at Leicester Square, almost made up their minds to escape through the open doors and follow the London banker and the world traveller, and settle on this delectable coast. Well, why didn't they? Some did. But for most, the mortgage, the children's schooling, washing machines, theatres and pensions were too much to give up.

It should be the function of the school not to marshal the young into mines and factories and offices nor to lure them with a fairy story about the Islands of the Hesperides, but to present the options open to them and the price to be paid for whichever choice they make. At Sandaig Gavin Maxwell entered enjoyingly into observation of wild life. 'There's an osprey,' he said one day as a fleeting tangle of cloud, very high, firmed into what might have been a bird and sent him running for his binoculars. But he told me that for the most part he was so busy writing books against a publisher's deadline in order to keep abreast of his expenses that he hadn't much leisure to enjoy these natural things. One of his expenses was a yacht. 'You could do without that,' I suggested.

'Indeed no,' he replied. 'I need a boat with a powerful engine to get up to the Kyle of Lochalsh to buy fish for the otters.'

What is it worth to us to have a nodding acquaintance with the natural world, to know when the wild geraniums and the little toads and the thistledown appear in their season; to row across from Coille Ghillie to the Eilean na Ba, the Island of the Cattle, and look down into the forest of tall upstanding seaweed fronds in the deep water of the landing-place and watch sea-urchins nibbling them, to be as interested in the seal who spies on them all the way back in the boat as the seal is in us? How much pay should we be willing to relinquish in order to have more time to watch the seal disporting itself in the water, playing a game of hide-and-seek, its head appearing briefly (like the head of a St Bernard dog if you could imagine its ears to be floated back) and then submerging for a long period, keeping us guessing about where its next surfacing will be. (Our hostess at Coille Ghillie had once sung to the seal when she was alone, but it was unresponsive.) There is the call of the eiders, the rough voice of huge black-backed gulls, the cries of small sea-birds restless at all hours like the surging waters of the Inner Sound. At night, lights from the lighthouses of the Crowlins and the south end of Raasay bring comfort and assurance like a night-watchman's message flickered out in visual morse, 'Three a.m. and all's well.'

In such out-of-the-way places in Scotland many Scots and many English incomers are gingerly revising their views on how to spend their time on earth. Their experience is worth paying attention to. Dissidence contains the seeds of gain for our society in the same way as incongruence in his calculations leads the scientific research worker to fresh discovery. Many people are learning to gather their own fleeces and spin and weave them into garments. Like our forebears, they delight themselves in colour, squeezing crimsons and scarlets and violet and orange out of lichens and vetch and bramble and sundew and bracken and bog myrtle and dock and willow bark. They rediscover the world of herb gardens and learn to season cream cheese with tarragon and garnish it with sweet celery. They vary their diet with edible fungi. (In France the local pharmacy will identify any fungus you are in doubt about.) They bake their own bread and discover that it tastes better. Forswearing chemical killers, they grow the poached-egg flower to attract counter-predators, and ingeniously direct the carrot fly away from the carrots. They keep bees.

If more people are interested in the movement to repopulate the

Highlands, they'll need to be supplied with the facts. On the twenty-five miles of the new coast-road from Applecross to Shieldaig I'd tell them the post-Culloden history of Wester Ross, the creation of a green desert without people. The tenacious House of Hanover digging itself in, in London, parading in rainbow uniforms, patronizing the arts (water-music on the Thames) needed money to support its life-style. It laid tribute especially on the peripheral, rebellious regions, reducing them to subsidiary status, de-grading a living space until today it is a sports ground for the rich, a development area for the Scottish Tourist Board and an experimental area for naval artillery. It's not all plain-sailing for the residual fishing-boats fishing out of these picturesque clachans; the government took away half of their fishing-ground, the Inner Sound, and gave it to the navy for the testing of torpedoes. We Scots would like to have some say in the disposal of our assets. We can face unpalatable facts. We know that it *is* a hard countryside from which to compel a living. In the past there was hunger and the long hours of toil imposed by an undeveloped economy. But we'd like to discover for ourselves, by trial and error, if this region is, as they say, *viable*, livable-in. Today there are better hostelries, bigger boats on the Sound, a helicopter landing-pad, listening-posts eavesdropping on the Hanoverians' enemies. Is that as much as can be expected, or can we generate a more comely community than that?

CHAPTER THIRTEEN

Strathconon

The internalization of the standards of the oppressor is the most serious affliction from which oppressed people suffer, and the most difficult to eliminate.   MARILYN FRENCH, *Beyond Power*

A road map of Scotland indicates most clearly where the no-go regions are, great chunks of mountainous countryside without through-roads, that keep us in touch with what natural life was like before sophisticated, industrial man was let loose on much of the rest of our island. The traveller, returning from Skye and Wester Ross, has to make a wide detour, an arc of a circle north-east through Achnasheen or south-east through Kintail and Glen Moriston, to reach Inverness. The traveller who follows the non-through roads from the east into this great skelp of highland terrain (to Glen Affric and Glen Cannich and Strathglass and Strathfarrar and Strathconon) sees a Caledonia different from the stern and wild stereotype. In Glen Affric there are midges, buzzards, pine martens, ermines, golden eagles and deer, blaeberries sweet to eat, sphagnum moss soft to lie on, sweet-tasting blaeberries, ancient accommodation of chambered cairns and brochs, and present-day kit-houses fitted with mod cons, a pleasing, smiling vale like Glen Moriston. In the Strathglass area there are what the Ordnance Survey calls 'settlements and field systems', 'enclosed fields' and forts on the craggy hillside. From the forts the view to the east is of opener country, a field of cattle and a field of deer, and woods. I imagine our forebears, between raids, lingering on the sweet-smelling red roses and orchids and speedwell, picking sorrel to chew, amused to watch twenty fat beetles foraging on animal dung, surveying the green fields. Like us they probably stopped to pick

205

chanterelles for their supper. Between here and Beauly is Kiltarlity. One of my early recollections is of a poem of the First World War which spoke of the Kiltarlity soldiers memorized on the graves of Neuve Chapelle and on a roll of honour beside the pumphel stair in the local kirk. In the poem there is no questioning of the dispensation which sent remote highlanders to die in distant Picardy.

Farther north the River Conon opens a way into the interior. On its lower reaches is the ruined Brahan Castle where the Brahan Seer lived. He forecast deaths and disasters and the coming of the railways. Scotland cannot make up its mind about him although the Highlands provide too many authenticated examples of the second sight for us to dismiss it out of hand. The schools are as devious about the second sight as about the New Testament miracles.

Strathconon is like a valley on the Spanish side of the Pyrenees. Like the Pineda it has no through road and the small river runs through it from the mountains. From the entering-into the strath at Marybank you pass through a noble avenue of tall sycamores, beeches, elms, chestnuts and oaks. The river widens into Loch Meig. The wind ruffles a triangle of water in the middle of the loch, leaving the rest of its surface in the lee of the banks a smooth shining black in which trees on the farther bank are clearly reflected. The air feels drier than in the west. We saw two Canada geese (Europe's largest geese), a buzzard circling overhead, its split wing-ends silhouetted, a crannog in a loch, a rowan-tree totally dependent on a boulder for its support and sustenance, two houses where they get no sun from October till Spring, and an early-warning structure on a hill.

The absence of through traffic has helped the twenty-mile strath to retain some of its identity although only delaying change. It's a good place for the Third World social anthropologist to come face to face with the reality of Scottish Highland life. All that's left now of the glaciers that furrowed out the glen is this small river, quietly flowing through a smiling, green valley but it continues the secular process, undercutting the banks, and the unsupported divots of earth depend on their grass roots to maintain their hold. In other places they have fallen into the river and will be swept away at the next spate. Like plant roots, the telephone and electricity wires have lately groped their way up to the valley's western extremity.

Deep ploughing runs acid water off the hills and a green blanket of fir trees has been thrown over some of the hitherto bare hills. A firwood gives the traveller a feeling of shelter. The force of the wind is dissipated by the dense trunks and branches, and the fallen pine-needles provide bedding.

This long beautiful valley is sparsely populated. There is a post office, but no shop. In 1851 a report on numerous ruined hamlets indicated that it was thickly populated once. Between 1840 and 1848 more than four hundred people were driven from Strathconon when it was the property of James Balfour (father of Arthur Balfour who became prime minister in 1902). These highland valleys couldn't support a population of that number, say the economists. I don't know about that. Once again it depends on what 'support' means. I doubt if it was all that frugal a life. You're not doing badly if you get meal from the mill, game, fish, honey, and secretly distilled whisky, together with the perks that the economists don't set much store on, the peace, well-being, the daily privilege of watching the drama of the natural world, often rounded off with a glorious sunset, the pleasure of using your ingenuity in the make-do-and-mend, the maintenance of the fabric that shelters human life. The *Scots Magazine* said that 'If it were a valley in Norway or in Italy, there would be abundant signs of human habitation.' Today only two of twenty-nine pupils in the school have a parent who was a pupil there.

On the first Saturday in August, however, the valley is a hive of activity. The visitor who knew the valley at other times of the year would wonder where all these people suddenly gathered from. The Highland Games, a recent innovation, is not just cabers and kilts. The day's outing starts with a stamina-testing hill-race. We spectators watched the start of the race and adjourned to the pub yard for a grandstand view of the antlike figures on the mountainside, watching them through binoculars while we drank a glass of beer. In the afternoon the St Andrew's Saltire flag is broken to the sound of the pipes, and a programme of athletics, hammer-throwing, shot-putting, clay-pigeon shooting, begins. It's a superb setting and people are not unaware of beauty of terrain. It's a social occasion, a chance to meet up with friends. 'Oh, hullo, I didna expect tae see you here . . .' Scattered rural communities depend on an occasion like this for maintaining their links with one another. At Luleå in Sweden up near the Arctic Circle they forgathered twice a year for the kirk sacraments in 'kirk houses' where they had an opportunity for a leisurely exchange of news and gossip and a renewing of friendships and for the young to make contacts outwith their own community. In the Transvaal, Boer families met in the same way for the sacraments, living in church houses and strengthening the ties of community. The telephone doesn't tie us closely together in a bond of community in the way that the kirk sacraments and the village Highland Gatherings did. There is a deep need to be reassured that we are members one of another, to check up on our lines of communication.

Thus the Strathconon Games fill a need. They are well organized and run with humour and understanding. The children's events create enthusiasm in the children and pleasure in the parents. Visitors comment on a local record, untainted by the commercialism of the big Highland Gatherings. The army is there, the police look in, a neighbouring pipe band marches and countermarches and is regaled with beer and whisky. Once, I would have felt it to be a national custom, freely evolved in an independent-minded community, but now I sense the constraints upon it. It is a reflection and confirmation of the power that rules the valley. Kipling and Baden-Powell would have approved of this opportunity to show the flag. The local people, upstanding, healthy-looking, friendly, relaxed, in all other things independent-minded Scots, are nevertheless loyal retainers, accepting their feudal status. A young Frenchman and his wife, from Rouen, follow the programme observantly, the tossing of the sheaf over a high bar, the pipe band's military-like uniform, the strength and knack of caber-throwing, the caste system. He was an anarchist, he told me.

He and his wife were at the dance in the local hall in the evening, taking stock of the culture of a Highland glen, the Gay Gordons, the Schottische, the Highland Fling, the fiddle music, the walls prodigally ornamented with deers' antlers, hundreds of them, the international pop music that filled the later part of the dance. On the way back up the glen we saw in the car headlights first a fox and then half a dozen deer.

The room where we ate had been part of a farm building. Two

young Englishmen had used a tractor to cart out decades of farm dung and then, with the aid of a *Reader's Digest* manual on building and occasional local advice, had transformed it into a comely house. In their modern kitchen they could sit comfortably at breakfast and look out upon the green mountain-slopes and the sheep, and the white pappus of the cotton-flowers bending in the wind. The English public school is much better at fostering that kind of initiative than our Scottish state schools are. But there are constraints.

Next forenoon there were drinks in an English visitor's holiday home. Round the walls there were paintings of birds. The *Sunday Telegraph* was already lying on a side-table. A good-tempered discussion arose. On one side the English country-house group, on the other the Scots. The two groups were differentiated by accent, attitudes and speech idioms. Like other minorities trying to keep their end up, such as the Scots in Manitoba, the English upper class cling to their separate identity. We are at a disadvantage because some of the reddest of us are tickled pink to be taken notice of by the gentry. And we don't want to appear churlish, because they are intelligent, sympathetic people. One of them spends a large part of each year helping in famine relief in Somalia. On this summer afternoon in Strathconon two cultures are seeking to maintain their integrity but to avoid collision. The English readily accept that 'there are faults in our society'. Then a Scot said, 'You've agreed that all these changes should be made but you won't do anything very much to bring them into effect.'

The English lawyer from a public school said, 'We're not serious enough for you.' The implication was that we Scots are a bunch of sobersides, a pedestrian, humourless lot, for ever insisting on drawing a debate to a clear conclusion. For them, conversation was a pleasurable activity like painting in water colours. It follows rules, avoiding solecisms that might lead to a clash of opinion. They are adept at deflecting crises. The lawyer's comments lightly dismissed the subject. There was no more to be said. Our glasses were filled up again and over the next half-hour we drifted away.

It could have been an illuminating discussion in which we got to grips with the things that divided us. How seriously did they take Burns's song, 'A man's a man for a' that'? It might have been the

Battle Hymn of the Republic but the royalists removed the fuse and anybody could sing it without feeling it would explode. For centuries the only alleviation of working class conditions has been that extorted from the ruling class and also that which an occasional more compassionate ruler has been prepared to concede. Now we're entering a new phase because we are demanding equality. That's something the ruling classes are not prepared to concede.

On the Monday we followed the track up the Scardroy Burn in the direction of Achnasheen. On the plateau at 1250 feet there was stillness except only for the trickle of the burn, the buzz of a fly, an occasional comment from a sheep and the cheeping of a small, slim black bird. The pink bells of the spring heather were withered to cinnamon. A deer that had fallen through the snow into a crevasse in the bitter winter was disintegrating. We separated out its skull, and the horns now adorn a house in Dundee. What would the anthropologist say about that? Is it atavism, a harking back to a closer communion with nature? Like geraniums in a window-box in Glasgow or the reproduction of a MacTaggart seascape in a livingroom.

Eastwards lay the wooded ravine of Gleann Meinich from which all the human beings were cleared by what are called the 'inexorable' laws of economics. Golden grasses were at their prime. Lichens on rock looked like daubs of whitewash or the graffiti with which angry Aberdeen youngsters disfigure the walls of Aberdeen institutions of which they disapprove. A stretch of black mud was shrunk by drought into crazy paving and the black earth was prodded by the hoofmarks of sheep and deer. We saw an eagle, slowly planing, and rabbits stimulated into quick movements, showing the white giveaway scut of their tails. In dry, black, peaty watercourses, white pieces of wood looked like bleached bones.

I'm setting all this down in the perhaps vain hope that a pattern will emerge from the details of a Highland glen and the life in it, the glacier sandpapered ravines, the eagle and the rabbits, the peace and quiet of the plateau, the laws of the valley, the English overlords and the Scottish underlings and the survival of the ancient terms of their co-existence. The visitor's impression is of hospitality and friendliness, the relaxed outpouring of Gaelic and lowland music, the ancient rich vein still prospected by the storytellers, the golden liquor and the August sunshine. And over and above all that, the belated discovery that Scotland more than I imagined is one of Europe's last outposts of feudalism. I sympathize with the urbane critic who will say that I am reading altogether too much into the weekend of a Highland Gathering. People raced, danced, sang, newsed among themselves, drank, enjoyed themselves, accepting a 'natural' order of things without fuss or question. I merely record how one highlander, brought up in the lowlands, perceived life in a Highland valley during a glorious August week-end towards the end of the twentieth century. The plateau, the high places where we get an eagle's eye view, encouraged the asking of basic questions about the nature of the power that hovers over the valley.

CHAPTER FOURTEEN

The North

Rocks that have suffered crushing, bending, breaking, and violent heat; have had molten granite thrust
against them from below and thousands of feet of
deposit laid on them from above.
                    JACQUETTA HAWKES, *A Land*

The itinerary I have been following in this often trackless territory
of the Highlands is that of those who as recently as two centuries
ago opened up the country, so as to get a rough-and-ready idea of
the lie of the land and the feel of its communities. At a later date as
opportunity arises, the traveller can quarter intermediate areas as a
hawk reconnoitres a limited sector, and then move on to another.
Given this sketch-plan, the explorer of Scotland is surprised at how
much detailed information homes in on him or her to fill in the
interstices. A newspaper article, a conversation in a train, a television programme or even a brief news item which previously would
have been free-floating and evanescent, is given a local habitation
and is fixed in the memory. A very vague conception like 'Scotland'
begins to gather definition and take shape. It can be handled, comprehended. And once they have got hold of the idea, the travellers
begin to feel competent to take a hand in the further shaping of
their country.

With this end in view I describe two journeys starting from
Easter Ross. The first took us by Loch Shin to the wild country of
Assynt and Coigach on the north west coast, then south to Ullapool
and back to the east. The second was by Strath Naver to the north
coast and back by Halladale and Kildonan and Helmsdale.

From the top of the Struie Hill road we got a panoramic view of
the Dornoch Firth. At Lairg we took the road that runs for twenty
miles alongside Loch Shin. Beyond Loch Shin we came into more

varied countryside. A tablet in a wall commemorates Lupus Grosvenor, first Duke of Westminster who died in 1899. 'He built lodges and dwellings, erected fences, made roads and paths through these forests.' It's a region of white houses, Land Rovers, anglers, and bright colours induced by the rain. At Laxford Bridge you can turn right to Cape Wrath which an American traveller called the most desolate place in Scotland, or left to Scourie where the palm-trees grow. We took the Scourie road and came south through peat and rush country to Kylestrome Ferry. Waiting for the boat we felt that these steep, mist-wraithed mountains are frowning upon us, threateningly. At Unapool we took the minor coast-road, narrow, twisting, climbing, and suddenly descending to the level of Eddrachillis Bay, sometimes at a gradient of one in four. A fox, like a golden labrador with a bushier tail, appeared on the road and ran in front of the car and broke off into the side. Beyond the clachan of Drumbeg where the houses huddle together to keep warm and safe, we came to Clashnessie and slept beside the sands. Throughout the night the sound of the sea could have been the sound of a distant express train. Eight large fishing-boats strung out their lights. Seabirds held a dark convocation throughout the night but, like the fishermen, they weren't there in full day. Clashnessie, explained a road sign, is merely an Englishing of Clais na easidh. In much of Europe a similar notice would have been more intelligible to me. I know a fair amount of French and German and a smattering of Spanish and Italian, more than I know of the speech of my own forebears. Did they know what they were doing, the dominies who cut us off from our roots?

What is a highlander, a stranger to Gaelic life and culture, exiled to the farmlands of Aberdeenshire, to make of the scene? There are deserted crofts, dark and forlorn, this reiterated plaintive quality about the clachan like the attenuated community that still clustered to the Antonine Wall when the legions retreated and the frontiers of Rome shrank. Its face has changed little since the retreat of the ice 13,000 years ago; occasionally new wrinkles gouged out. Recent rain, making the river come down in spate, caused it to cut a corner and change its course and rush against a drystone dyke and then chew into a sandbank at the edge of the sea. We walked upstream to a huge deep-thundering waterfall whose fine spray was blown back like smoke when it emerged into the reach of a small wind and then went round in whirls. Economic power, capricious like water power, altered its course and came pounding against the aborigines which were damming its flow. Ultimately they gave up the struggle and withdrew. An advance party of strange new colonists replaced them and built a fort in a new kind of Antonine Wall, listening post on the bill between the clachan and the waterfall, and manned it. So there are two places here. One is Clashnessie, an outpost of the Westminster metropolis manned against the Russians by soldiers who are, I imagine, most of them as reluctant as Rome's legionaries on the Antonine Wall, and populated in the tourist season by comfortable incomers who own the white cottages that had no lights in them last night. The other is Clais na easidh, a village in a region of green, green grass, ferns, mosses and lichens, blue scabious and the black terminal flowers of reeds, of soft colours and soft air and ancient rocks, Torridonian and Archaeic, and some Old Red Sandstone, a community whose people had consumerism and its values imposed on them.

In the morning we resumed our journey. There were smashed-up hedgehogs on the road and, off it, a dump of wrecked cars. Smoke rose from a white chimney. Lochs filled in the spaces between the ancient rocks. And then we came down to the trees, ash, and rowan, their berries very red, the ancient trees of Scotland, and larch; and to Lochinver. It is populous enough to be free of the beleaguered air that encompasses smaller places in the wilderness. The shops are busy, the harbour active with fishing-boats, the white houses trim and reassuring and withal it retains one of the advantages of remoteness, the morning newspapers reached Lochinver at half past four in the afternoon and that delay, like a spring, buffers the community against the impact of the newswriters, the breathless urgency and immediacy. An American tycoon told his reporters that they weren't doing a good job unless their readers said 'Gee-whiz' as they read every item. By the time the newspapers reach Lochinver, they have lost their excitement and potency and people are freer to get the news into perspective. London assumes less importance.

The road from Lochinver back into the interior of Scotland runs first alongside a rushing river and then Loch Assynt. The old road, tarmacked but now weedy and unused, crosses the new road and winds about and returns to it as a dog scampers away into diverting sights and sounds and smells but always returns to the direction of its more-singleminded master. Even more than at Clashnessie I was aware of the modern world's change of emphasis, symbolized by the new road's entrepreneurial determination to deliver, its Roman-like directness. Roads are to get us speedily from one major staging-point to another, not to encourage us to dilly-dally on the way as our forebears did. Near Inchnadamph there are caves and heaps of stones where early man lived. In this wild province between Ben More Assynt and the Minch there are bright blinks of sunshine lighting up the soft, tan, heathery covering of the hummocky ground. The colours are intense. But low cloud lowers menacingly on the mountainside, and the light disappears as if a capricious god had switched off a smile and suddenly the terrain is feelingless and remote and vaguely hostile.

The distinctive peaks of Canisp and Suilven were shrouded in cloud and only the lower slopes of the mountains of Coigach were visible. In this inhospitable country an occasional but-and-ben has been modernized, there were stacks of recently cut peat, and black and brown and white cattle grazed. And there was another listening device on a hill.

At Ledmore we came in clearer sight of the other dramatic mountains of Wester Ross. The landscape and its people are dominated by these gaunt, jagged mountains. Elsewhere many of the Highland mountains qualify for the word *meall* which means a shapeless lump. But these frightening shapes of Assynt and Coigach are different. They bestride the world like colossi as daunting as their names, Quinag, Canisp, Suilven, Cul Mor, Cul Beg, Stac Polly. Sometimes they disappear in mist like a convocation of gods hiding their faces. None of them is up to the 3000 feet ranking which is the bar excluding claimants to the title of Munro. But they are not the less imposing. In descriptive writing there is a temptation to overdo it. The reporter sees Valkyries in blown rags of mist. But if I lived at Achnahaird and woke every morning to the towering presence of these giants I'd be aware of the power stored within the earth that explodes into such cataclysmic geological change. It is imagination-provoking country calculated to produce children different from those nurtured in the softer, serener farmlands.

Above the village of Achiltibuie, strung along the shore, you can see the Ullapool-to-Stornoway ferry after it emerges from the fleet of east European fishing boats in Loch Broom. These are factory ships into which Scottish trawlers decant their catches direct. Nearly two centuries ago Telford's boats and canal and harbours and roads hosed Scottish fish into Russia and Germany. His enterprise, a highlight of Scotland's story, fed eastern Europe. The tradition continues. Who would have foreseen these fish-processing plants within ships' hulls moored in Loch Broom? Strolling the deck after breakfast before they get into their day's work, factory employees speaking Russian and German look out on the Summer Isles, Tanera Mor (the biggest of them) nearest the mainland and, on the other side of the shipping route, Priest Island. Ullapool is an unbelievably white and clean and well-ordered town. It's much more in the swim than Lochinver. The Scottish newspapers come in early, the English papers a little later. English accents and the sharp Buchan accent mix with the soft local lilt. Huge lorries, their refrigeration motors running while they are filled up with mackerel, edge away from the quay and roar up the hill to feed the world. Here and there a dozen split mackerel lay on the cement floor, some of them squashed and their blood mixed with the rainwater. Their colour is as intense as those of the landscape. Among them was a discarded haddock that had got into the wrong company. In the harbour a seal swam about leisurely and unafraid. A Peterhead boat manoeuvred itself into a narrow space between another boat and the harbour wall with the deftness of a good car driver parking in a limited space. The skipper leapt ashore and I commented on the clever movements. 'We've two side-propellers, for'ard and aft,' he said.

We set off on the crossing of the kingdom, Loch Broom to the Cromarty Firth, following the lorries that pounded up the hill. The road runs close to the Falls of Measach and the fifty-yard-deep Corrieshalloch Gorge, a slice through the integument of Scotland as through a many-tiered cake. At the bottom of Scotland's Grand Canyon the water is still chiselling away the bedrock. Scotland's native trees flourish here, birch, rowan, hazel, bird-cherry, wych elm, Scots pine. After that we went through wild, desolate country. A buzzard was sitting solitary on a post. Poles, marked off in feet, line the roadside to guide travellers in times of heavy snow. A new road was being blasted through ravines. East of Garve there are sheltering woods and open cultivated country dominated by Ben Wyvis, and at Dingwall we are in the different climate of eastern Scotland, on the edge of the rich farmlands of the Black Isle. It is a circumspect town of over five thousand inhabitants and low, prosperous buildings. The shapely curve of the academy on a site that would have graced a Greek temple suggests that it has the same subliminary function, to discourage people from asking unseemly questions.

From Dingwall the thoroughfare to the North follows the shore of the Cromarty Firth past an area which, when the tide is out, could accommodate several farms. To bring it under cultivation would be a minimal effort in comparison with the breath-taking enterprise of the Dutch in enclosing the Ijsselmeer with a twenty-mile motor causeway and starting to raise food from the whole region down to Amsterdam, or the even more audacious land reclamation farther south, equivalent to building a causeway from Tarbat Ness to Findhorn and pumping out the water. What is it in the Dutch, their upbringing, their knowledge of their history, maybe their religion, that commends intellectual audacity to them and the ingenuity and realism that converts ideas into accomplished fact? For sheer confrontation of nature and the extortion of benefits to mankind, the epic achievement of the Dutch, in the past with their windmills and in the present century with their causeways, has no equal in recent history. The Scottish Education Department might be looking into the source of the energy that stokes that powerhouse.

On the other side of the Cromarty Firth rises the television mast at Eassie. Near the mast there is a tablet to the memory of a forester who was responsible, between the twenties and fifties of this century, for planting most of the woodlands of the area. We teachers should be telling young Scots more about such characters. He was in the Dutch tradition.

* * *

All of the Highlands were cleared of people as Hamelin was cleared of its infestation of rats, but the most poignantly recorded clearances were in the north. The publication in 1962 of Ian Grimble's book, *The Trial of Patrick Sellar*, and in 1963 of John Prebble's book, *The Highland Clearances*, were a milestone in Scottish education. It took well over a century for the Clearances to rise into the full Scottish consciousness. These books alerted us to the insufficiency of our instruction in the annals that concern us nearly. The story was filled out by Neil Gunn's *Butcher's Broom* (1934) and James Hunter's study (based on a thesis for an Aberdeen University doctorate) *The Making of the Crofting Community* (1976). Iain Crichton Smith contributed to our enlightenment with his novel, *Consider the Lilies*, an (in the best sense) artless story making known to us what it is like for an unremarkable old lady to slip from the short and simple annals of the poor into a national trauma. But if we are to envisage fully the desolation we have to go and see the valley for ourselves. The grass grows greenest where townships were, except where spruce and fir were planted over them. It is only by journeying through the valley that we can feel what the Achness minister, Donald Sage, felt when, a week after the clearance, on his way from Kildonan to Tongue, he saw the houses still smouldering, and the banks of loch and river, formerly studded with cottages, a scene of desolation. I wanted to see three of the Clearance valleys that Prebble described, Strathcarron, Strathnaver and Kildonan.

When we left the A9 (Inverness to Wick) road at Ardgay and struck westwards up the Carron valley, we were in new territory. The October sun lit up the russet bracken on the low slopes which contained a medium-size black river and its occasional waterfalls in a shallow valley where birch-trees grew. The landscape contained, against its old background, some black cattle, many sheep and some new white houses. Well-maintained stone dykes, reinforced by wire fencing, separated the fields. I'd like fine to bide there and make sorties along Glencalvie and the Alladale River and Strath Cuileannach far into the interior, sleeping in random bothies, and piece together a few words in Gaelic and, on a basis of rocks and stones and fields, raise a reconstruction of how our forebears lived before disaster hit them in the 1840s. In 1840 Queen Victoria had been three years on the throne and married Albert of Saxe-Coburg-

Gotha; Abraham Lincoln was 31 and Karl Marx was 22. Middle-aged men bored their grandchildren with their memories of Waterloo. Railways were pushing their tentacles over the country. A Reform Act had slightly dented the perimeter fence of the aristocracy and the word 'socialism' had been used for the first time five years earlier. In this remote valley people lived under an ancient dispensation, helping themselves to a deer from the hill, a salmon from the river or a tree from the wood. I wish I could penetrate to the intimmers of that life. I doubt if it was all that different from the rural Aberdeenshire of my childhood eighty years later. They enjoyed the summer, and tholed the winter as they tholed the political system. The keenest arguments were about rival interpretations of what that Nazareth joiner had really meant; for example did he want the ministers to be chosen by the lairds or by the folk themselves? Life had gone on like that in the Ukraine and Switzerland and Wessex, seedtime and harvest, for centuries. Even in winter harshness, people felt safe. Subterranean economic rumblings, like thunder, were no great cause for concern. Then came the cataclysm, sudden, inexplicable, inexorable.

The *Times* man was there, and wrote an unexpectedly compassionate story, totally supporting the people against their oppressors. It had not the slightest effect. Croick church, which was at the core of the *Times* man's story, is a comely, dignified place of worship, built by Telford. It lies at the west corner of a shallow basin, near the hills. The sound of water is never absent. Chestnuts new-fallen lay among the graves and some of them had split open, revealing their fruits glossy brown with the sheen of polished furniture. A stove sends its warmth through a pipe into the church. It was outside the church, on the east side, that the dispossessed homeless put up tarpaulins, rugs and plaids and blankets to get shelter. They scratched messages in English on the church window-glass, 'Glencalvie people was here', 'Glencalvie people the wicked generation'. They made a fire, and two cradles with babies were placed close to the fire.

Like most of my fellow-countrymen I had been brought up to believe that highland valleys, like those opening up from Croick, had always been like that, green, beautiful, empty, plaintive. It was news to me that the desolation was man-made. Today it is difficult to envisage several hundred people living in these depopulated valleys. We saw few holdings. There were red-marked sheep, some curly-horned rams, some skeps of bees, buzzards, some cottages, roofed with rusty corrugated iron, silage under black perspex held down with car tyres. A wooded gorge breaks through the north slope of the mountains and the triangle between the lodges of Amat, Glencalvie and Alladale is variously wooded and there are blaeberry bushes.

At Bonar Bridge we rejoined the road north to Strathnaver. Telford's bridge over the Kyle of Sutherland, part of the programme to alleviate the poverty caused by the clearances, was succeeded in 1972 by an eye-catching steel structure. A memorial alongside to the two twentieth-century world-wars makes a visitor wonder how so sparsely populated a region could have nourished so many soldiers. Beyond Lairg the flat road runs between fields of rushes and black earth upturned to make wet, peaty trenches, the desolate, neglected periphery of empire. A river's surface is garnished with berry froth. Blue plastic sacks containing the cut peats stand out of the biscuit-coloured monochrome of dry reeds and grass. Then the plain was broken by Ben Kilbreck on the east, as geometrical a cone as Schiehallion in Perthshire and, ahead, Ben Loyal, a great rhinoceros of a mountain.

It was a relief to come to Altnaharra, an oasis where people have squeezed colour out of the desert. There was emerald grass, a lawn and a pool and a small rock-garden, trees and rhododendrons. Altnaharra has a school and a mart and a hotel and shed post-office. It's like a laager within whose circle of covered waggons the sojourners protect themselves from the dangers of the night and the wild country, warming their spirits with the comfort of colour and homely, known things.

We followed the twisty lochside road through open country where alders and birches and rowans grow. A notice in English, French and German forbade fishing. Strathnaver begins at the end of the loch, a smiling valley, wider, greener, more fertile, more beautiful than I had imagined. The river is wider and deeper than I thought. Prebble as guide pulled the curtain a little back and I got a glimpse of what was happening in my country these one hundred and seventy years ago, in these communities strung like beads along the river Naver, nourished on milk and butter and cheese, flesh and fish and fowl, potatoes and kail, song and dance and stories, and kirk doctrine. Across the river, on the opposite slope we saw the rickles of stones, relics of farm-touns dinged doon by the sheep-men, the obliterated community of Rossal. There was a roadside memorial to Donald Macleod who chronicled the devastation. His report, *Gloomy Memories*, was read by Kark Marx in the British Museum where he dug out the detritus of our history. We Scots need the persistence of Marx if we are to uncover the reality of the crime. We knew as little of these recent events as we knew of the lives of the Picts who built the longer-enduring brochs and cairns with which this smiling valley is littered. Grimble quotes evidence about the houses burned, given to the Napier Commission by a witness, eleven years old at the time of the burning. 'All from the River Owenmalloch and another river coming into Strathnaver on the east side, down to Dunviden burn.' Cross-questioned about the attitude of the people, she replied, 'You would have pitied them, tumbling on the ground and greeting and tearing the ground with their hands.'

A detail like that stabs our school-anaesthetized senses into sharp awarenes. In the old Tolbooth in Tain, where the Glencalvie folk waited trial, Prebble found writs of removal issued in Easter Ross. 'Sixty years of tragedy are bound in strong tape and buried in dust.' A summons of removal applying to Glencalvie tenants quoted in a 1756 Act which stated that if a tenant hadn't been under an obligation to flit (that is, get out), the landowner could use a 1555 Act to eject him. I had been nurtured in the Scottish mythology of the justice of the Law, which I saw as a venerable heritage incorporating the wisdom of our forebears and broadening down from precedent to precedent. I had no idea of the nature of law-making, what an arbitrary exercise it is. The young should know the circumstances of the making of the 1555 Act, the room in which it was discussed, the people who wanted to make it law and the material gains which it would confer on them. We have not been alerted to the real nature of our past. That helps to explain why, as an unusual news-reporter of the Clearances claimed, the middle classes of Scotland were accessories to the extirpation of a people. The *Inverness Courier* editorialized on the Clearances in the way that the London tabloids editorialized on the miners' strike.

In Strathnaver, Nature comes to the support of our elders in covering over the painful evidence of the past. I saw moraines of yellow-white stones and yellow sand, some cattle and sheep, rabbits, a dead deer in the back of a van, great Swiss rolls of straw, occasional new bungalows, a peat-stack, farm tractors, a good road, Gaelic place-names sign-posted and, beside the road, a monument commemorating the raising of the Argyll and Sutherland regiment in 1860.

A sandbar blocks the exit of the Naver into the northern sea at Bettyhill. The comfortable hotel we stayed at was the substantial manse with which the family of Stafford (later Duke of Sutherland) rewarded the Rev. David Mackenzie for his services in easing for them the course of the evictions and translating their orders into Gaelic. On an October evening the pub was a cheerful place where a score of people relaxed. Before we left in the morning a seal was bobbing up and down in Farr Bay, watching us crossing the beautiful white extent of sands. The twisting road eastwards along the north coast of Scotland goes through a green-brown moorland carpet, patterned with reedy lochs. Grey rocks show through the carpet. A triangle whose apex is Strathy Point contains croft-houses such as I remember from my earliest days in Aberdeenshire but which are now rarely seen there. In the Strathy pub are pictures of the Clearances in Uist and of last century's gold-diggings down near Helmsdale. This is the area to which some of the Strathnaver crofters were evacuated. Ten miles across the bay is the white sphere of the Dounreay nuclear station and, opposite it, the mountains of Orkney. They say that children in the Strathy triangle have died from Dounreay pollution. But for the Dounreay construction and a few broken dykes and rusty shed-roofs and a few communities, this is the same bleak face that the southern land presented to the Vikings as they pulled their longboats up on the shore and set off inland to explore and plunder.

Here we are near the boundary of Caithness, which is a lowland shire and takes pride in maintaining its distinctive charcter. One of the best books I ever read in my life, Neil Gunn's *Morning Tide*, is about life in one of the Caithness east coast fishing-villages.

Another village, Clyth, near Gunn's birthplace, is the scene of Donald Campbell's play, *The Widows of Clyth* (1979). In his introduction, Campbell says, 'I must add the strongest qualification that, *on no account whatsoever*, must a conventional "Highland" accent ever be used in any performance of this play.' He says he has avoided the very distinctive dialect, but used Caithness idioms worded in standard English, and a few dialect words like 'Weeck' for 'Wick'. Down in the Means, Lewis Grassic Gibbon adopted the same policy. If we are going to make clear to young Scots the nature of their countrymen we must tell them about these communities which, although on good terms with other communities on the other side of the mountains or the shire border, are fiercely insistent on their own identity and, as part of it, their local speech.

At Melvich, staying in Sutherland we turned south into Glen Halladale. We passed a mill, its water-wheel still in use. Hawks harry the open country. From Forsinard the road is in a tight embrace with the railway through Kildonan to Helmsdale. There are stone sheepfolds. Kildonan was a particularly good feeding-ground for the new breeds of sheep that the developers brought in. In April there was cotton-grass. When it faded there were pastures of fresh deer-grass. Then in August they could depend on harvest-moss. We passed the sites of last century's gold diggings and saw two amateur prospectors, furnished with a pan and a narrow shovel and bucket and a narrow seat, padding for gold in the Kildonan Burn. Most of Kildonan's history is covered over. There are small piles of stones, so little trace. Splotches of light-brown bracken vary the heather mantle and the hillside is corrugated with furrows that run off the acid water. Near a cottage a brown hen wandered about leisurely, staking out a tiny area of domesticity in a lonely place. At Helmsdale we turned north to the Ord of Caithness to see the ruins of Badbea, a village built on a slope above steep sea-precipices by local people evicted by Sir John Sinclair. Children and animals had to be tethered for safety. Today it is a windswept tract of heather uniformly brown like a worn rug but in places varied with bracken and whins and grey boulders, green-lichened, and heaps of ruins and an enduring stout circular enclosure, probably for animals. From this high platform the evicted crofters looked out across the wide Moray Firth to where the land, light blue, receded towards

Fraserburgh in Aberdeenshire. The low sound of the sea was constantly in their ears. Here you get a god's-eye view of Scotland as a solid sited in water, and the uncomplicated panorama pushes you into asking basic questions about what sort of drama was scripted for this stage, or if there was no script and the characters just appeared and ad-libbed. The foreign traveller, piecing together such evidence as this landscape offers, to try and visualize a pattern, to get an inkling of the civilization that expressed itself in these artifacts, would be puzzled, no doubt in the same way as we have been puzzled and non-plussed to account for some extravaganza of Asiatic culture and conduct. What manner of men were they whose inner thoughts and compulsions issued a manifestation like Badbea? The author-producer of the Badbea scenario lived in the Castle of Dunrobin, twenty miles down the coast. On the top of Beinn a'Bragaidh near the castle the Duke's family raised a 76-foot pillar and on top of the pillar is a 30-foot statue of the Duke. His remaining tenants were forced to contribute to the statue fund. The Duke on his mountain is a picture of what happens when the desire for mastery reaches manic proportions.

The Highland landowners, said Telford (who had dealings with them, particularly when he was building the Caledonian Canal), were the most rapacious in Europe. Some of them, descendants of merchants and property-dealers, were on their way up, buying commissions in Sepoy regiments in the East India Company and in the Black Watch, marrying into what are still called the 'great families' and gilding their dusty pretensions with coats of arms (silver wolves' heads, a right arm holding an imperial crown) and Latin mottoes (saying that glory is the reward of courage). To diagnose the forces that led to the Clearances, 'one of the grand crimes of modern Europe' as Scottish journalist Neal Ascherson described them, we have to look not only into economies and such-like but also into the magic and mystique of heraldry and Latin. An educational psychologist said that when a pupil steals money you must look at what he does with the money. When the landowners stole the land they spent a considerable amount of their gains on heraldry and Latin. Thomas Gray's warning about the boast of heraldry and the pomp of power didn't cool their ardour.

There is much digging out to be done concerning not only the motives that drove the landed proprietors but also the real nature of the Highland crofters. In his introduction to Ian Grimble's *The Trial of Patrick Sellar*, Eric Linklater said that war was a natural exercise to these Gaelic speakers. Some Gaelic poetry supports him. But I have my doubts about the theory that most Highlanders in cold blood would naturally elect for a soldier's life and stick a bayonet in a French or Boer belly for the hell of it, exultantly driving back the enemy at Waterloo and Magersfontein. Some of them were forced to enlist because the Highland chiefs burned their parents out of their houses when they didn't, others because of unemployment and hunger. The 'martial spirit' of the Irish peasantry was used against the Highlanders, and the 'martial spirit' of the Highlanders against the American colonists. The *Times* reporter, accepting Walter Scott's stereotype of the fierce, fighting spirit of the Highlanders, was puzzled at their docility at Croick and said that in England there would have been a riot. The discrepancy between the Scott myth and the Croick reality indicates one area for spadework.

And there is much digging out to be done, many questions to be answered clearly, before the Scottish young can get their recent history into perspective. James Loch, Sutherland's commissioner, listed the improvements that his sheep-based economy had brought to a poor country. For some evicted crofters there was employment in herring fishing and gutting and coopering. The wool trade flourished. Coal was struck at Brora and lime quarried. Roads, bridges, harbours and inns linked lonely communities into the rest of the nation. How can we help our pupils feelingly to set these assets against the liability of dispossessing Kildonan crofters, to feel what it was like to be a crofter in Kildonan? Such issues *are* comprehensible to the majority. We would have no difficulty in understanding the issues that will determine the future of the Kildonan valley. As James Hunter explained, the Highlands and Islands Development Board was set up by Labour in 1966 to hold the balance between economic and social advantage, but it tiptoed away from that philosophy and said that land settlement in Kildonan couldn't be economically justified. That debate is crucial for Scotland.

The towns on the broad firths of the north east are different characters from those on the narrow, remote western sea-lochs. Dornoch has a cathedral where the Earls of Sutherland are buried. Andrew Carnegie, the Pittsburg rail-king from Dunfermline who lived in a local castle, contributed richly to its upkeep. I don't suppose the young of Dornoch notice the large shield, decorated with pictures of a wild cat, a horseshoe and three gold stars which declares WITHOUT FEARE. Elsewhere the motto becomes SAN PEUR and, inconsequentially, DREAD GOD. The tabards and blazons and coats of arms, the beasts and boasts of the Heralds, may have impressed the soldiers of the time. In Dornoch you never get far from the profession of arms. The Seaforths commemorate their 8432 comrades in ten battalions of the regiment who died in the 1914–18 war, and underneath are the words, SCOTLAND FOR EVER. Dornoch is a fine town of stately streets and it has a glorious expanse of sandy coast. The Witch's Stone on the gold course tells that it was in Dornoch that the last execution for witchcraft took place.

'So what?' say the irreverent young as we earnest pedagogues seek to interest them in local history. It's a box of beads without a string to link them together. What does it all add up to? Tain, across the Firth, is also a royal burgh full of ruined chapels and tenuous connections with saints and kings. It has a market cross and a Bastille-like Tolbooth. East of Tain, the strip of level land that fronts the Moray Firth from Tarbat Ness down to the Cromarty Firth's opening has a comeliness of its own. It has springy seaside turf, lark song, seapinks, tormentil and sheep sorrel. Portmahomack, facing the Dornoch Firth and the rougher country beyond it, is a sunny, sandy place and is in the area of Scotland's lightest rainfall.

The smell of the sea comes into Cromarty on the wings of a north-east wind through the Sutors, the headlands that guard the opening into the Cromarty Firth. It's a tidy, cheerful backwater of white houses and houses of red sandstone. In Cromarty the National Trust looks after Hugh Miller's house. Like Telford, he was a stonemason. Telford's experience of handling rock, his knowledge of its nature and constituency, led him to the powerful manipulation of it, excavating it, moulding it into building blocks in the making of canals and harbours and roads. He was called a

Colossus of Roads. He linked together communities separated by the wildness of Scotland's earth-crust. His mental make-up was that of the explorer, enquiring into what is possible for us in our covered waggons seeking alternative ways of spending our time-allowance on the planet. Miller's handling of rock made him an explorer, too, going far back into earth-history, using his knowledge of the Old Red Sandstone of the Black Isle to dynamite its secrets out of the universe and learn how to live comformaly to our evolution. The difference between them was that Telford started from scratch, unencumbered by the rubble of earlier generations. The stonemasons and village blacksmiths who initiated the industrial revolution in Scotland had a clear field. They knew much more about steam engines and engineering than the Greeks did and didn't have to waste their energies referring their explorative mechanisms to colleges of learned men. Miller was weighted down by centuries of Scottish philosophy and religion. He was an explorer who forever had to look back over his shoulder to check that he was in line with kirk teaching. The strain broke him; he committed suicide. If he like Telford could have had a clean unhandicapped run at using his knowledge and understanding, he could have made as big a contribution to Scotland's culture and the upbringing of the young as Telford made to our trade and transport and communications.

His house exhibits his correspondence with Darwin and Carlyle, his anti-Pope books and copies of the twice-weekly paper, *The Witness*, that he edited. It contains close-printed reports about whether the French President would be pushed into accepting the title of Emperor; his troops were pushing him hard into acceptance. It is from a quarry like this that we school-teachers should be blasting out the building blocks of Scottish education. The French Bastille having been dinged doon, power-hungry men were trying to raise it up again. Teenage Scots, impatient of restraint, should understand the nature of the power that restrains them, the ideas that the tolbooths cemented into Scottish life.

The shadow of the past lies heavily over Fortrose as over these other towns. Fortrose Cathedral was the burial place of Seaforth chiefs. It weathers well, parts of the Old Red Sandstone changing to an attractive fawn. The town is full of ecclesiastical names. The chiefs and the bishops stamped their imprint on the town so indelibly that, to the visitor, life in Fortrose at the tail end of the twentieth century looks like a postscript to a fifteenth century religious play. These confident, enterprising characters knew where they were going and were ruthlessly determined that for unforeseeable centuries the people of the Black Isle would follow their direction. The building of that beautiful cathedral was the main event in Fortrose in the second millennium of the Christian era. The churchmen knew how to make the artists serve their purpose. The Old Red Sandstone was moulded into vault and font and tower and chapterhouse as men's minds were moulded into homage and worship.

The old railway line from Fortrose to Avoch is an example of the failed initiatives which litter Scotland. The amount of energy that went into it is phenomenal. To make a railway they dynamited cuttings through rock, removed earth, built up ancient burn-eroded valleys with earth and rock, cemented culverts, slowed up the currents of rainwater to preserve the track undamaged. There were daily inspections, signalling systems, attractive stations. And then a 'business' man came along, declared them 'uneconomic' and wiped many of them off the face of Scotland, impoverishing the country. The track still shows the corrugated pattern made by the removal of the sleepers. The scalloped leaves of the oak-trees cover the track. Self-seeded trees grow along the side of the track, those that seeded themselves in the middle having been trodden out. Green lichens are growing over carefully cut, shaped blocks of Old Red Sandstone at a place where there was probably a railway halt. On the slopes above the lineside, hazels, oaks, ivy, brambles, broom and whins flourish.

On a June night we slept in the van on the top of the hill above Fortrose and Rosemarkie. A Scottish panorama was open for inspection. At the limits of visibility eastwards, on the southern coast of the Moray Firth, a grey whiteness indicated the Culbin Sands. Nearer, Nairn was tucked into a nook. Just across the Firth rose the gigantic leg of an oilrig under construction at Ardersier. Beside it, the dark smudge of Fort George fading into the grey light as it is fading into history. Then the stretch of coast round to Inverness, containing in its hinterland Cawdor and Culloden. But from our eminence, the play of light and shade in the sky, the massing of the clouds, was the eye-catching thing, the earth being only the footstool of the firmament, just a bright strip of coastline still, and hodden-grey earth backing away from it. By the time we had read the Sunday papers and their extracts from an Australian's rhyming couplets on 'Charles Charming's Birthday Ball', the lights had appeared, outlining coastal communities. There were especially garish lights at the Ardersier fabrication yard. It was like a stage spectacular, all spectacle and episode and no identifiable plot. The audience might ask, 'What's going on down there?' A poet a thousand years hence might like to know the details that I'm setting down.

Where does all this noting down of phenomena lead? We identify siskins and greenfinches and tits on a birdtable at Fortrose, learn to discriminate between alder and hazel leaves, between willow and hazel catkins, peer into the garden-soil world of beetles, cockroaches, grubs, millipedes, learn about the joint housekeeping of mosses and lichens, appreciate the limpid quality of the water and light at Avoch and out on the Firth, a crystalline quality that is found in Switzerland. We savour a word like opalescent to fix it in our recollection. We are like detectives, card-indexing the clues, piling them up, but getting no forrarder in solving the mystery. Maybe I'll have a theory to offer, a hypothesis, by the time I get back to Aberdeen again.

Munlochy Headland sticks out into the Firth between Fortrose and Inverness. It's easy walking on the carpet of heather and rushes, cropped probably by the wild goats. Their crooked paths wind through the heather and their stamping ground reeks of shit and urine. Down at the base there are unexpected rich ploughlands but the goats have the run of the plateau, making the high places their own. This is goat territory. They can survey the town of Munlochy and its commodious churches of Old Red Sandstone, and, nearer, a ruined cottage and croft-steading and a restored cottage; pine-trees, wind-flattened in their youth, now resuming their vertical growth; far below, cormorants perched statuesque on tree branches immediately above the Firth, holding this outstretched-wing pose; planes above Inverness airport just across the water; and barges of timber lying off Inverness, on their way to Scandinavia where the Scottish trees will be made into wood pulp for us to buy. The ploys of the goats are less complicated and contrived than those of the busy and ingenious human beings down there. James Stephens made an uncanny appreciation of the goats' point of view. They pause to crop here and there, stare on the roving sky, wind about in the heather paths, run away from trespassing humans and couch down again to brood, 'quietly in quietness'. This is the most relaxed poem in the English language. Its implication is that the goats have got something that we've lost. In a sunny solitude, says Stephens,

> I would think until I found
> Something I can never find,
> Something lying on the ground,
> In the bottom of my mind.

The Scottish schools don't take poets seriously. Stephens was an eccentric Irishman who had a talent for rhyming jingles and a question about him might possibly come up in the Highers. But the idea that the way of life of the goats on Munlochy Headland might give us something to think about is not one that enters into the calculations of our mark-earning pupils.

Inverness is an unexpectedly unromantic place for a Highland Capital, but its picturesquely sited theatre, beside the Ness, brings a mellowing of romance to the region. Its new Kessock Bridge is the gateway by which we leave the North.

CHAPTER FIFTEEN

Inverness to Aberdeen

The people here has of late broke very loose.
letter (1796) in Darnaway

The hundred-mile journey from Inverness to Aberdeen, from one physical and cultural landscape to another, is marked by subtle transitions. At first we are still in the Highlands or their hinterland. A short road goes off to Culloden. Even those Scots who are usually insensitive to atmosphere speak of a brooding presence that haunts the battlefield and its marked graves. All that unutterable suffering and waste of Highland and Lowland lives, is there nothing for it but that we must dree our weird? Was it an inexorable rendezvous? In his poem *Culloden, The Last Battle*, George Mackay Brown tried to handle this filmy stuff. It is like Morag at her wheel turning the fog of wool into a thin swift line of light. Out of the shadowy mists of time, undefined, insubstantial, something took shape that was very defined, very substantial, a terrible battle. For one clansman it meant three wounds 'heavy and round as medals'. 'Red shapes drifted about me in the drifting smoke.' They played this game of ghost on the long moor and when it was over travelled homeward on the old lost roads, twilight by twilight.

The postscript to Culloden was Fort George, seven miles away, on a Moray Firth headland. In today's money it cost a billion. Its theme was the total subjection of the Highlands. The ramparts are nearly a mile round. It was completed in the year when Napoleon was born. When Bonnie Prince Charlie was drowning his sorrows in Paris and Rome, the clansmen were herded into Fort George to train to fight for King George. Down the centuries the Scottish people were expendable, deployed to further the claims of one dynasty one day and of the enemy dynasty the next. I think this attitude is an outrage on human personality but we have been brought up to regard it as the natural order of things.

Inland from Fort George, on the other side of the Inverness to Aberdeen road, is Cawdor. It has thick walls, a moat and draw-bridge and, on the September day we were there, a huge fire roaring up a formidable draught of chimney. Its curios include a flint-knapping hammer, cowhide fire-buckets and Dali's picture of Mac-beth. It's a fine place and peaches ripen in the garden but it sheds less light on Scottish history than Darnaway, the home of the Earls of Moray on the other side of Nairn. One of the Moray chiefs planted trees of which eight million are still growing. The tenants were compelled to use the earl's mill for grinding their corn. The custom was called *thirlage*, a word and a habit of mind that has sur-vived the practice, and the payment was called *multure*. The bene-fiting feudal superiors hung on to the vassalage conception of human relationships. In 1796 a letter, on exhibition in the Visitors' Centre, written by a land agent to the absent laird, said that 'the people here has of late broke very loose. Murdoch younger in Cooperhill I have found out stealing wood.' Darnaway, like the other 'great houses' of Scotland, was well to the fore at the 1822 George IV reception in Edinburgh. The Sword of State was carried by Morton, the Crown by Hamilton, and the sceptre by a younger member of the Moray family, later earl.

The curator of the Forres Museum invited us into his back room to answer the question I had asked him about the date when dis-aster overtook the Culbin Sands, the girnal of Moray. 1694, he said. Then he started us on an identity quiz of some of his curios. He picked up a blackened clamp which might have come from a Forres science-room. 'Any ideas? . . .They fitted a dry, rosity stick atween the two lips and set a light to it. And this?' He was pointing to a small metal rack which looked like an oatcakes-toaster that I've seen fitted in front of an Aberdeenshire grate to finish off the quar-ters of oatcakes when they had been taken from the girdle. 'Aye, maybe. But it's listed as a grill to dry the sticks before they used them as lights.' He struck a spark off a flint and a 'fleerish', and made a piece of saltpetre paper smoulder and lit his pipe with it. 'A great thing, flint. We used to import it from France. Fire, arrow-heads, hammers. Aye, it was a major industry.'

'That drum there. It was beat every weekday morning to waken the folk of this town. If the drummer failed to beat the drum, that was accepted as an excuse for not turning up to your work.'

He had been a gardener and brought to the museum's problems the same practical enquiring attitude as he might have brought to the problem of preventing spinach from shooting too early. He picked up a garnet that had been cross-sectioned, and pointed to faint lines that looked like those in the cross-section of a tree. 'This is a local stone. It took me a long time to figure out what these lines might be.' I pictured him sitting contentedly in his workroom reading Hugh Miller and searching for an explanation that would satisfy his practical turn of mind, and then going on to the problem of the faint Mezozoic fossil embedded in the stone. Maybe it took as long as he had taken over the identification of a Persian woodpecker. In a Scottish classroom there is the pressure of the examinations, speed and abstract thinking and preoccupation with the manipulating of words. In the museum there was a leisurely, almost timeless, spirit and the exhibits don't let you get far from concrete, three-dimensional reality. Scotland would be a better place if we had more realists like the Highland Lady from Rothiemurchus and the Forres curator to do the independent detective work of digging out clues on our earthly sojourn and putting them together.

Here and there in Scotland I have found areas that are particularly luminous, like Arcady in Greece, that open up vistas of rural peace and happiness. The railway from Elgin to Keith offers a journey into such an interior, the enclosed, protected valleys, wooded river-basins shining in resplendent sunlight, an old mill, a fine bridge over the Spey, hummocky ground, grassy, Hiawatha country.

Elgin was the western limit of the railway that tied the north-east of Scotland into one region. It is a trim and tidy place. It has dignity, maybe because its ruined cathedral influenced later builders. An acceptable ambition was realized in the Great North of Scotland Railway station at Elgin. The GNSR was a wee railway but they called it 'Great' and built that lordly terminus. I believe it was something more than interest on their investments that shaped their instructions to the architect. They were ignoring the widely accepted idea that saving money is the most important consideration and that any shed would do for the locals. Elgin's GNSR station illustrates the ups and down of the wayward Scottish spirit. Today that fine building has been remaindered. A cheaper building, the station of the former Highland Railway a few score yards to the west, is more economic. In those days the chairman of the GNSR, the laird of Kinmundy, insisted that no Sunday trains would be run by 'the Company'. The Sabbatarians have been replaced by the Economists, Moses by Adam Smith.

All of that is the daytime world of north-east Scotland. If you travel from Inverness to Aberdeen by road in the darkness of a November night, you are in a transformed world, unrecognizably different from the spread and clarity of the landscape presented by solar illumination. The earth illuminations concentrate their spot-lights on selected corners of the stage, totally blacking out the rest. At Inverness a Chinese restaurant is seen to be doing a steady night-business, and street-lights along the Moray Firth and the River Ness are brightly mirrored in the water. It's a significant word, *mirror*. The Latin word *mirari* means *to wonder at*. It's a wonderful thing to see a reflection, especially for the first time. The early spirit of wonder, of novelty, is recaptured when a visitor to Inverness sees all that effulgence of electric light duplicated in the water, two night-lights for the price of one.

On the Nairn road we meet many oncoming cars. At Ardersier powerful lights illuminate a rig under construction, a nightmarish shape. Across the Firth lesser lights pick out Avoch and Fortrose. During the hours of daylight they melt into their hinterland; at night they have clearly defined identities, communities asserting their independence against the kingdom of the dark, pinpointing themselves as clearly as the constellations overhead. In a night jour-ney we realize more forcefully the amount of earth-energy that is prodigally consumed by our desire not to go to bed with the sun but to remain waukrif until the early hours. Wee flecks of light automatically switching on and off like fireflies warn us of a road-obstruction. Bigger lights illuminate the tall green blackboards of roadsigns that smash themselves into our field of vision. The orange glare of the street lights of Forres indicate the continuing activity of the town. Kinloss aerodrome is lit up like a fairground; the pilots are practising night-flights so that they won't be caught napping by the Russians. Eight high red lights mark the Burghead transmitter and warn the Kinloss pilots to keep clear. Traffic lights mark road holdups and town intersections. A world of ingenuity has gone into the pictograms that tell the traveller about a nearby abbey or battleground.

Traffic decreases but there are more people still on the move after dark than I would have expected. More house lights have gone out, the goodman and his wife being in bed, and the few that remain give us a sense of comfort that other human beings are keeping us company in a dark landscape in the watches of the night. Now that the stage is going dark my thoughts move inwards. This onward movement, through a tunnel of woods, across an open space and into a rocky ravine, then through a sleeping village, recalls the monotonous beat and changing harmonies of Sibelius's *Night Ride and Sunrise* in which he recorded his feelings about a journey through the night in Finland. Unbidden, Robert Frost's lines come to my mind,

> The woods are dark and deep
> But I have promises to keep
> And miles to go before I sleep
> And miles to go before I sleep.

On and on and on winds the road, the headlights flooding the biscuit-coloured winter grass of the roadside, growing halfway up the fences. In this light, concentrating on the road and the immediate roadsides, I see the trees as much more individual figures than in the daylight, many of them contorted into gaunt, knobbly-kneed shapes, stark and cold since the frosts pinched the already slight attachment that the leaves had to their parent branches. Here and there a late chip-shop is filling a need, ensuring that its late customers don't have to go supperless to bed.

On a night journey the lowland roads hold as much of the unexpected as a cunningly lit-and-obscured stage. But in daytime I always feel it as a come-down to emerge from the poetry of the hills into the prose of the more profitable farmlands. It is indistinctly round about the town of Keith that I feel I am back to aul claes an porritch. The town itself is pleasant. It has unexpectedly broad streets, for which it is indebted to the foresight of its eighteenth-century Earl of Fife lairds. It has a makeshift railway station which looks as if it had been rigged up as a temporary shelter by people who were here for a day and a denner and tomorrow expected to move to richer pickings elsewhere. On an August Sunday afternoon two combines are prairie-harvesting the oats and barley, mining the good earth. But there's always the bogland, here since the Ice Age, and the barley skirts it in a curve. The old bluebells of Scotland maintain their hold, like the Celtic people during the Roman and Anglo-Saxon invasions, in the places that the tillers don't want.

A railway carriage gives the traveller a privileged view of the countryside, back-gardens and all, and a wider view since he is higher off the ground than in a motor car. To sit with a cup of coffee or a glass of whisky and see the north-east lowlands of Scotland flash past and the changes that time has wrought on the face of the landscape, is not this happiness? A white kirk has been converted to a house. (Scottish evangelicals, who have their own usage of the word *conversion*, would demur at its use in that sense.) Everything is in a process of change. A young, attractive, trade union secretary is translating shorthand notes direct into a tape-recorder without the intervention of alphabetical writing. We rattle through country stations that the train used to stop at, but we manage to see that the drinking fountain is still there at Wardhouse station. It wasn't worth anybody's while to take it away. Wardhouse? It was really Wardes (two syllables) but the name was anglicized. The colonizers made us feel that our speech was uncouth like an unwashed face or a garden overgrown with weeds. Kineddart on the Macduff line was changed into King Edward and the fishing village of Fittie became Footdee. I think it is worth while stoking up the recalcitrance of our teenagers by pointing out to them the ridiculous devices by which our misguided elders sought to teach us to think and speak proper. *Fittie* is a Gaelic word meaning marsh; *fit* is the Aberdeenshire word for *foot*; the ancient fishing village of Fittie lies at the mouth of the River Dee; therefore the cultural colonizers changed it to Footdee. It was a desperate effort at derivation; nobody ever talked about the *foot* of the Dee.

We rattle through railway stations with a Pictish name like Pitcaple or a Gaelic name like Inveramsay. The Macduff line, for which Inveramsay was the junction, is closed. We still stop at Inverurie which James IV used to visit for a day's sport with his falconers. The best-kept station of the north-east, Kinaldie, is weeds and piles of sand. Dyce, the railway station beside the airport, has lupins growing on its platform. And with that we are back in the welter and sprawl of the city of Aberdeen.

CHAPTER SIXTEEN

Scotland Turned Upside-down

There exists a fundamental human urge to make
sense of the world and bring it under deliberate
control. MARGARET DONALDSON, *Children's Minds*

On the completion of this circuit of Scotland, like Crusoe after
reconnoitring his island, I sit down to take stock and draft a report.
What follows is an attempt to integrate the details, to read them
into the continuity of world history, the plot that gives some intelligibility to the drama, and finally to rough in the role that the majority of us Scots could choose to play in the development of our story.

In our early-twentieth-century Aberdeenshire parish we were
presented with western civilization as a many-splendoured multinational, its national headquarters magnificently housed in private
estates. As we grew up we were afforded glimpses of the soaring
architecture of the Loire châteaux, the ogives and corbelling (words
that we had always to look up in the dictionary) of magnificent
churches, its brocades, the Titian pictures, the cardinals and
madonnas and Dutch merchants, its heroic literature and its
heroes, Roland and the Black Prince, its chroniclers Froissart and
Petrarch and Boccaccio. Arts education in Scotland was an induc-
tion into its worship. The honorary directors of the firm were Soc-
rates, Jesus Christ, Michelangelo, Shakespeare and Beethoven. A
figurehead called God was its president. It propagated its wares all
over the world; in the west it controlled everything. We trusted
them implicitly as we trusted the local doctor who looked after our
health. No need for us to trouble about these complex things.
Underneath were the everlasting arms, the firm's support system.
In Scotland the firm was accorded almost total acceptance; in it
we lived and moved and had our being. The rarity of dissidence
emphasized the power and glory of the system.

Even the slaughter in the First World War created no great visible stirrings. Plowtering through muddy fields at home, often soaked as they turned over the furrow, the farm-servants were inured to the mud and suffering of the trenches. The terror was accepted with dour passivity. If they ever heard of the English upper-class anti-war poetry, the Gordon Highlanders would have regarded it as fist-shaking at a volcano, another 'act of God'. Glasgow teetered on the edge of revolution but we didn't know anything about that either. Our lives were permeated by the current ideas and attitudes. (But who can say what most people were really thinking? Only a minority of people were regular attenders at the kirk. Maybe Scotland was never really Christianized.)

Petrol engines, telephones and cream separators didn't alter the immemorial rhythm of seedtime and harvest. Life went on at two main levels; there were the people labouring in the fields and there was the warrior class directing them. Every glen and strath (or so it appeared to me) had its Lieut Col dominating the community as hon president of the ploughing association and the village hall, director of the bank and the railway and the daily newspaper, representing our interests in local councils and in parliament, selecting kirk ministers and school teachers and donating a Christmas tree to the Sunday school. Between the wars some of the officers, become MPs, retained their military designations; but no MP referred to himself as Sergeant Smith.

The 1939–45 war brought a clarifying of ideas, and an expansion of knowledge. After initial disadvantage, the postman understood the Theory of Flight as well as the university graduate, and the clerk asked basic, concrete questions about a cold front that made the met. officer scratch his head. The war presented to us the contrasting experiences that made us look again at our own, stirring us into new awarenesses. Soldiers' minds were fertilized with ideas that had their origin in the ends of the earth. In South Africa I was trained as an RAF navigator. One night returning by a short cut through a deep valley to the Air Force station at Grahamstown, I overtook a black worker employed at the station who was slightly drunk and singing snatches of songs. We walked together, he sometimes talking and sometimes breaking into song. Then, suddenly sober, he said in a deep voice, 'I am a Zulu. Once I believed

A Search for Scotland

that Jesus would make everything all right. I believe it no longer.'

Equipped with wider experience, clearer understanding and a new confidence, we returned to civilian life. Radio and then television scattered the seeds of ideas widely, as printing had done in Europe five hundred years earlier. In the mid-century an optimist, plotting the course of people's thinking, would have forecast a quickening of life throughout the western world and especially in Britain. In a surge of optimism we delegated Labour to take the initiative, and a spirit of good-natured reform was abroad. There would be better health, better housing, more incisive enquiry. We thought we were standing on the top of golden days, gazing on a prospect of liberty, equality and fraternity. And then over two decades we perceived that we had dreamed a dream.

It wasn't until the last part of the century that the deluge came, pounding through the valleys like a Cairngorm river in heavy spate. Judges were seen to have made mistakes more often than we had guessed. A Scottish earl promised Scotland that his party would enact a bill to give devolution to Scotland, and then forgot about his promise. When Hugh Greene presented him with the scripts of a series on Suez ten years after, saying, 'The truth will presumably come out one day,' Lord Normanbrook, chairman of the BBC replied, 'Damned good care has been taken to see that the truth never will come out.' A civil servant was sent to see a psychiatrist because she expressed doubts about the methods employed by MI5. A cabinet minister spoke of 'the grovel count' of his colleagues. Academics crumpled before the government's attacks on their values. Oxfam produced proof of the shady dealings of the pharmaceutical companies in Third World countries. An American expert on air accidents said on the BBC (1/6/87) that 'If it's cheaper to kill people than to fix it, it's likely that people will die.' Anabolic steroids are consumed not only by international athletes but also by middle-rating athletes because of the consuming and all important desire to win at all costs (although they know the damage the steroids do to them). A London editor sacked a photographer who returned without pictures of a riot, having stopped to help a man who had been cracked on the head. Forty per cent of North Sea fish have been poisoned by chemical discharges. Old people died from the cold and niggardly grants were made to help against extreme cold. There were queues for hospital beds and patients died who might have been saved. Scientific research was being run down and scientists were emigrating. Hospitals were being run down and doctors and nurses were emigrating.

Ecological disasters were perturbing humanity. Rain forests were wiped out, the Sahara was extending, droughts became more frequent, Canadian lakes and German forests died, industrial and nuclear pollution increased, fish, sheep, reindeer and people were poisoned. Our food was doctored. Little was done about the leaded petrol that was attacking the intelligence of the young. A thunder of alarms reverberated in our ears. Reagan followed in the Nixon tradition. In the Stock Exchange and Lloyd's of London and Guinness the walls of integrity came tumbling down. The Theatre and Sport brazened out their dependence on their beer and tobacco patrons. The Commonwealth Games at Edinburgh came to us by courtesy of Guinness. World athlete and teetotaller Daley Thompson wasn't allowed to compete unless he advertised beer on his jersey. The Wimbledon tennis-players were demeaned by the gaudy advertisements they flaunted on their clothes. The Olympic spirit had travelled a long way since its *Chariots of Fire* decade. Eric Liddell, Scottish athlete who came to talk to us at Gordon's College in Aberdeen in the 1920s, belonged to an outmoded world.

Governments were unabashed when they were caught out telling lies. London was Babylon and the writing was on its Palace of Westminster walls. Obscurantism was creeping back like a fog into education and religion. The USA stopped some of its students from learning about Darwin and evolution. The Pope revived ancient references to the Devil as a rebelling angel, a serpent, a dragon and a goat. That he was quoting from the gospels didn't make his speech less reactionary. Hundreds of Americans gathered every sunset to view what they believed to be an image of Jesus Christ on the side of a soya-bean storage tank in Ohio. 'Ohio needs a miracle,' somebody explained. Throughout western civilization religious priests, rational in other communications, defended the belief that Jesus 'descended into hell' and that there is cleansing power in the blood of the Lamb.

Mountains of food and lakes of milk accumulated. The earth itself is sick. The supply of oxygen, our breath of life, is decreasing.

Nuclear bombs proliferate like cancer cells. Politicians regard economic wealth as the only wealth and exclude non-economic values from their decision-making. Our politics is untroubled by awareness of an ecological crisis.

One of the corollaries of élite rule, unmodified by old values, is the ruthless mining of the earth for the purpose of gaining consumer satisfactions. After the scientific revolution of the seventeenth century, the earth came to be regarded no longer as Mother Earth, but as a commodity to be exploited, squeezed to produce teeming harvests more than it could naturally sustain or its colonists consume. The majority of us listening nightly to some new twist in their tortuous story were being pushed into farther-reaching questions. Axioms of western civilization were coming under the microscope. There was that comely Greek doctrine of the mean, the middle way, the Rule of St Basil who was father of the orders of the Eastern Church. This was how he said a monk should behave.

> The middle tone of voice is best, neither so low as to be inaudible, nor ill-bred from its high pitch. He should be amiable in social discourse, cultivating gentleness in kind admonitions. Harshness is ever to be put aside, even in censuring.

His influence continued in Scotland right up to the early days of the twentieth century. I was brought up to believe in wise counsellors, amiable in social discourse, calmly adjudicating in our affairs and reaching just conclusions. Up until about 1970 I could persuade myself that there might be something in this gospel, the trust that deep down there is an essential goodness in those placed in authority over us. But the evidence of the political efficacy of St Basil was wearing thin. Maybe it had seldom been all that efficacious. The church-going Chartists believed that the decorum with which they conducted a mass-meeting at Paisley would strike terror into the hearts of their enemies. In *A Century of the Scottish People*, Professor Smout commented, 'Under these circumstances the workers posed much less of a threat to the ruling order.'

Other axioms of western civilization were coming under scrutiny. Our *literature*, for example. We had been brought up to regard it as a basic record of human aspiration. But writers, like other artists, were dependent on the patronage of the upper classes. Robert Burns had to go cap in hand to the great lords and had to watch his step. In a book entitled *Life in Nineteenth-century Grub Street*, Nigel Cross said that 'the writing, production and reading of books was a middle-class monopoly'. You were handicapped unless you had education, social status and monied leisure. With the monopoly went the doctrine that literature is 'above' Politics. Many writers distanced themselves from political participation, but a Nigerian writer, Ben Okri, said, 'Literature that is apolitical is to me incomprehensible.' The Medici conception of a kept culture is under scrutiny.

We had been brought up in the belief that power was the proper goal of all Caesars, Kaisers and Czars because power, like gravity, was a law of the universe. Their natural role was to extend their power and centralize its administration in a grand metropolis. The Dark Ages (we were led to believe) were dark because they suffered from lack of centralization. We're putting all of that age-old orthodoxy under the microscope. How did we get caught up in this obsession with power and powerful men (more rarely, women)? Does the exercise of power give an extra zip to life, like the consuming of whisky, and is it not possible to live a full life without it? And were the Dark Ages all that dark? In *Creating Alternative Futures*, Hazel Henderson says that the people of the Dark Ages devised labour-saving equipment, a better plough and harness, better windmills and watermills, introduced rotation of crops and respected manual labour.

An upbringing based on the belief that the pursuit of power is natural and admirable led writers, frequently acting as public relations officers for the kings, to fill their books with battles. The *Iliad*, I was told, was one of the world's Great Books. I read it twice, willing to be impressed but I emerged puzzled. It's a story about Greek thugs, a death book. The heroes we are to admire are those who kill most people. To this day the blood-lust is never for long absent from the media. In the USA it is estimated that young people will have seen 18,000 murders on television by the time they are sixteen. The aristocratic contempt for the majority of human beings, the brutish soldiers, has continued on parade from the plains of Troy to the playing-fields of Eton. From school history and literature I learned that the folk I belonged to were of little account, sacrificial pawns in the noble chess-game. They have been tortured, diddled, bribed, laying down their lives for causes not their own, lauded for being docile, execrated as 'the mob' when briefly they rebelled. The main medium through which the ideas of a master-class have been lodged in the minds of Scottish children is the school.

In Scottish schools there is a premium on 'leadership qualities' which is probably a spin-off from the pursuit of power. Because we ourselves have been brought up to be power-hungry, we put pressure on the young to seek control over others. Allied to 'leadership qualities' is the esteem given to toughness. If people enjoy climbing the ice-slopes of Bidean in January, that is fine. But if they are driven to endure extremities of cold and fear in order to prove something, the motive is suspect. When we tell the young the derivation of the word *Spartan*, we should describe in detail the sufferings which the Spartans inflicted on their children in order to make them tough, so that when they became soldiers they would be better able to maintain the power of Sparta. In Scotland it was in the rural areas, where there was the greatest incidence of Lieut Cols, that the institution of flogging (long after it was abolished in the army) was most widely continued even in infant schools. Aberdeenshire five-year-olds were told that when they went to school they would 'get their licks', which means that they would be belted with the tawse. A teacher at Insch school told about a youngster who was asked on returning home after his first and second day at school, 'Did ye get your licks?' On the third morning he went up to the teacher and asked, 'When do I get my licks?' The North-American Indians were shocked at the severe whippings which the Puritans inflicted on their own children. Corporal punishment in school, abolished from Europe's schools, continued in Britain, Australia, New Zealand, Canada, South Africa, the USA, Barbados, Kenya, Singapore, Sudan, Swaziland, Trinidad and Tobago. All these were colonized by Britain.

Dismantling a political system's basic ideas, we learn how its parts are interlocked. What we have been taught to regard as axioms, self-evident truths, articulate with one another. The doctrine of power depends on a belief that the majority need an intelligent élite to guide them. The élite spread the axiom that the majority of earth-dwellers are unintelligent and, to justify the assertion, flood the educational system with incomprehensibility. The majority of children, obviously failing to comprehend, are adduced as proof of the majority's limited intelligence. The lesson is 'Leave it to the élite'. If now we investigate what it is in the school work that makes it incomprehensible, we find it coagulated with abstract thinking. It's not a new device. In the Old Testament, Job asked, 'Who is this that darkeneth counsel by words without knowledge?'

Here is an example of how the schoolbooks use words to conceal reality. The BBC produced an excellent film on Culloden. 'This is grapeshot,' said the commentator, indicating a pile of spheres the size of tennis balls. 'And this is what grapeshot does;' the film showed a clansman's hideously mangled leg. Now I'd read about grapeshot many years earlier in a school history-book. When the citizens of Paris rebelled against Napoleon, he cleared the streets (the book said) 'with a whiff of grapeshot'. In so far as I pictured it at all, I imagined it to be a particularly powerful kind of smelling-salts. School history masks the bloody truth. No time to fill in the sickening details as the teacher hurried us on to the further adventures of Napoleon.

Throughout most of the century the schools and universities, by dwelling on generalizations and abstractions, hid from us the realities of war. An incident in my early days in the RAF broke in on my ignorance. Up till then I had been insufficiently on my guard against the spell of the pipes and drums, the trooping of the colour, the spotless white spats of the Gordon Highlanders, the regimental flags hanging romantically tattered in dark corners of cathedrals, the poetry, the medals. One fine day in 1941 we were doing bayonet drill, sticking the bayonet into straw-filled sacks, pulling the bayonet out and advancing against the next row of sacks. The corporal explained that it would be much more difficult to extract a bayonet from an enemy belly. That was because of the suction. You had to kick the bayoneted belly with your left foot and at the same time pull with all your might. That piece of realism had been missing from the dictated answers we memorized to pass the examination in Higher History.

Seventy years after the battle, I visited Verdun and was shocked at the tortured moon-landscape now grassed over and treed, and at the extent of countryside covered with white crosses. A white-haired woman of Alsace, on a bus trip from Metz, was devastated and came across to give utterance to the words that were choking her. 'How can we believe in God when he allows this to happen?' And then, as if taken aback at her own outburst, she said, 'But if we don't believe in him, what hope have we?' She paused and continued, 'I have two grandchildren, both of them very good musicians. But what hope is there for them?' It was the concrete detail that stabbed the woman from Metz and us from Aberdeen into shock, the myriad names and crosses, the moraine-like heaps unsmoothed by time, the concrete pill-boxes cunningly positioned to cover flanking movements, the empty space where a village had been blasted off the face of the earth, the points of bayonets and the barrels of rifles still protruding from the top of a filled-in trench in which soldiers had been buried as they stood, grasping their rifles. The failure to communicate to our young the reality of war (as of so much else in our civilization) is a deliberate failure on the part of educators. They have cleaned up the wounds, wiped away the blood and spilled guts, pulled a drape over the awful suffering and the terror, sanitizing it all, turning it into abstract, uncomprehended words.

That was one of the faults in our society that the political optimists of 1945 didn't take into account, the incomprehension that clouded much of the history lessons and political essays. It wasn't real. Neither was the culture disseminated by the academics. It had little to do with our lives. We were invited to regard culture as the great park of a noble lord which we were graciously permitted to stroll through and admire. In his play on Hitler, Steiner asked if all this high-minded culture might not come between us and reality, preventing us from hearing the cry for help in the streets.

It is time to recap this sketch of what we Scots were thinking during the twentieth century. We started off accepting our rulers who said, 'Leave it to us. We know where we're going.' The 1939–45 war caused a broadcasting of ideas, a fertilizing of questions. That brought Labour to power in a spirit of optimism and goodwill. Slowly disillusion grew. Then suddenly we began to be bombarded with reports of pollution, political corruption, manipulation, regression. The trust in a caring minority weakened. Questions, once activated, proliferated into doubts about the axioms on which western civilization had been believed to take its stand, doubts about culture and the role of literature, power-hunger, the function of the schools, the arbitrary division of the young into 'academic' and 'non-academic', the deliberate wrapping up of education in obscure, abstract words.

That brings us up to the end of the eighties. Where do we Scots go from here?

CHAPTER SEVENTEEN

The Pedigree of the Scottish God

I would thou wert cold or hot.   The Revelation

A record of what the Scots were thinking this century should try to trace where our convictions and prejudices and hopes and fears come from, through what wild centuries rove back our creeds. To some extent we have to disencumber ourselves of the legacy we have inherited. In her book, *When Things of the Spirit Come First*, (*Quand Prime le Spirituel*) Simone de Beauvoir (born 1908) said that the young aren't confronted merely with the toil of learning what life is like; they have painfully to unlearn a blueprint for life which has initially set them on the wrong track. She described in Europe 'the vast, soft, tough octopus of Catholicism institutionalized and secularized into the bourgeois ethic of a whole race'. Presbyterianism held me in its tentacles long after I had left the kirk. How do we free ourselves from some of the more oppressive effects of a Scottish religious upbringing? We have to understand our own past, not the chronological events only but the ideas and feelings from our lurid, dowie, nightmarish, bloodshot, fitful, sordid and occasionally resplendent history, that haunt and control us, the ideas trickled deep into our subconscious when we weren't looking.

Our teenagers would enter with gusto into the exploration of what H. G. Wells called 'the vagueness, the monstrosity and the incoherent variety of the first gods' in the shape of hawks and hippopotamuses and cows, pieces of meteorite, strangely shaped lumps of rock. There were hang-ups on self-mutilation, circumcision, tattooing, magic murder to placate the gods, the killing of a loved one under some terrible psychological compulsion. There is an unconscionable amount of residual magic in western civiliza-

248

tion. Ancients and moderns share the worship of sacred stones. The English carried off the Stone of Destiny from Scone and lodged it in their temple at Westminster. In a daring manoeuvre it was repossessed by Scottish Nationalists in the middle of this century and laid in the ruins of Arbroath Abbey where the Declaration of Independence had been made. It was repossessed and conveyed to the vaults of Westminster. The English rulers were re-enacting the ancient belief that conquest was finalized when the image of the god of the conquered people was carried away and lodged in the temple of the conquerors. Our ideas are at a more primitive stage of evolution than we were led to believe.

That's a territory that we should be helping the young to explore, explaining where our beliefs had their origin. In the same way as the Canaanites in the Bible (the Arabs) smelted and moulded their gods from gold, silver, wood, hammered brass and nails, the prophets of Judah (says Dan Jacobson) manufactured their gods out of words. They invested the word *Jehovah* with magic. Of all the boring books imposed on Scottish youth, the Bible is the most boring. But it needn't be so. Punks whose unconscious promptings issue in exotic hair styles are pre-disposed to enter imaginatively into such a hallucinatory book. If scholars would recreate for them, preferably in films, the horrors of what went on in the sacred groves, the sickening ostentation of Babylon, the simple village life, the crises when they had to reconsider how they should be spending their allocation of years on the earth, then the young would be fascinated. And particularly by some of the sayings. Be still. Let not your heart be troubled. Take no thought for the morrow. Lay not up for yourself treasure. Ye must be born again . . . It describes many a critical juncture in a people's history, like ours, when people felt a need to alter their perception of reality.

After that I'd like to tell the young about the weird story of how some tribes, nearer our own day, interpreted the Bible story in a manner congenial to themselves and appropriated its ideas to support their own policies. The Children of Israel were a small tribe fighting for survival against more powerful neighbours, the Philistines (Arabs). The Scots, the New England colonists and the South African Boers were small tribes fighting against strong, sometimes overwhelming, enemies, the English, the North American Indians, and the Xhosas and Zulus. These small, threatened groups identified with the Children of Israel and made the Jewish holy book their own.

A holy book can be used to still the promptings of your own nature and gives you carte blanche to commit atrocities. Armed with the scriptural injunction, 'Thou shalt not suffer a witch to live', the Scottish and New England zealots set fire to human beings. As Miller's play, *The Crucible*, showed, the good folk of Salem went crackers on witchcraft. I can feel how a tribe like the Scots, when minister-dominated, could be caught up into a community hysteria. At an evangelists' service for children in an Aberdeenshire village hall at the age of eight I stood up and publicly acknowledged the Lord Jesus Christ as my Saviour. I was born again. That enthusiasm (which by derivation means possessed by a *theos*, a god) was the same kind of hysteria as possessed Salem (Jerusalem) in Massachusetts.

For us Scots, suckled on the Jewish Bible like the New England colonists and the Boers, like them seeing our national destiny as a pilgrimage through the wilderness, a battle with the heathen, which would lead to occupation of the Promised Land (for us Scots none the less potent for being metaphorical, the New Jerusalem) to read their story is like following the career of your twin who has emigrated. It's like looking at a mirror image, recognizable but in part distorted. In the Dutch Reformed Kerk at Laingsburg in the Cape I felt at home. We also put on our best clothes which we called always our 'Sunday clothes' to go to the kerk, which was pronounced in the same way as they do. The Laingsburg Kerk has beautiful pews of imported oak. It is a decent, dignified building, spotlessly clean, sunny, simple after the style of opulent Quakers. The Predicant is head of the local community, he has a free house, free hens and vegetables, sits on committees, exacts tithes and controls the neighbourhood. It is a community of god-fearing people like the Aberdeenshire of my early days. I was steeped in the same culture, its usages and beliefs. I would have felt far more at home in a Dutch Reformed Church in the Cape than in an Episcopalian church in Aberdeenshire whose Anglican rituals were alien to us. The idiom of the Old Testament was intimately intertwined in their daily speech as in ours. Like theirs, our perception of reality was that which was filtered down to them through the medium of the Bible. A century ago David Livingstone felt at home in a community of Boer farmers in the North Transvaal, or nearly at home. In the Boer War, fighting at Aliwal North in the Cape, Dingwall crofter's son, Major-General Sir Hector Macdonald, said what a pity it was that they should take up arms against such a godly people.

Outside the Laingsburg Kerk a foundation stone is inscribed 'JEHOVAH-Nissi Exodus 17, 15b'. JEHOVA-Nissi means the Lord my banner. The *Exodus* context is a battle in which 'Joshua discomfited Amalek and his people with the edge of the sword'. The verse referred to on the foundation stone and the following verse say

> And Moses built an altar, and called the name of it
> JEHOVA-Nissi;
> For he said, Because the Lord hath sworn that the LORD
> will have war with Amalek from generation to
> generation.

Scottish national poet Robert Burns was as familiar with the story as the Boer farmers were. In *A Cotter's Saturday Night* the big family-Bible is taken out and

> The priest-like father reads the sacred page,
> How Abram was the friend of God on high.
> Or Moses bade eternal warfare wage
> With Amalek's ungracious progeny.

The twinship ties had been closer than I expected.

The Voortrekkers, fleeing oppression in the Cape, used the Bible as a manual for their pilgrimage, a King's Regulations for their campaign. Few religious tribes in the history of the world can have obeyed holy books which so closely reproduced their own experience. The English in the Cape were like the Egyptians, rich, arrogant, irreligious oppressors. The native Kaffirs were hostile like Amalek; the journey was through a wilderness. The Voortrekkers, a Chosen People like the Children of Israel, shared the troubles recounted in the Book of Exodus – shortages of food and water, skirmishes and pitched battles against the local inhabitants, loss of heart, murmurings and signs of revolt against the expedition's leaders. The Voortrekkers would not have found it extraordinary that the desert that the Israelites' pilgrimage took them through bore the name, 'The Wilderness of Sin'. The mirror reflection of their daily experience confirmed and reinforced in them the faith that they walked with destiny, the Lord's Elect, like the Scottish Covenanters and the Pilgrim Fathers.

Like the area of Rephidim near Mount Sinai where the battle with Amalek took place, the area round Laingsburg was fought over. The descendants of the Voortrekkers who made the exodus from bondage to seek a Promised Land were vividly aware how closely their history followed the history of the Jews making the exodus from Egypt. I found myself in tune with the Boers' Voortrekker Memorial outside Pretoria. It's like a laager, the main building protected by a circle of outspanned ox-waggons. Inside are murals of the Great Trek. A circle in the roof lets the midday sun shine on a sarcophagus below the floor. At midday on 16 December, the date of the Battle of Blood River in 1838, the ray of light strikes on an inscription. In the lower half of the building a perpetual flame burns to symbolize the light of civilization, white civilization. The nearby museum fortifies the imaginative impression and the intended political indoctrination with details of life in a canvas-covered ox-waggon.

Each waggon contained a Bible, a baby's bottle of narrow, cylindrical glass, saddles, thongs, tools to make the felloes of waggon wheels, cooking pots, home-made clothes and home-made shoes, the basket that swung below the waggon. There are pictures of parting scenes, of the use of a raft to float a waggon across the Orange River, a letter from a young man urging his parents to join the trek. Like the Americans in their covered waggons, they developed confidence in their skills to defend themselves and to improvise, and, I expect, in their skill in creating a self-governing community. And their descendants who built the memorial were, I am sure, aware of the injunction of Moses in that Exodus passage, 'Write this for a memorial in a book, and rehearse it . . .'

They were re-living Biblical history. Like the Jews in the Sinai Desert, they made hard bargains with their god, which they called covenants. The Scottish Covenanters, searching the Scriptures, were sustained by the same metaphor of life. When the

Voortrekkers came to a place in the Orange Free State where they got supplies of wheat, they called it Bethlehem, knowing that Bethlehem means 'the place of bread'. The same detailed Biblical knowledge is found to this day in Aberdeenshire. A favourite name for a fishing boat is The Fruitful Bough. The reference is to Genesis 49, 22. Joseph was a fruitful bough because his roots were in the water.

Down the hill from the Memorial, in Pretoria, Paul Kruger's house, now a museum also, has evidence showing how close he, a Bible fundamentalist, was to the spirit of *A Cotter's Saturday Night*. The statues of the members of Kruger's cabinet in the station square in Pretoria have the bearded, patriarchal, righteous, god-fearing appearance of an Aberdeenshire school board at the beginning of the century. Their clothes are the same. The elders that we were schooled to look up to were dour, forbidding, reproving, tholing, Sabbatarian, shunning sex. Boer speech sounded guttural like farm speech in Buchan and some of the words, like breeks for trousers, were the same. The metropolitan Dutch regarded their speech as uncouth, just as the English regarded ours. The Boers and we Scots disliked the posh speech and fine manners of the English upper class. Like the Children of Israel, the Covenanters and Pilgrim Fathers and Boers were oppressed minorities and therefore they responded to the promise that the Old Testament god made to his Chosen People, 'I have broken the bands of your yoke, and made you go upright.' The promise helped them to cling to their faith and cultural identity and stand out against the compromisers whom St John and the Scottish Covenanters exercrated as 'the Laodiceans'. I can visualize a Boer farm-kitchen reading from the Revelation of St John the Divine as clearly as I can visualize the same reading in an Ayrshire cotter house or the ante-room of an Aberdeenshire village hall. The members of the church in Laodicea, one of the seven primitive Christian churches in Asia, were backsliders and St John was commanded to write to them:

> I know thy works, that thou art neither cold nor hot: I
>   would thou wert cold or hot.
> So then because thou art lukewarm, and neither cold nor
>   hot, I will spue thee out of my mouth.
> I counsel thee to . . . anoint thine eyes with eye-salve,
>   that thou mayest see . . .

> To him that overcometh will I grant to sit with me in my
> throne, even as I also overcame, and am set down with
> my Father in his throne.
> He that hath an ear, let him hear what the Spirit saith
> unto the churches.

The nearest we can get at the end of the twentieth century to entering into the spirit of those heady words is to hear them thundered with total conviction from a Belfast pulpit by the Rev. Ian Paisley. In Northern Ireland they reverberate with their ancient force. In a Transvaal farm-kitchen these words would be followed by a prayer and a benediction, and the Boer family would go to bed sustained in their resolution to stand firm for their faith, its message and its idiom incorporated into their being, a gospel for the conduct of life. But a century later the children of the Voortrekkers are losing their attachment to the gospel. No laager can exclude foreign signals flashing from television aerials seductively presenting the case for Economic Man. Mammon lured many Boers into the affluence and influence of the boardrooms of Johannesburg. The landscape round the Voortrekker Memorial was desecrated by orange manganese smoke belched into the air from their own ISCOR chimney. Having overcome the anglicizing elements in their country, the Boers were relishing industrial power, but still trying to reconcile the practices of multinational capital with the precepts of the Old Testament.

An account of how the Scots were thinking this century can be illuminated by taking note of how our twins, the Boers, were thinking. But only up to a point. After that the paths diverge. We go our separate ways and it is no longer helpful, it no longer sheds light, to compare the stories. It was more difficult for the Scots to escape from anglicizing influences. Ulster respected longer the traditions followed by the Boers, but Scotland, influenced not only by English economics but, ironically, by the freer-thinking English culture, followed a different course. The questions we asked were different. When I went to South Africa I saw life differently from the way a Boer farmer saw it. In the veldt, black labourers were poorly housed at a hygienic distance from the white baas's stoep; in the Aberdeenshire of my childhood the cotter houses, 'potato-pits of houses', were similarly sited. Black 'locations' were like slums in

Glasgow and Edinburgh. Black pupils were segregated from white pupils as in Scotland 'non-academic' from 'academic' pupils. 'They are so stupid, man,' exploded the rulers of South Africa when speaking of the blacks; The Scottish rulers spoke of 'the limited pool of ability'. The history of Scotland that Scottish pupils was taught, star-billing a succession of acquisitive chiefs, was no more the history of Scotland than the adventures of European-born expropriators was the history of Xhosas and Zulus. Both ruling minorities talked about *scroungers* amongst the majority.

I talked to a senior class in an English public school about the disadvantages encountered by working-class schools in Scotland. In Fife we had had to sell pupil-made canoes in order to buy a tyre for the school bus. I asked them if they thought it was fair. 'Yes,' answered all of them except one; 'Britain depends on its future rulers and it is important that we should have educational advantages so that we can be educated to be good rulers.' They were in the tradition of the seventeenth century Earl of Clarendon who said that 'It is the privilege of the common people of England to be represented by the greatest and learnedest and wealthiest and wisest persons that can be chosen out of the nation.' He said that people in 'great towns and corporations' had a 'natural malignity'. 'The common people in all places' showed 'barbarity and rage against the nobility and gentry'. The MPs opposed to the Royalists, the Parliamentarians, were 'dirty people of no name'. He said that in the long run the economic power of 'the natural rulers' would prevail. But these were the tones in which Robert Burns had spoken of the Philistines, the Palestinians, whom the Children of Israel had dispossessed. 'Amalek's ungracious progeny'. Two centuries after Burns, we Scots were asking questions different from those he asked. Unlike him, we weren't accepting the Bible's opinion on Amalek.

The best text I know for bringing home to pupils of a Scottish school the lesson on Amalek comes from a school in Soweto. Eight years ago in Johannesburg a Soweto headmaster told me the story. A black teacher was teaching a lesson on citizenship, and a white inspector was sitting at the back of the classroom. A black pupil asked, 'Sir, am I a citizen of this country?' The black teacher answered with care. 'You have heard what was said about the rights of citizenship and the duties of citizenship. I must leave it to you to decide the answer to your question.'

Before then, most black parents in Soweto, like ambitious working-class parents in Scotland, were eager that their children should 'better themselves' and do the lessons and pass the examinations. It's different now. They've lost faith in the schools. They have discovered that the master race uses the schools to discipline its work force without conferring on them the dignity of citizenship.

The same idea is beginning to dawn on the minds of some Scottish pupils. Apartheid is clear in South Africa because it is a matter of black and white. In Scotland it is masked, white and white; but it is apartheid just the same, the privileged rulers and the majority who work for them. After all those years in Scottish education, it is only now that I have become aware that the schools are not on our side. They are the agencies of the rulers. They bring us up to do what we are told, and not to speak back, to learn our lessons and pass the examinations. Above all not to ask questions. Another surmise like a new planet swims into our ken. Is that our appointed role in history, playing the part of Amalek?

CHAPTER EIGHTEEN

The Conclusion of the Whole Matter

On what we do now will depend the future of the
earth, for thousands or even millions of years.
PROFESSOR EHRLICH (1987)

I started out on the search for Scotland with the encouragement of
the traveller Freya Stark in my mind. 'There are too few people in
our age who choose to use their own wits in an honest endeavour
and, with the facts in a tangle before them, sort them into a pattern
of their own.' This final chapter is an attempt to make some sort of
pattern out of the tangle.

At the end of the second Christian millennium Scotland is at an
eerie, apathetic stage in its history, maybe like the immobility of the
water at the turning of the tide. One dispensation is losing its force
and the other has not started into motion. We have come up
against the bankruptcy of capitalism and materialism, its lack of
resources to satisfy our end-of-century needs.

Capitalism made an immense contribution to the development
of Scotland. In Aberdeenshire, resourceful but responsible railway
entrepreneurs transported lime to neutralize an acid soil, leather,
flour, horseshoe nails, letters and world news to enrich local life,
and carried cattle to the Aberdeen and southern markets. It eased
and embellished life for my forebears by sharing the product of
the ingenuity of people otherwise far outwith their ken, binding
the community together in a larger partnership. I thought that the
system and its rail roads would last for ever. And then as the
branch lines, and even main lines, began to close, we wondered
what was happening to our way of life. 'Our little systems have their
day, they have their day and cease to be.' Capitalism was passing
its peak, becoming a little desperate, somewhat unscrupulous. The

257

entrepreneurs, under the pressure of their own system, became less responsible and made concessions on their values. They mined the earth and looted the sea in the singleminded pursuit of profits. They grew more and more insensitive. In some regions of western civilization the effects were extreme. As long as Christianity was a power, its teachings tempered the claims of the controlling group. But in the last century of the second millennium AD, Christianity was losing its hold and its values were being abandoned. In his *Ecrits Corsaires* (1975), Pasolini said that 'the abandoning of old values was the humus in which Nazism grew'.

In Scotland at the end of the century, the eclipse of capitalism's power to cope with our accumulating distresses was like the fading out of the light at the close of a midsummer day, so gradual that until it was nearly dark we hardly noticed it. In his *Study of History*, Toynbee said that when the going gets tough for a civilization, and the ruling minority is seen to be failing to cope with gathering problems, a new *religion* rises out of its proletariat. It was in the twilight of the Roman civilization that Christianity emerged and spread. Maybe a similar surge is going to issue from the feelings and thought of the Scottish proletariat. 'But such a tide as, moving, seems asleep, Too full for sound and foam.' Aberdeenshire country and city people feel that there is 'a vrangness' (a wrongness) in things. Life shouldn't be like that. We weren't born to cheat and be cheated, to be worried, to be unemployed, to be powerless to make changes in our society, to be catalogued in a computer, to be mugged by youngsters who are themselves drugged, to be alienated from our children, to be absorbed in the accumulating of material goods, to join a long queue for a hospital bed, to be stampeded down a steep place into extermination.

But none of the major religious or political gospels on offer in Scotland measures up to these deep needs and longings. Labour, for example, has been weighed in the balance and found wanting. This despite the votes it gathered in the General Election of 1987. These were unenthusiastic votes delivered without great hope. When the bright hopes of Labour's 1945 government slowly dimmed there was (as Browning said in his poem about the Lost Leader, Wordsworth) doubt, hesitation and pain. Burns, Shelley, were with us, they watched from their graves. We in Scotland had been especially caught up in the dream. We were in on its begetting.

One reason that Labour sank into the twilight was that it got stuck with consumerism. Its realistic policymakers insisted that it is hope of material gain that makes people put their marks in the Labour square in the ballot paper, and that it is enough if they buoy up their supporters with the hope of a new order of society this year, next year, sometime. Under Labour the majority of us would be materially better off but Scotland wouldn't be radically different. Labour cancelled its journey to the Celestial City, preferring to tidy up the City of Destruction and make it more habitable.

Two Scots personified the initial vision and the modified version. The difference between two Highlanders, John Maclean and Ramsay MacDonald, goes deep into our psychological make-up. In the Covenanter tradition, Maclean had a craggy independence of personality which couldn't be corroded by the need to placate friends just as he was proof against the suffering inflicted by enemies (except for the extreme suffering in Peterhead prison). I encountered this unbendable quality in our home in Aberdeenshire. I felt uncomfortable when my father disagreed with the friendliest of neighbours, maintaining what felt to me an uncomfortable integrity. He had a vision of inner truth to which he was totally loyal, even if its expression hurt a friend's feelings. I, however, longed for accord, protection, friendship, reassurance. It was part of a north-east upbringing. We were brought up to be 'respectable', doing the right things, not being uncouth in any way, throwing under a cushion the socks that were drying at the kitchen fire when somebody knocked at the door. I wouldn't have admitted that we slept four to a room and that we had a dry privy at a corner of the garden. We maintained the façade that was considered respectable. I felt vulnerable, dependent on the good opinion of neighbours. We had a reluctant admiration for the local aristocrats who could afford the luxury of relaxing and being themselves, untroubled by the need to court the good opinion of the neighbourhood. In the middle of an address to a Women's Rural Institute meeting, a Scottish baroness felt her bra coming loose. Without fuss or concealment she pulled it up inch by inch, continuing nonchalantly with her talk the while, and put it into her handbag. I envied her her indifference to the village's opinion. In the freedom from fear that Euripides set up as a major aim for humanity, we have to include the freedom from fear of others' opinions.

I understand how a north-east man, Ramsay MacDonald from Lossiemouth, ultimately failed because he shivered at the prospect of standing alone, of seeming to be churlish or uncouth. Scottish Labour MPs at Westminster succumbed not to hostility but to friendliness. They were in the tradition of the Laodiceans who angered the Covenanters. They played the role of 'good House of Commons men', compromising when they should have opposed. They were unwilling to stand up to the money men and equally unwilling to let the majority in on the problems which they themselves had so signally failed to solve. As in the USSR after 1925, the new tribunes of the people had become merely a variation on the old governing minority. They at first permitted and ultimately relished honours and pomp and ceremony. George V said that he would be happy to have the members of the first Labour Cabinet presented to him wearing dark suits, but Ramsay MacDonald insisted on full-dress uniform. Sixty years later a Labour ex-Prime Minister, James Callaghan, said that he was 'overjoyed' at the prospect of becoming a Knight of the Most Noble Order of the Garter. We wouldn't have expected that strapping on a king's garter, even symbolically, was a proper ambition for a democrat. The Labour Party is still living in the shadow of Ramsay MacDonald's knee-breeches.

The Party was acculturalized to capitalism, its models of art and literature and education, its examinations, its life style and accents. In his book *Ecrits Corsaires* (1975), Pasolini reported on the same phenomenon in Italy. The left in power, he said, seeks development on the lines of bourgeois industrialization, it assimilates to the mode and quality of life of the bourgeoisie.

In 1972 Paulo Freire diagnosed the pressures that were influencing left-wing politicians. The left, he said, tempted by a quick return to power, strays into 'an impossible *dialogue* with the dominant élites. It ends by being manipulated by these élites, and not infrequently itself falls into an élitist game, which it calls "realism"'. The populist leader is inoculated by the dominant group with the bourgeois appetite for personal success. He becomes an *amphibian*; 'shuttling back and forth between the people and the dominant oligarchies, he bears the marks of both groups.' An American writer supplemented Freire's diagnosis. 'The labor movement was created by people at the bottom, by the courage and idealism of working men and women; once established, it made itself an élite governed by an élite.'

Self-interest and material comfort play a larger part in the lives of most of us than we confess to. No minority can for long be trusted to submerge its private interests in the general good. In this country it has been a slow disintegration, sometimes unnoticed because there were good things, too, to set against the fall from grace. For the most part it was not a dishonourable phase in the evolution of Scotland. It didn't measure up to the faith of Rev. James Barr MP who at a Christmas service in the North Kirk in Aberdeen in the nineteen-twenties told the congregation that a new star had risen in the east, the Labour Party. It could have caused a political reformation comparable to the religious Reformation four centuries earlier. But the dream became a dwaam. Unless Labour can develop new modes of thought and a change of heart, the Party is over.

The general election of 1987 was seen as a sporting entertainment like the Eatanswill election that Dickens described in the year 1827. Candidates kissed babies to woo voters and the hidden persuaders from the advertising world moved in to promote competing brands. Dickens had the artists Seymour and 'Phiz' to help popularize the *Pickwick Papers*; in 1987 the television cameras were exploiting 'photo opportunities'. Same old stage, same old play, re-enacting the knockabout of Pitt and Fox.

Labour's chiefs in Westminster see the regiment of Scottish Labour MPs as auxiliaries from the periphery brought in to try and restore the lost balance at the centre. We Scots will remain their colony as long as they are so hard-pressed for Labour MPs in England. The Scottish political scene is further befogged by the Scottish National Party. Perversely they have insisted on tying themselves to a detailed programme which is irrelevant to the main aim of Scottish independence. In an effort to alienate neither their Tory nor Labour adherents, they have appeared as anti-Labour in one constituency and anti-Tory in another. Nobody is going out on the barricades for such a lukewarm message, but they will gather support as Labour fails to deliver and the electors become more desperate. If they emerged as a movement for Scottish independence which nationalists across the political spectrum could unite to support, they would gather nationwide momentum.

Apathetic, perplexed, we watch the oil running out, the shipyards closing, the dole queues lengthening, and feel frustrated, powerless, like a man tied up and watching his house being ransacked. A car-sticker in Aberdeen said, 'Oh Lord, send another oil boom. We'll promise not to piss it all away this time.'

The rule of élite minorities is at the source of our distresses, alike in most capitalist and communist countries. Lenin's wife, Krupskaya, said that many communists 'still cannot throw off the old view of the mass as an object of the intelligentsia's care, like a small and unreasonable child,' and she added, 'Our job is to help the people *in fact* to take their fate into their own hands.' Rosa Luxembourg said, 'As long as theoretic knowledge remains the privilege of "academicians" in the Party, the latter will face the danger of going astray.' And Barbara Lerner said that a society in which the majority do not fully participate is a sick society; 'systems and institutions with authoritarian structures cannot effectively mobilize the therapeutic potential of any community'. Two German psychiatrists, Alexander and Margarete Mitscherlich, who studied Nazi Germany, argued that the chances of survival for the human race depend not on preserving the methods of thought intimidation by which for millennia the individual was domesticated but on educating the critical understanding of every single person. The individual, they said, 'can attain independence only if, in his first attempts to practise initiative, he feels himself securely supported by the sympathy and understanding of those close to him'. They called for 'nothing less than a revolution in child rearing'.

The richest of the resources that Scotland is wasting is her young. We would be immeasurably richer for their cooperation, and their reintegration into the community. Many years of dealing with these edgy youngsters of industrial Scotland have convinced me of their intellectual ability and potential goodwill as well as their spiny independence. I suspect that our prolonged schooling of them is to hold them down, to protect us adults from their explosive initiatives. Keeping them into their late teens memorizing swathes of barely comprehended information takes the steam out of them. Maybe schools aren't the best way of bringing up the young. All the politicians in the last election thought that excellence in education is better examination results. Our rejection of the majority of pupils and extended tutelage of the rest have turned them to violence and drugs and suicide. We adults should confess our obtuseness and give them the most potent of cures, our affection.

Bruno Bettelheim confirmed in me the intuition on which I based this book and my attitude to Scottish school-pupils. He was a Viennese psycho-analyst, imprisoned in Dachau and Buchenwald for a year, who set up in Chicago a school for severely disturbed children. From his study of the effects of brutality on the prisoners, he deduced that the psychoses of his patients had been produced by the same kind of painful experience. He further claims that all children act out of an innate logic. Whatever a child does, however outrageous, he has excellent reasons for doing. The homicidal and suicidal urges, the fantasies, are logical conclusions from the child's experience, particularly of his parents. The child's fear may be not only of being hurt but of being destroyed. Bettelheim's success in bringing salvation to severely disturbed children is evidence that his theory works. Scottish education is based on the opposite hypothesis; juvenile delinquents indulge in juvenile delinquency for the hell of it. There is no future for Scotland in that diagnosis of its ills.

The Germans had identified a principle concerning the terms necessary for our society's health. A revolution in child rearing is essential to a widespread cultural change. Without it there will be no rule of the majority, that is to say no democracy. With it there will be a new perception of the nature of intelligence as a fusion of thinking and feeling into a deeper understanding; a new perception of how to live our lives; and the healing (the making whole) or our sorely riven society. Wholeness starts from below, for example in classrooms without the apartheid of class or colour or intelligence quotient. Already in Scotland and notably in Fife a start has been made to welcome pupils of all abilities into the same classroom, learning together, growing together. Free from the divisiveness, the intense individualism of examinations, the pupils will feel free to frame in words, and share, their ideas and feelings however clumsy and ill-fitting the expression. Practice in articulating their ideas helps intelligence (and confidence) to grow. There is a nourishing warmth. (For most of our young in Scotland it remains education in a cold climate and it is growing colder.) A quarter of a century ago the staffs of two Scottish secondary schools tried to bring that about. A generation later both groups of former pupils held a reunion to tell us that, as a result of what we had sought to communicate to them in school, they were rearing their own children differently from the way in they had themselves been reared.

There's market for that kind of education. The young Scots are brimming with questions that the intelligentsia thought they alone articulated, weighing consumer satisfactions against a simpler life-style and contemplating new frameworks of society, new makes of chassis to replace lumbering institutions. Many of them are out of sympathy with the temper of present-day Scotland. 'No longer at ease here, in the old dispensation, with an alien people clutching their gods'; T. S. Eliot put it bleakly in *The Journey of the Magi*, who also were trying to penetrate the truth about living. Mediaeval Scottish students (Scotus vagans) wandered over Europe, endlessly engaged in what I thought was academic disputation, but maybe they were like the young Scots of today, probing to *feel* what life could be about. The young are looking far beyond the bounds of the political parties and the kirks for something that can be described only as a rebirth. We adults would do well to be in on this parturition, helping them as they query the feelings and beliefs that have been in occupation of our minds and hearts. For example they look at Bannockburn and the Reformation and ask, were these genuine movements welling up from below or were they stratagems imposed from above? They are capable of weighing wisely a programme for the quickening of life in Kildonan, balancing the economic arguments against the social arguments. They could make Scotland a clearinghouse of ideas. They haven't a hangup like us adults on whether it is the will of the elected Westminster parliament or the will of the Scottish people that is sovereign and paramount when we talk about government. They don't try to undo that tangled knot; they just cut it. They have a tenderness towards all natural life and are closer than we are to understanding the terms on which we will be permitted to abide on the earth. Extended sojourns in their natural heritage, the land of Scotland, confirm in them their perception of what is sound and sweet.

The alternatives are drastic as never before in our history. Either we will be exterminated and Scottish history and earth history come to an end for homo sapiens. Or there will be an awakening out of our Scottish dwaam into rebirth. I'm not optimistic. Toynbee in his *Study of History* said that a suicidal urge comes over civilizations as their ills approach a climax. There are enough symptoms of that yielding up of the ghost in Scotland, a feeling of powerlessness in the face of rampant money-making.

But there *is* a chance, the possibility that things might go the other way. All over the earth, people are realizing that if we stick with our masters (in Scotland described as 'a tight circle of politicians, business men, civil servants, lawyers, trade unionists, churchmen, academics and a nostalgic sprinkling of titled gentry') they'll be the death of us. We're on our own, dependent on our own efforts to find a way out. The majority of ordinary people world-wide are looking as if they might just possibly take over the running of their community. Everything is up for revaluation as never before in human history. It's like leaving the lunar module and stepping on to the moon's surface. It would be a giant step for mankind.

INDEX

Index

Index

Index

Index

Index